The Hillforts of Cardigan Bay

Discovering the Iron Age communities of Ceredigion

The mighty coastal hillfort of Pen Dinas, Aberystwyth, seen from the south across former wetlands near Tanybwlch. (T. Driver)

For Aric and Charlie

The Hillforts of Cardigan Bay

Discovering the Iron Age communities of Ceredigion

Toby Driver

Logaston Press

LOGASTON PRESS
Little Logaston Woonton Almeley
Herefordshire HR3 6QH
logastonpress.co.uk

First published by Logaston Press 2016
Copyright text © Toby Driver
Copyright illustrations © as per credits and acknowledgements

ISBN 978 1910839 03 4

Typeset by Logaston Press
and printed and bound in Poland by
www.lfbookservices.co.uk

Front cover: Main image: Castell Rhyfel. (Crown Copyright); see page 141.
Stone head. (Michael Freeman. By kind permission of Amgueddfa Ceredigion Museum);
see pages 108-109.
Pottery jar found at Pen Dinas hillfort, Aberystwyth. (By kind permission of the National
Museum of Wales); see pages 60-61.

Rear cover: Pendinaslochdyn hillfort. (Toby Driver); see page 152.
The Pencoed-y-foel neck-ring. (Permission of the National Museum of Wales; image courtesy of
Bristol Museums, Galleries & Archives); see pages 48-49.

CONTENTS

ACKNOWLEDGEMENTS

For many years I have been intending to write a guide to the hillforts and prehistoric settlements of Ceredigion (Cardiganshire). Along the way I was distracted first by PhD research on the north Ceredigion hillforts and then by an academic monograph on the same subject. It is good, finally, to see this book finished. The content and approach have been shaped in large part by the many questions I have been asked when presenting or taking part in lectures, talks or guided walks. These questions have always forced me to explain myself more clearly, or to stop and think about the interpretations that I have just put forward. I hope the information in these pages will shed some new light on what we know about the Iron Age communities, hillforts and prehistoric farmsteads of Cardigan Bay – and just as importantly what we *don't* know. My aim is to encourage readers to visit these fascinating sites, to keep their eyes and ears open for new finds, to help in making new discoveries and to contribute new thought about the distant past of the land embracing the great sweep of Cardigan Bay. There is still so much to learn.

A host of friends and colleagues have enlightened or encouraged me over the years. My mother and father pursued the ancient sites of Gwynedd on childhood holidays and inspired my love of these places from a young age. My wife Becky has always encouraged me – without her I would never have started my PhD research, let alone finished it. I still learn much every year from our two boys, Aric and Charlie; they are never short of questions. I have gained immeasurably from working at the Royal Commission on the Ancient and Historical Monuments of Wales over the years, especially from specialists such as Stephen Briggs, David Browne and Chris Musson. In my research work I was fortunate enough to be supervised by Professor Andrew Fleming, who constantly prompted me to develop new ideas and to broaden my outlook. In recent years I have been lucky enough to carry out fieldwork, survey and excavation and have never stopped learning. I have explored wild coastal promontory forts and complex hillforts with Louise Barker, always sharing new ideas. I have spent many happy hours tramping over Ceredigion hillforts with Keith Haylock, and exploring the prehistoric field systems on Skomer Island with Louise, Bob Johnston and Oliver Davis. My excavation work with Jeffrey Davies and local volunteers at the Abermagwr Roman villa has been constantly rewarding, especially through the commitment and fellowship of a stalwart band of local volunteers – I may even have started to understand a little about the Romans!

This book would not have been possible without the unfailing support of Andy and Karen Johnson at Logaston Press. They believed in the project from the outset and gave me invaluable editorial steers along the way. I cannot thank them enough. In preparing the text and illustrations I have received invaluable comments and suggestions from a number of willing 'readers', especially Michael Freeman and Chris Musson, who have both shared their knowledge of Ceredigion and various aspect of prehistory and have given up their time to edit and improve the text of this book; their particular contribution to the text has been invaluable. Jeffrey Davies helped me with Chapter 6, Scott Lloyd and Louise Barker with Chapter 1. Adam Gwilt refined and modernised the Timeline at the beginning of the book and provided detailed information on the remarkable Pencoed-y-foel neck-ring.

Many others have contributed time and expertise in answering queries or providing information, notably Gail Boyle, Bill Britnell, Barry Burnham, Carrie Canham, Jackie Chadwick, Stuart Evans, Andrew Fitzpatrick, Fiona Gale, Erika Guttman-Bond, Iestyn Jones, Ken Murphy, Harold Mytum, Marion Page, Alison Roberts and Simon Timberlake. Gillian Clarke, the National Poet of Wales, kindly allowed me to use her Pen Dinas poem in my Foreword. Sally Evans – Sally Parcybedw – passed on her family memories of the 19th-century discovery of the Pencoed-y-foel neck-ring. To many landowners and tenants I offer my thanks for letting me undertake archaeological fieldwork on their land, especially Ceredig Thomas and Wendy Crockett at Castell Grogwynion, Teifi and Jenny Davies at Castell Nadolig and Huw and Ann Tudor at Llanilar. My thanks go to them and many other landowners who over the years have allowed me access to the hillforts and ancient settlements that have fallen within their care.

Many individuals, archives and organisations have provided images for this book. I am particularly grateful to the Royal Commission and the National Monuments Record of Wales, the National Museum of Wales, the Dyfed Archaeological Trust, Denbighshire County Council, Amgueddfa Ceredigion Museum and the Bristol Museums, Galleries and Archives for letting me enliven the following pages with stunning images from their collections. In particular I am grateful to Penny Icke for permission to use numerous images from the National Monuments Record of Wales in Aberystwyth which have been expertly scanned or digitally improved by Fleur James. Individual acknowledgements can be found in the captions to the images themselves. Notes on the contributing organisations are included in Chapter 9.

Without the help of all these individuals and organisations the book would have been far less complete and well informed than it is now. My sincere thanks go to all of them. Any remaining omissions, errors or misinterpretation are of course entirely my own responsibility.

Editorial Notes

Geographic scope of this book
This book principally deals with the later prehistoric and Romano-British hillforts and defended settlements of Ceredigion, formerly Cardiganshire, on the west coast of mid Wales. The northern and southern extents of Cardigan Bay – from Gwynedd in the north to Pembrokeshire in the south – are touched upon at various points, including in the list of 'Gazetteer of hillforts to visit' in Chapter 8.

Access to sites
Unless otherwise stated all of the sites described or illustrated in this book should be assumed to lie on private land, to be visited only with the permission of the landowner (and at the visitor's own risk). Details about attractive and easily visited sites are given in Chapter 7, with others listed in Chapter 8, together with information about access and safety. Visitors should always strictly observe the Countryside Code.

Dates
Most dates in this book are given in calendar years BC and AD, for the purposes of clarity. Where radiocarbon dates are described, the date ranges are given in calendar years without discussion of calibration issues and the underpinning percentage probabilities. Readers wishing to further explore the quoted dates should consult the published sources listed in Further Reading and References near the end of the book.

Terminology
Throughout the book the terms '**hillforts**' and '**defended farmsteads**' (or close synonyms) are used to denote the Iron Age settlements of mid and west Wales. Archaeologists tend to think of **hillforts** as the larger, more monumental and conspicuously sited settlements, often positioned to dominate the local landscape and commanding wide views; they will have one or more lines of defensive rampart, with flanking ditches and defended gateways. **Defended farmsteads** (or 'defended enclosures') tend to be less monumental and less conspicuously sited in the landscape, though usually still enclosed by one or more ramparts, palisades or ditches. As in all things there are grey areas: one can find large but lightly defended enclosures on hilltops or impressive defences around relatively small lowland or hillslope settlements. Some sites identified as 'forts' or 'farmsteads' may have served other functions such as for the corralling of stock, the holding of seasonal fairs or the conduct of ritual or religious ceremonies. Without excavation on a fairly extensive

scale it is impossible to be sure about such things. In Pembrokeshire defended farmsteads tend to be called 'raths', in Gwynedd more commonly just as 'homesteads'. While most of Ceredigion's hillforts and defended settlements were probably built and occupied during the so-called Iron Age, between about 800 BC and 50 AD, some at least may have had their origins in the preceding Bronze Age while others remained in use well into the Romano-British period or even perhaps beyond.

FOREWORD

In these galleries of glass
reflection and transparencies
under Pen Dinas skies
our Iron Age forebears' glance
give us good governance.

© Gillian Clarke, The National Poet of Wales. (By kind permission of Gillian Clarke)

These lines of modern verse, prominently displayed in the foyer of the glass-and-steel office of the Welsh Government at Rhodfa Padarn in Aberystwyth, reference the brooding presence of the mighty Pen Dinas hillfort on the hilltop nearby, and ask our Iron Age ancestors to give the blessing of good leadership, across two millennia, to the politicians and civil servants of the present day. The verse tells us that this long-abandoned and grassed-over hillfort still has a role to play in modern Wales, to fire our imagination and spirit of enquiry, to enhance our sense of time and space and to inspire both staff and visitors when entering this regional seat of the present-day government of Wales.

Hillforts are the greatest monumental legacy to survive from our prehistoric past along the coastal plains and inland hills that front onto Cardigan Bay; some are among the finest to be seen in Wales. This book aims to provide an introduction and guide to the more than 200 Iron Age farms and hillforts in the county of Ceredigion, formerly Cardiganshire, a region bounded to the north and south by the rivers Dyfi and Teifi, to the east by the Cambrian Mountains and to the west by the great sweep of Cardigan Bay.

The impressive earthen banks and stepped terraces of the hillforts of west Wales are testament to the sweat and toil of our Iron Age ancestors. They have long attracted fanciful stories, fables and legends. Commanding rocky hilltops, standing silent within dense woodland or clinging to eroding coastal cliffs and headlands, these ancient earthworks were once thought to be the work of giants or the castles of Romans. Views have changed, of course, in more recent centuries and decades. During the interwar years, for instance, they were seen by many archaeologists as 'military' camps, attributable to invading peoples and cultures arriving from Continental Europe. Others saw in their complex defences a later response to the attack strategies of the Roman armies. In recent decades, however, a different and more nuanced appreciation has emerged as a by-product of large-scale excavation programmes in many parts of Britain. Environmental analyses and radiocarbon dating have also played their part in this transformation of ideas. Hillforts are now understood rather as a 'home-grown' reaction to changing circumstances in the first millennium BC, some at least having indigenous origins in the preceding Bronze Age. For the most part, however, Iron Age Britain was not dominated by a uniform 'culture' but presented a complex regional mosaic of interacting peoples and cultural groupings. Communities along the sweep of Cardigan Bay may well have differed from one another in a variety of ways but there is material evidence to show that they were nevertheless well connected to the wider cultures and traditions of the rest of prehistoric Britain, the Irish Sea and even continental Europe.

It is questionable whether all hillforts fulfilled a wholly military or defensive role. Most fighting in the pre-Roman centuries probably took place between rival families or neighbours, in the form of competitive 'display behaviour' or raiding rather than pitched battles or frontal attacks. Bulky ramparts and complex gate-structures were no doubt intended to impress and intimidate neighbours and attackers, but weaker defences and flimsy 'back doors' elsewhere around the circuit hint that neither the hillforts nor the defended farmsteads were intended to withstand sustained attack. How, then, were the hillforts used? As they span many centuries it is likely that their functions and chronologies were as diverse as their physical form and siting within the landscape. Along with the lesser settlements they probably ranged in function from complex defended villages, through political centres or seats of family or tribal power, to prosperous or humble farmsteads or even ceremonial or ritual centres. Some of the less impressive examples may have served primarily as enclosures for corralling stock or for holding seasonal fairs and markets. All of these possibilities will be discussed and illustrated in the following pages.

Some of the prehistoric finds from the region are very special indeed. Many are on display to visitors from around the world in Britain's great museums yet remain unfamiliar to the people who live in Ceredigion today. Of particular note is the earliest gold object from Wales (the Banc Tynddol 'sun disc'), a glorious Late Bronze Age ceremonial shield (from Rhos Rydd, Blaenplwyf) as well as a pair of Iron Age 'divination' spoons from Castell Nadolig, Penbryn, one of only fifteen pairs yet known from the whole of Britain.

That said, there has been a relative lack of fieldwork and excavation in Ceredigion compared with other parts of western Britain. Even so, many new monuments and finds have been chanced upon through excavation, field survey or aerial photography in recent years and many more will be discovered in the future, each one with the potential to enrich our understanding of prehistoric and Roman west Wales.

Although the names of Ceredigion's early leaders are long lost, we can still visit the sites of their homes and look out across the hills, valleys and coastlands that once fell within their gaze. We can ponder, too, the allegiances and power struggles, the building styles and beliefs which united – or drove apart – the prehistoric communities of Cardigan Bay. There is indeed plenty to see today. At many sites, especially in the winter months when the vegetation is low, one can still make out roundhouse platforms or glimpse ancient stone walling protruding through grass-covered banks. Over the centuries many of the smaller sites have been lost to the plough, only to be rediscovered in recent decades through aerial photography. This book will take the reader back to the landscape and prehistoric inhabitants of Ceredigion, exploring the latter through the surviving traces of their hillforts and defended farmsteads, poignant reminders of a shared legacy from two millennia and more ago.

Toby Driver, Bontgoch, Ceredigion, 2016

Timeline for Cardigan Bay

4000-2900 BC
Early-Middle Neolithic: The first farmers. Stone chambered tombs, causewayed enclosures, polished stone axes, leaf-shaped arrowheads. *Garreg Fawr, Llanbadarn.*

2900-2500 BC
Later Neolithic: Earlier tombs are blocked, great stone circles and henge monuments built. Appearance of new pottery styles. *Settlement evidence at Llanilar.*

2500-1150 BC
Early-Middle Bronze Age: Inhumation and then cremation burials in cairns and round barrows. Appearance of distinctive funerary pottery and grave goods. Seasonal metal mining at Copa Hill, Cwmystwyth, and at other north Ceredigion mines. *Banc Tynddol 'sun disc'. Llanilar Urn.*

1150-800 BC
Late Bronze Age: Climate colder and wetter. Disappearance of burial evidence. Early hillforts and field systems established. Swords and high status weaponry. *Rhos Rydd shield.*

800-600 BC
Earliest Iron Age / Llyn Fawr period: Appearance of Halstatt material culture elsewhere in Britain.

600-400 BC
Early Iron Age: Simple, large hillforts established with early palisaded defences. *Ffynnonwen enclosure, Tremain, constructed on the coastal lowlands of Ceredigion.*

400-50 BC
Middle Iron Age: Expansion and development of hillforts. Rise of high-status smaller hillforts. Rise of La Tène European decorative style and its influence on Iron Age metalwork from Wales. *Construction of Darren Camp near Pen-bont Rhydybeddau and Caer Cadwgan near Lampeter. Deforestation around Cors Caron and the Ystwyth valley.*

50BC-50 AD
Late Iron Age and the Roman conquest of west Wales: Occupation of hillforts and defended farms continues. Severe deforestation and clearance of lower Ystwyth valley linked to expansion of agriculture and settlement. Development of complex hillfort architecture. *The Castell Nadolig or Penbryn spoons.*

43 AD
Roman invasion of Britain by Emperor Claudius at Richborough, Kent.

47-78/80 AD
Latest Iron Age /Roman Campaigning period: Aspects of Iron Age identity and culture continue into the early Romano-British period. Roman conquest of west Wales finally achieved through the campaigns of Governor Frontinus in 74-77 AD.

77-78 AD
Brutal suppression of Ordovices tribe in north Wales by Agricola, followed by capture of Anglesey. *Manufacture of Tal-y-llyn shield (50-80 AD). Pencoed-y-foel neck-ring.*

125-130 AD
Roman forts at Trawsgoed and Llanio abandoned and dismantled. Continued occupation of Romanised defended farms including Troedyrhiw, Y Ferwig. Prominent local leaders accrue wealth under Roman rule.

200-340 AD
Construction, occupation and final abandonment of the **Roman villa at Abermagwr.**

383 AD
Magnus Maximus (Macsen Wledig) becomes Emperor of the Western Roman Empire.

410 AD
End of Roman rule in Britain.

411-1066 AD
Early Medieval period or 'Dark Ages'. Re-occupation, or construction, of a number of Ceredigion's hillforts and defended farms

Reconstruction of Hen Gaer hillfort near Bow Street, drawn for Ysgol Rhydypennau School at Bow Street by Dylan Roberts in 1980. The view perfectly captures the life of a small Iron Age hillfort or defended farmstead, in this case sited on a steep hillslope. Recent research has suggested that the rampart at Hen Gaer was in fact stone-walled. There may also have been more open space within enclosures of this kind, for assembly, working areas, small-scale gardens and even the corralling of stock. Despite this the drawing vividly evokes the character of daily life in such a settlement and depicts the type of timberwork and gateway one might expect at a small hillfort or defended farmstead. (By kind permission of Dylan Roberts)

Chapter 1

EXPLORING THE HILLFORTS OF CARDIGAN BAY

Chapter frontispiece: Pen Dinas hillfort, Aberystwyth, commanding the confluence of two regional rivers and looking out across Cardigan Bay.
(Crown Copyright RCAHMW AP_2012_4264)

THE RISE OF HILLFORT STUDIES IN CEREDIGION

The [Iron Age]…was one of intensive hill-fort building and here Cardiganshire has a rich inheritance[1]

Giants and folktales

Hillforts in Britain are so numerous and visible that they have long attracted the attention of antiquarians and archaeologists. Among the earliest references to the hillforts of Ceredigion were those made by Sion Dafydd Rhys in his defence of Geoffrey of Monmouth's *Historia Regum Britanniae*.[2] This detailed 16th-century literary geography of Welsh giant lore describes the sites of their strongholds, including a number in 'the country of Aberteifi', present-day Ceredigion, that we now know as hillforts or medieval castles. Not all of them, however, can be securely identified today. Castell Moeddyn near Cribyn is mentioned thus: 'in Llanarth there was Moythyn the giant, and his abode is still called Castell Moythyn'. Pen Dinas, at Aberystwyth, is mentioned as the abode of '… Maylor the giant, and the place in which he dwelt is still called Castell Maylor, which is built on a high hill or high bank named "y Dinas" on one side of the river Ystwyth within the common lands of Aberystwyth.'

The fort of 'Castell Maylor' is linked to an elaborate folk tale about Maylor the giant, held captive twelve miles from his castle. Before being put to death he was allowed to blow on his horn three times. His son Cornippin, out hunting on an 'immensely large horse', heard the horn whilst on 'Cefn Hiraethog', possibly the moorland of Mynydd Hiraethog in present-day Denbighshire. Cornippin rode so fast to the rescue that his bloodhound's head tore from its body, leaving only the head and mouth in the leash at a now-unlocated place called 'Bwlch Sabn y Ci'. These early references tell us much about 16th-century perceptions of Ceredigion's prehistoric earthworks as old and unusual structures, once the homes and fortresses of the powerful people of mid Wales.

Antiquarians and pioneers

Hillforts and encampments in Ceredigion are mentioned from the late 16th century onwards by gentlemen travellers and antiquarians. Edward Lhuyd, a native of Ceredigion, was one of the earliest in Wales to make reliable records and surveys of ancient monuments. He also sent out a list of questions to each parish asking for information about antiquities, with the returns summarised in his *Parochialia*.[3] In the north of the county the late 18th-century mine surveyor Lewis Morris included fairly detailed sketches and

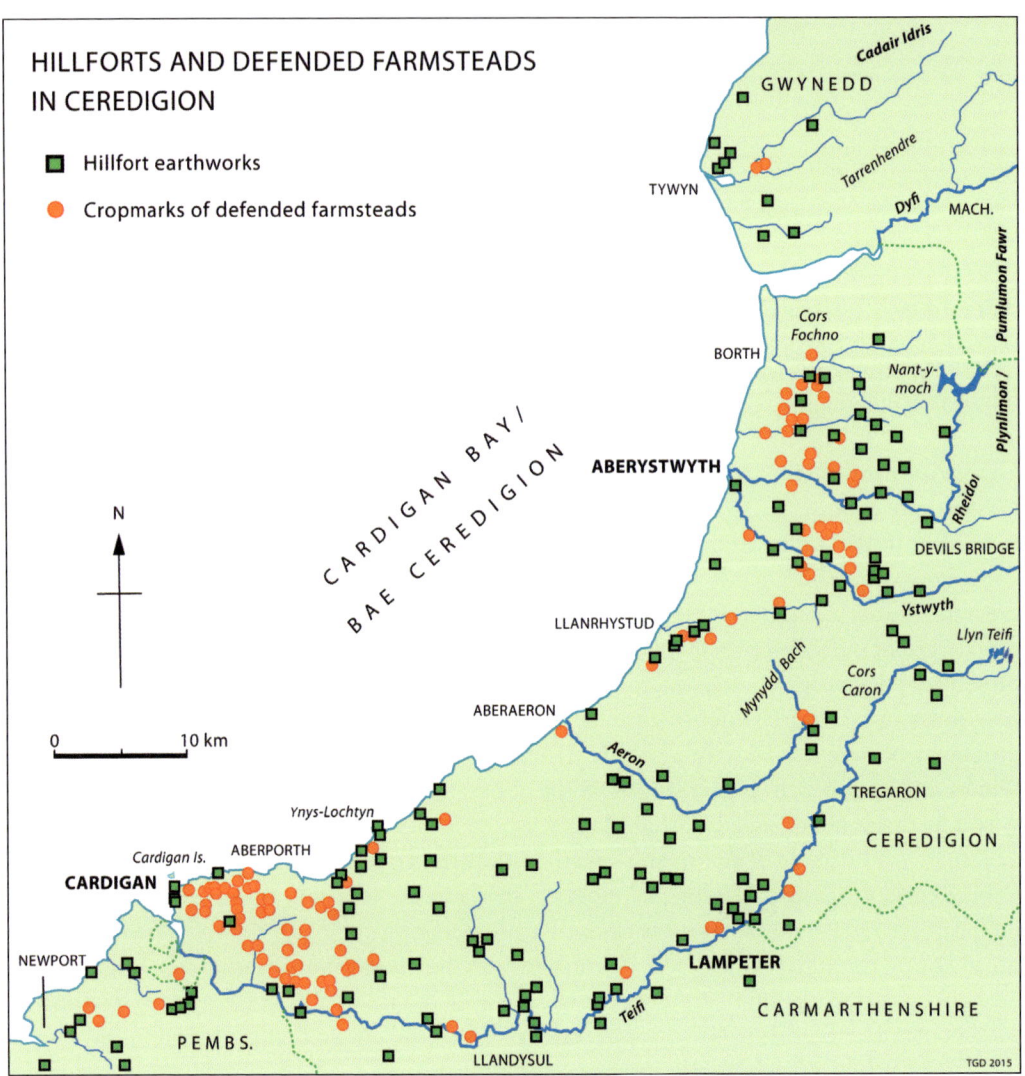

Figure 1.1. Distribution of Iron Age hillforts and defended farmsteads in Ceredigion, showing those which survive as earthworks and those which are known only as plough-levelled cropmarks recorded from the air. Note the numerous plough-levelled enclosures in the extreme south and far north of the county. In dry summers cropmarks are often revealed on the better-drained arable soils of lowland Ceredigion; they are far less frequent on the inland grasslands and uplands, though periods of exceptional drought have revealed cropmark enclosures along the upper reaches of the Aeron and along the Teifi around Lampeter. Potential unenclosed settlements, perhaps indicated by prehistoric finds, are not shown. For the identification of key sites see Figures 1.11 and 1.12. (T. Driver. Information derived from the Dyfed Archaeological Trust's Defended Enclosures Survey and the Historic Wales Portal)

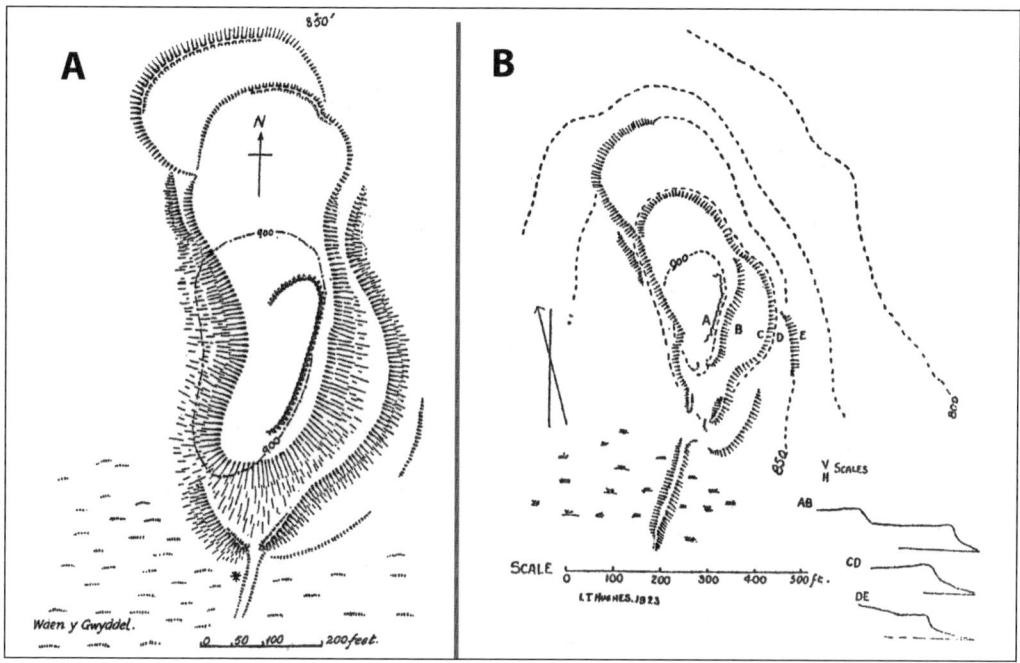

Figure 1.2. Archaeological pioneers. Comparative plans by Frank Wright (A, 1914) and Ieuan Hughes (B, 1926) of the multi-phase hillfort of Pen Dinas, Elerch, sited on high ground between Talybont and Bontgoch. The Royal Commission and Aberystwyth University recently carried out new survey work at this complex and interesting 'mountain fortress' shown in Figure 1.17. (A: Copyright Reserved B: Courtesy of the Ceredigion Historical Society)

plans of hillforts north of the river Rheidol in his map and perspective views of the metal mines of the 'Mannor of Perverth'. Interest in all things antiquarian developed during the 19th century, with the Cambrian Archaeological Association visiting Castell Nadolig during their 1859 summer meeting to observe the remnants of recently excavated cremation burials. In 1867 J. Graham Williams published a paper on 'Ancient Encampments near Aberystwyth' in the journal *Archaeologia Cambrensis* and drew attention to place name evidence and topography suggesting that hillforts had been built to defend the working of local metal ores.

Hillforts have been interpreted in a variety of ways over the years. During the Victorian period they were often seen as military works involving the Romans, Danes or other invaders. The era of 'modern' Iron Age research in Britain arguably reached a critical stage with the publication in 1931 of an influential paper by Professor Christopher Hawkes, entitled simply 'Hillforts'. Public imagination was also captured by early hillfort excavations of about the same time, including Mortimer Wheeler's campaigns at Maiden Castle in Dorset. By 1931 work in Wales had already begun to adopt a more scientific approach. Willoughby Gardner's earlier address on 'Hillforts in north Wales and their defences', delivered at the 1926 meeting of the Cambrian Archaeological Association, discussed a number of new ideas about the distribution, defensive siting and construction of hillforts, as well as the lives of their inhabitants.

The first decades of the 20th century had also seen the publication of two important regional surveys of Ceredigion. Frank Wright's 1914 paper, 'Some Ancient Defensive Earthworks near Aberystwyth', included descriptions and ground surveys of eleven hillforts. Ieuan Hughes' 1926 'Regional Survey of North Cardiganshire Prehistoric Earthworks' described a further fifteen omitted both by Williams in 1867 and by Wright in 1914. Both Wright and Hughes were forward-looking in their views. Hughes, for instance, included plans because they '… possess a value which is two-fold. They help to interpret the earthwork; they remain as reasonably accurate records of sites liable to destruction.' Here was a call, already in the 1920s, for better interpretation and conservation of Cardiganshire's hillforts.

In July 1933 Professor Daryll Forde of the then University College of Wales, Aberystwyth, answered Hughes' calls for an excavation on a large hillfort by undertaking exploratory work over a period of six weeks at Pen Dinas, high above the town. Excavation was continued for a further four seasons until 1937, eventually being published in the journal *Archaeologia Cambrensis* in 1963.[4] For the most part Forde used long sections through the defences, an idea favoured at the time, but he also opened wider trenches across the major gateways and a roundhouse in the south fort. This allowed structures to be examined in plan, rather

Figure 1.3. Looking sun-tanned and relaxed, Professor Daryll Forde (seated, right) poses with colleagues for a photograph in August 1933 at the excavated south gate of Pen Dinas, Aberystwyth. Striped ranging rods stand in former postholes either side of the wide gateway passage, seen here from inside the fort. The tented excavation camp is visible in the middle distance above Penparcau. An external view of this gateway is reconstructed in Figure 4.19. (Pen Dinas excavation archive, National Monuments Record of Wales)

than trying to work out complex building sequences from very narrow sections and small trenches. This is the way that archaeologists explore sites today.

Remarkably, these excavations still represent one of the most sustained programmes of work on any prehistoric site in Ceredigion, comparable to excavations in the 1980s at Caer Cadwgan hillfort, Cellan. Forde's campaign mirrored Mortimer Wheeler's hugely popular explorations at Maiden Castle, Dorset, in progress between 1934 and 1937. In the post-war years knowledge about the archaeology of the county was further boosted by the 1955 publication of W.J. Lewis' *Ceredigion: Atlas Hanesyddol* or '*Historical Atlas of Cardiganshire*'. This book is still notable for its illustrated distribution maps of stone implements, Bronze Age tools and weapons and Iron Age hillforts. This modest publication has inspired genera-tions of local people to appreciate the richness and depth of the county's prehistoric past.

Celts and invaders

In the first half of the 20th century most archaeologists were sure that the tradition of hill-fort building arrived from overseas. Many viewed developments in the British Iron Age as evidence of successive waves of 'invasion', with the arrival and assimilation of 'immigrant cultures' on British shores. Hillforts were seen as a 'new culture', developed first in the south and east of Britain by new settlers from the Low Countries, the ideas then spreading west and north as immigrants moved overland or charted the western coasts by ship. Excavation campaigns at hillforts were designed to establish evidence for these 'invasions' as well as to date regional cultural sequences.

The idea of invading cultures was nothing new, continuing a narrative first popularised in the 19th century when hillforts were often interpreted as 'native' responses to bands

Figure 1.4. Pen Dinas, Aberystwyth. This view shows the approach to the south gate.
The entrance passage (centre), now partly infilled, was originally much deeper and would have been crossed by a timber bridge flanked by a massive projecting bastion on the right-hand side, as shown in the reconstruction drawing in Figure 4.16. An interior view of this gateway under excavation in 1933 can be seen in Figure 1.3. (T. Driver)

of invading Danes and others. The First World War may have stoked such ideas. Indeed, the invasion hypothesis lasted well into the 1950s and 1960s. A popular guide to Wales, written in 1939 and revised in 1969, summed up the prevailing popular view: 'In the late Iron (La Tène) Age, i.e. the last centuries B.C., came another wave of Nordic invaders, constructors of hill-top entrenchments and talkers of Brythonic.'[5] These ideas were finally abandoned in the face of growing excavation evidence for the emergence of regional Iron Age cultures within Britain, rather than a single invasive culture from abroad. This radical change of view was supplemented by a clearer picture of dating and hillfort development. New evidence suggested indigenous rather than foreign origins for British defended settlements, and far more complexity than a simple cultural spread north and west from the south-east coast.

Homegrown hillforts

It is now clear from excavation evidence that Iron Age hillforts in Wales originated in social and cultural changes taking place between about 1100 and 800 BC during the preceding Later Bronze Age. There are several dated hillforts with evidence of this origin in eastern Wales, while recent excavations in north Pembrokeshire and south Ceredigion have demonstrated late Bronze Age beginnings for many defended forts and farmsteads, with occupation sometimes lasting onward into Roman times. In the hills of north Ceredigion there are at least two early hilltop enclosures which may date back into the Early Bronze Age or even earlier.[6] The spread of new ideas from Europe through long-distance trade undoubtedly played a part in this start to defended settlement, but was not the origin of the building style. The British Iron Age certainly benefited from a flow of cultural and artistic ideas from the Celtic heartlands of Europe, especially from around 300 BC, as shown by the increasing incidence of the characteristic swirling patterns of high Celtic or 'La Tène' art. Undoubtedly these artistic ideas influenced the way local craftsman styled their jewellery, horse-gear, weapons and decorative fittings so that by the later part of the Iron Age in Wales, from about 50 BC to the Roman conquest in the 70s AD, objects such as shields, bracelets, brooches and chariot fittings of the indigenous aristocracy reflected the wider international art styles of Celtic Europe.

Advancing our knowledge: the 1960s to the present day

Following the Pen Dinas excavations, similar work was not seen in the county for nearly 50 years. Meanwhile, however, the hillforts of the region were systematically surveyed by the Ordnance Survey during the 1960s and 1970s as part of the UK national mapping programme. During the 1960s, too, small-scale excavation took place on Hen Gaer hillfort near Bow Street under the aegis of the Cardiganshire Antiquarian Society. By the 1980s there was a renewal of archaeological interest in Ceredigion's past through the Ceredigion Archaeological Survey,[7] established at St David's University College, Lampeter. A key project saw several seasons of relatively intensive excavation at the nearby hillfort of Caer Cadwgan, Cellan. New plans were also made of Pen y Castell, Bontgoch, and Pen y Daren (Darren Camp) hillforts during ambitious parish surveys. A parallel project also studied the archaeology of Ceredigion's coastal parishes between Newquay and Tresaith, resulting in a travelling exhibition, leaflets and local heritage signs which still remain in place today.

The formation of the Dyfed Archaeological Trust in 1975 saw a rise in archaeological activity across the newly constituted county, including rescue excavations in advance of development and aerial prospection for cropmark sites during dry summers – a task continued by the Royal Commission from 1986 onwards. Ken Murphy directed excavations at the ritual and burial ground at Plas Gogerddan, north of Aberystwyth, in 1986 and at the Odyn Fach defended enclosure near Talybont in 1989; excavation work was also undertaken at Pendinaslochdyn hillfort, near Llangrannog, in 1992. Describing the Odyn Fach project in 1989 Murphy[8] noted that '… the work at Odyn Fach … is published here to highlight what little is known of Iron Age settlements in mid-Wales.' He has since gone on to co-direct – with Professor Harold Mytum – large-scale excavations at the hilltop settlement of Castell Henllys in north Pembrokeshire. In south Ceredigion the Trust also investigated cropmark enclosures at Troedyrhiw, Y Ferwig (2005), and Ffynnonwen, Tremain (2006), both of them discovered, with many others, during Royal Commission aerial reconnaissance above the rich arable farmland east of Cardigan. During recent decades new finds from elsewhere in Ceredigion have added significantly to the growing archaeological collections on display in the Bowen Gallery at Amgueddfa Ceredigion Museum in Aberystwyth.

Figure 1.5. A modern archaeological excavation is a major undertaking, requiring meticulous planning and execution. This view from July 2006 shows the excavation of part of the inner ditch of the Ffynnonwen defended enclosure, near Tremain, by the Dyfed Archaeological Trust and the University of York. This enclosure ditch was 4.2m wide and 2.2m deep, with almost vertical sides cut through the solid bedrock. Creating such a ditch must have been brutal work – elsewhere at Ffynnonwen the builders abandoned the effort at an early stage after finding the bedrock simply too hard to conquer (see Chapter 4).
(Copyright Dyfed Archaeological Trust)

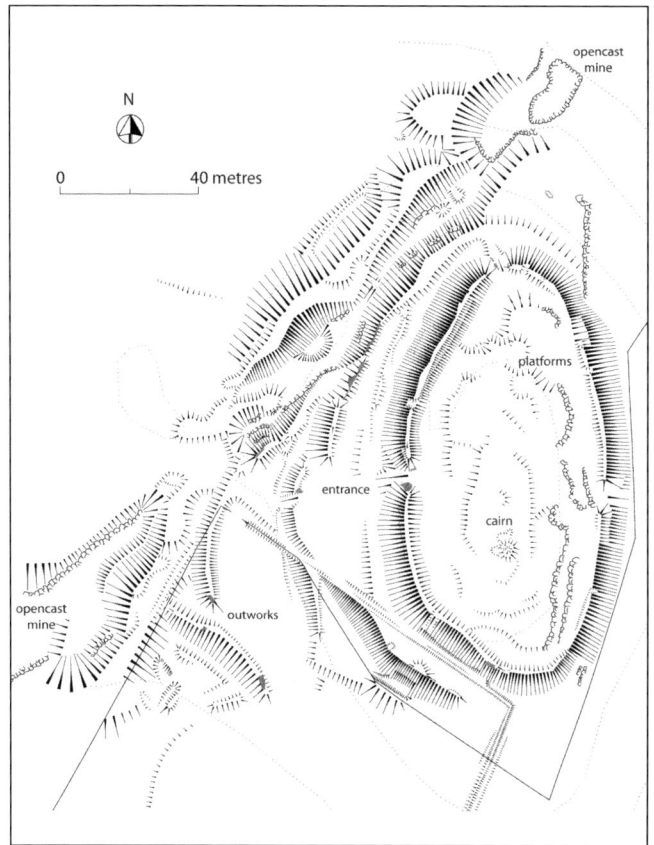

Figure 1.6. This 2005 survey of Darren Camp, above Pen-bont Rhydybeddau, was made by Louise Barker of the Royal Commission. It shows the western outworks of the hillfort slighted by later 16th-century opencast lead mining. Prehistoric house platforms and a Bronze Age cairn survive within the hillfort. Note the contrast between the complex defensive outworks and entrance-way to the west, and the virtually undefended 'rear' gate to the east. Excavations in 2005 by the Early Mines Research Group showed that the western ditches of the hillfort had intercepted the mineral vein[12] but whether this saw the start of prehistoric opencast mining on the hilltop is still not clear. (Crown Copyright RCAHMW, DCM09).

In 1994 a milestone was reached with the publication of Volume 1 of the *Cardiganshire County History*, containing sections on the Iron Age and Roman archaeology of the county brought together by Jeffrey Davies and A.H.A. Hogg.[9] This scholarly work, many years in gestation, provided an authoritative statement following nearly two centuries of survey and recording, yet confirmed how little research had up to that time been done during the 20th century. More recently, in 2005, the present author completed his PhD research on the hill-forts of north Ceredigion,[10] raising the total of known or probable prehistoric settlements to nearly double the number recorded in the County History. Since 2005, other work on Ceredigion's hillforts has included new detailed surveys by Louise Barker of the Royal Commission, excavations by the Early Mines Research Group, the Dyfed Archaeological Trust and University of York, and PhD research on Iron Age metal working and hillforts by Keith Haylock of Aberystwyth University.[11]

Hillforts in Ceredigion today: exploration and discovery

Ceredigion is rich in traces of prehistoric defended forts and farmsteads. In 2006 a survey of all hillforts and defended enclosures in the county by the Dyfed Archaeological Trust recorded nearly 230 within the county, dating back to between 2,800 and 2,000 years ago. Of these almost half were known only as cropmarks recorded during aerial survey, demonstrating the huge impact of this technique in the discovery of Iron Age settlements along Cardigan Bay during the 20th and early 21st centuries. As shown in Figure 1.1, in the far south-west of the county, where arable crops predominate to the east of Cardigan, there is a striking imbalance between a few upstanding earthworks and the known extent of plough-levelled settlements. In a triangle from Penbryn on the coast, south to Newcastle Emlyn and west along the Teifi to Cardigan, there is only a handful of upstanding hillforts, including Castell Nadolig and two coastal promontory forts. Yet following 40 years and more of aerial reconnaissance a further 60 or so defended farms have been discovered, revealing a more complete prehistoric landscape, much of which is now barely discernible at ground level.

It is highly likely that currently unrecorded defended farmsteads – and perhaps even genuine hillforts – will continue to be discovered, filling gaps in our understanding of prehistoric settlement patterns within the county. As we will see with the discoveries of the Bronze Age Banc Tynddol 'sun disc' from Cwmystwyth, or the Romano-British villa at Abermagwr, persistence and serendipity are likely to play a significant role in the discovery and interpretation of the county's archaeological legacy from the thousand years or so before Romans arrived on the shores of Cardigan Bay.

Aerial survey and hillforts
Archaeologists have been studying the British landscape from the air since the 1930s, but the Cardigan Bay coast was first studied in earnest during the 1960s by aerial archaeologists from Cambridge University, as part of aerial surveys which in time covered almost the whole of the British Isles. Before aerial survey, our knowledge of Iron Age settlement was limited to surviving hillforts and upstanding earthworks. Many of the plough-levelled cropmark sites along Cardigan Bay were once significant defended farms or small hillforts, almost erased since their final desertion by centuries of erosion, clearance and ploughing. This is a process which has been ongoing since pre-medieval times, particularly following the advent of mechanized ploughing in the 19th century and its intensification in the 20th.

So-called 'aerial archaeology' can reveal previously unrecorded sites in two main ways – through *shadowmarks* or *cropmarks*. Once impressive settlements can, over time, become virtually levelled by ploughing. However very low sunlight in winter, perhaps combined with a dusting of snow or melting frost, may yet reveal the denuded earthworks as a contrast between highlight and shadow; hence 'shadowmarks'. Alternatively, in dry summers, ripening crops will change colour in response to the sub-soil features, producing 'cropmarks'. After prolonged dry weather crops of various kinds growing over buried ditches will grow taller and ripen later, their roots responding to moisture and nutrients still present in the buried ditch. Conversely, those growing over stony material such as a Roman road or a plough-levelled rampart will ripen early, turning bright yellow or, in the case of parched grass, almost white. These dramatic colour differences are strikingly obvious from the air – almost like an 'x-ray' of the summer fields. This remarkable phenomenon may only last for a week or so in a dry summer, for following rain the crops will quickly return to a uniform colour. Since the early 1980s archaeologists from the Dyfed Archaeological Trust and, a little later, from the Royal Commission have carried out regular sorties over Ceredigion to rediscover these near-vanished sites in the ripening fields and dry grasslands bordering Cardigan Bay.

Figure 1.7. How cropmarks form. An Iron Age hillfort in about 200 BC (top) has a stone-built rampart and external ditch dug through rock or subsoil. By the 1960s (centre) the fort has become a low earthwork under pasture, now regularly ploughed for arable crops. By the present day (bottom) the fort has been completely flattened and there is nothing to see at ground level. However, in dry summers arable crops (or even grass) will grow tall and green over buried ditches, pits or postholes, but will ripen early and turn yellow over buried stonework or other impervious surfaces. These striking colour variations, along with differences in the height of the crop, can occasionally be recognised from ground level – as seen in Figure 1.8 – but can most readily be identified and photographed from the air, for subsequent documentation and mapping (Drawing by Charles Green after T. Driver. Crown Copyright RCAHMW, DI2006_1443).

Geophysical prospection

Other modern techniques that can reveal buried archaeological sites include geophysical prospection. Passing electrical currents through the soil or measuring tiny disturbances of the earth's magnetic field can reveal buried features with surprising clarity. Plotting these 'anomalies' across an entire field as a photo-like image can effectively 'map' lost or buried archaeological sites, often showing fine detail of ditches, wall footings, pits and postholes. These techniques have been particularly effective in south Ceredigion where the Dyfed Archaeological Trust and the University of York have systematically surveyed over 20 plough-levelled settlements within and just beyond the county before selecting a smaller number for targeted excavation.

Figure 1.8. A cropmark seen at ground level. The Glan Fred promontory fort in July 1999, showing the dark green grass over the buried northern ditch, contrasting starkly with the yellowing pasture in the rest of the field. The coloured ranging poles measure 1 metre in height. Compare with Figure 1.18. (T. Driver)

Figure 1.9. The dramatic green cropmarks of the Cawrence enclosure (SN 226 456), north of Llechryd in south Ceredigion. This late Iron Age farmstead had a main entrance at the left and a 'back door' marked by a simple gap in the outer ditch at top right. Just inside the main entrance were two minor gates giving access for livestock into the outer part of the enclosure, essentially a protected 'infield' alongside the farm itself. Geophysical survey and test-pitting by the Dyfed Archaeological Trust in 2011[13] revealed a possible prehistoric circular structure – very likely a house – within the inner enclosure and confirmed that only some 30cm of ploughsoil survives above the bedrock into which the ditched features had been cut. (Crown Copyright RCAHMW, DI2007_1989)

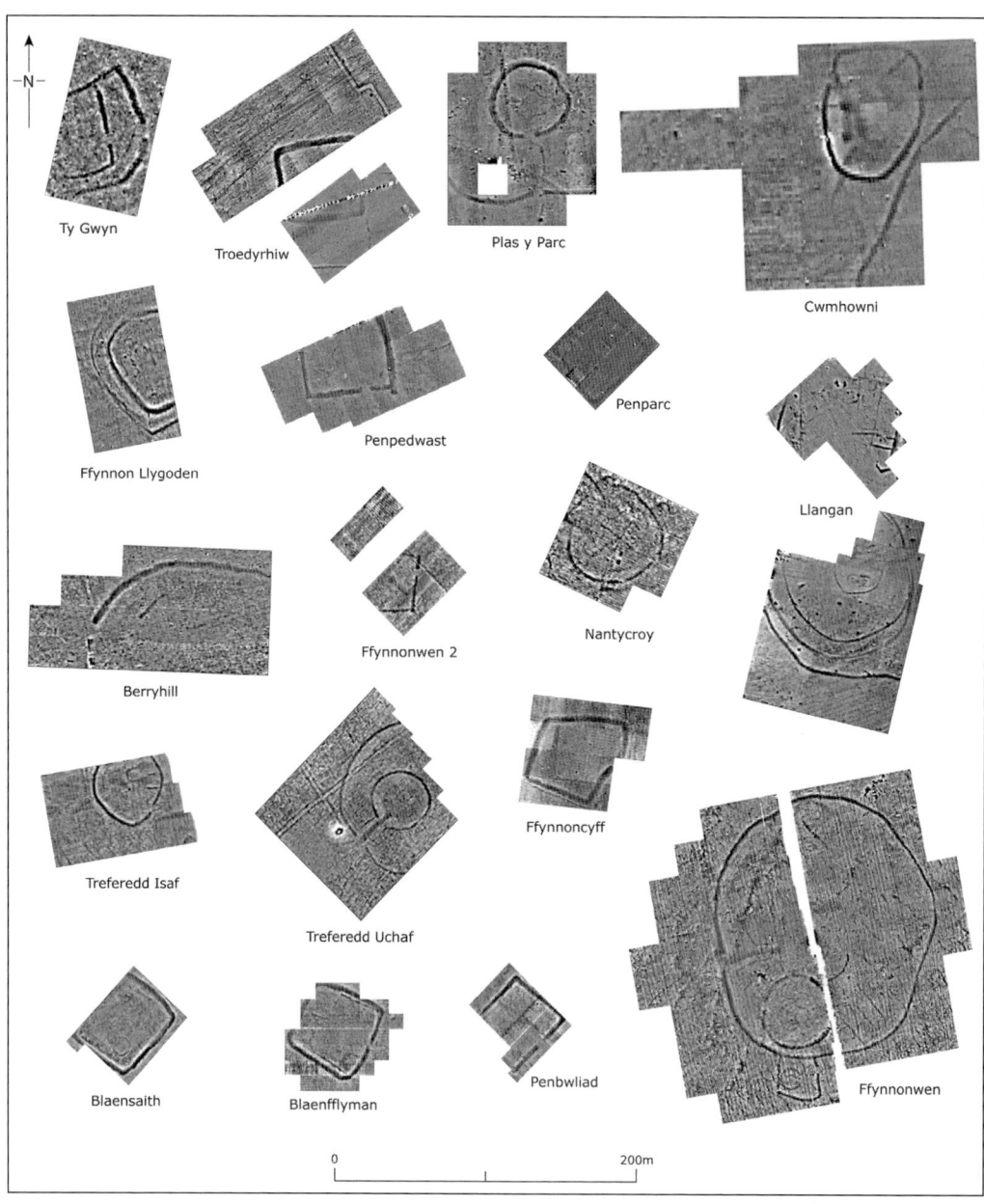

Figure 1.10. Seeing beneath the soil. An astonishing array of Iron Age and Romano-British defended farmsteads revealed during geophysical survey of known cropmark sites across south-west Wales. Llangan and Plas y Parc are in Carmarthenshire, and Penpedwast and Berryhill in Pembrokeshire. The remainder, from south Ceredigion, reveal the great hidden heritage of Cardigan Bay. Note the excavated Ceredigion enclosures at Ffynnonwen (bottom right) and Troedyrhiw (top, second from left). (Copyright Dyfed Archaeological Trust)

Airborne laser scanning and 3D imaging

Over the last decade another advanced survey technique has proved invaluable for archaeologists – LiDAR (Light Detection And Ranging). A specialized aircraft with a scanning laser device passes over the land collecting millions of points a second, building a 3D digital height model of the land surface, accurate to a few centimetres. Not only is the scan a valuable tool for archaeologists studying earthworks and other archaeological sites in fields or on hilltops, but through sophisticated digital filtering of the collected data the lasers can also 'see through' trees and undergrowth, revealing the previously obscured earthworks of heavily wooded hillforts and other archaeological features in stunning detail.

While LiDAR remains an expensive survey tool for archaeologists, recent developments in digital photogrammetry mean that anyone with a camera and appropriate software can now produce a 3D virtual model of a monument of their choosing. A 360⁰ array of photographs, taken either from the ground or from a drone, can be processed in a computer to build a rotatable 3D model using a process called 'structure from motion'. Even ten years ago this was unheard of. The pace of change is incredibly fast with new and cheaper ways of accurately surveying and recording archaeological sites becoming available almost every year.

What were Hillforts?

Typical hillforts were monumental enclosures defined or encircled by earth and stone banks, often with one or more external ditches, sited on hill summits or in strong and commanding positions. The gateways were often the most elaborate point, where ramparts and ditches were more massively built and at their most visually impressive. 'Promontory forts' were structurally similar but were sited so that the ramparts and ditches cut off coastal cliff promontories or inland ridges, allowing large areas to be defended with a minimum of effort.

The many 'defended farmsteads', built close to farming territory on coastal plains, hillslopes or valley bottoms, were usually less monumental and were mostly set in less commanding positions. That said, many quite small farmsteads were nevertheless ringed by impressive defences, as seen in the deep rock-cut ditches and quartz-walled entrance of the Troedyrhiw enclosure near Y Ferwig in south Ceredigion (Figure 4.11). In truth the distinction between a 'hillfort' and a 'defended farmstead' is often a fine one.

Hillforts and defended enclosures served a variety of functions. Few could be thought of as 'military' strongholds built for outright war. Many in mid and west Wales *looked* impressive from the front, but had few practical defences at their rears, suggesting that they could not have withstood a sustained military attack. Even if they served little purpose for conflict, impressive ramparts were tremendously effective as a 'show of strength' and as a display of wealth and power to all those who approached the fort, whether as friend, foe or stranger. Perishable elements which formed essential parts of the defensive system will by the present day have effectively vanished, including timber palisades formed of upright stakes, planks or tree trunks. Wattle fencing or even carefully managed hedges might also have played a quite effective part in ensuring that predators such as wolves (or even unfriendly raiders) were kept at a distance even where physical ramparts were slight.

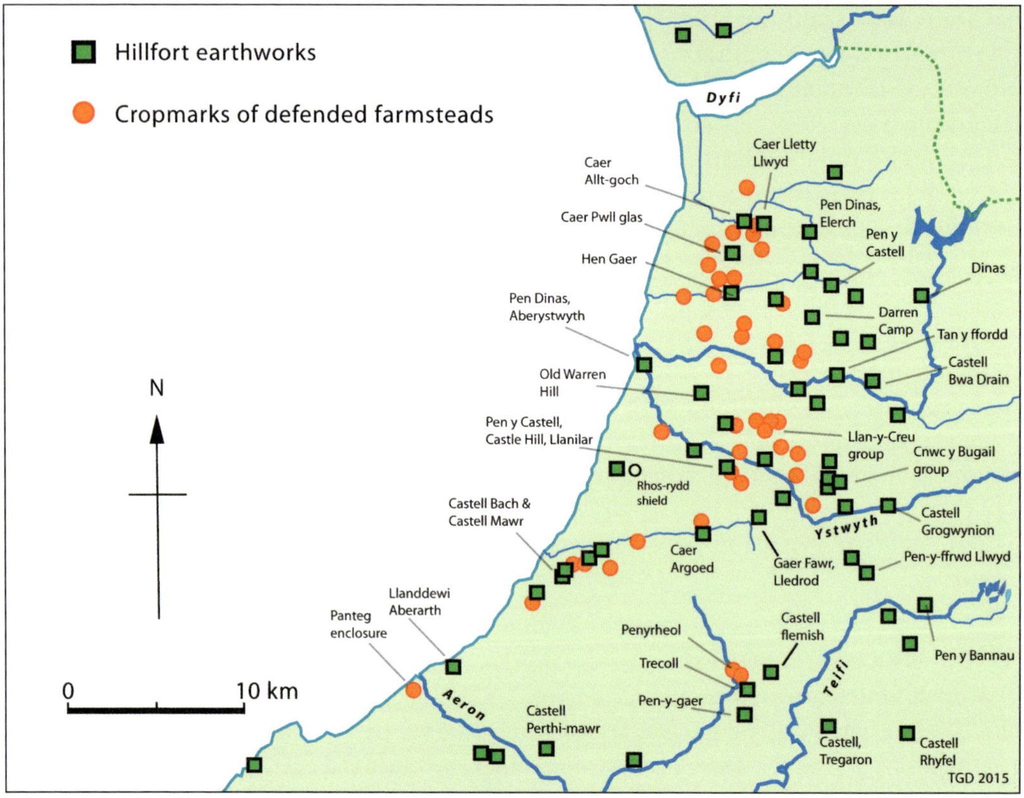

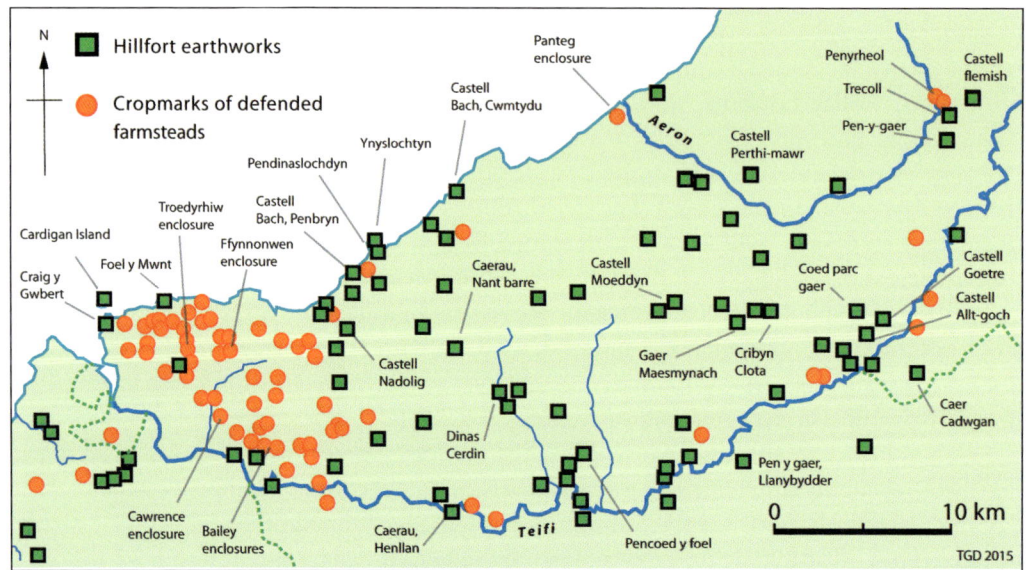

Figure 1.11. North Ceredigion. Key hillforts, defended farmsteads and prehistoric sites mentioned in the text.

Figure 1.12. South Ceredigion: key hillforts, defended farmsteads and other sites mentioned in the text. (T. Driver. Information from the Dyfed Archaeological Trust's Defended Enclosures Survey, with additions).

Place-names and prehistory

Welsh place-names are full of topographical and archaeological meaning. They can be useful when interpreting the name or landscape setting of a hillfort, or even when looking for as yet undiscovered sites in the countryside using only place-name evidence. A short list of some of the most common topographic or archaeological terms is given below:[14]

Allt	hillside or wood
Bach	small
Banc	mound, bank or hillock
Bannau	beacons
Bedd	grave
Braich	promontory
Bryn	hill
Bwlch	gap or pass
Caer	fort
Carn, Carneddau	cairn, cairns
Castell	castle
Cefn	ridges
Cerrig	stones
Clawdd	bank, hedge, ditch
Cnwch	small tump
Coch	red
Craig	rock or crag
Crug	mound, cairn
Du	black
Dinas	fort or camp (now 'city')
Disgwylfa	watching place
Esgair	mountain ridge
Foel (moel)	bare-topped hill
Hen	old
Llys	court or mansion
Mawr	large
Mwnt	mound or hill
Mynydd	mountain
Nant	stream or small valley
Pant	hollow or valley
Pen	head of, or top
Tan	below
Tomen	mound

The majority of sites were smaller defended family homesteads and working farms containing thatched roundhouses, raised granaries, a working yard, and other buildings serving as byres, stores, workshops or smithies. Some of the larger and more monumental hillforts are far beyond what a farming family would have been able to build; they may instead have served as the residences of Iron Age leaders and their extended clans and retainers, in effect local or regional centres of politics, power or trade. These centres of power no doubt controlled the surrounding land and resources as well as perhaps 'governing' the farming communities living in the smaller settlements. In return for stable political control, with rival clans hopefully kept at bay, the occupants of the smaller farms would probably have been required to pay tribute to the chieftain in the form of food, farm produce, workmen or indeed young warriors, fulfilling 'debts of obligation' or labour whenever required.

Many larger forts, such as Pen Dinas at Aberystwyth, had secure annexes or 'terraces' outside the main gates or sheltered within ramparts set back some distance from the innermost defence. These were probably used as safe grazing for livestock, and on occasions as places for markets or fairs, reinforcing the role of the hillfort as a regional centre of power and trade. In this scenario visiting traders and strangers would have been able to exchange news and greetings, and to buy and sell (or more likely barter and exchange) foodstuffs and other goods without necessarily being permitted to enter the inner spaces of the hillfort proper.

Interpreting hillfort earthworks: then and now

Figure 1.13. Modern-day earthworks give only a general impression of how an Iron Age hillfort looked in its heyday. But there are clues to indicate what is buried beneath the present surface. (A) **Main gateway**. The entrance may now appear as no more than a hollow way, worn through centuries of use but now partially refilled by erosion. A particularly deep hollow way between high rampart terminals may indicate the former existence of an entrance passage crossed by a timber bridge or even a gate tower. (B) **Facing walls of stone** ('revetments') may be exposed through the turf that has been eroded by the actions of livestock. Stonework at the main gateway may be more impressive, and of a better build than elsewhere around the hillfort. (C) **Ditch and counterscarp bank**. The 'counterscarp' bank, on the outer lip of the ditch, was formed by the frequent clearing of the ditch deposits but sometimes became (or was originally made as) a defensive feature in its own right. (D) **Quarry pits.** These can be seen at several Ceredigion hillforts; they show where soil and stone were excavated and then thrown forward to form the defensive rampart. (E) **House platforms** cut into the hillslope to provide a level platforms for roundhouses or other buildings. (F) **Iron Age roundhouse.** (G) **'Four-poster'** with a raised floor for the storage of grain and other foodstuffs away from damp and rodents. **(H) Earthfast boulders and rocky outcrops** may once have formed integral features of the interior in Iron Age times. (I) **Plough ridges** are often found within long-deserted hillforts. Irregular or sinuous ridges may indicate medieval ploughing while straighter ridges may result from steam-powered or tractor cultivation in the 19th or 20th centuries.

Figure 1.14. The rock-cut base of one of the roundhouse platforms excavated in 1936 within the south fort at Pen Dinas, Aberystwyth. The roundhouse would have measured 9.75m across at its maximum extent, with a curving 'gully' at the rear of the platform, either for drainage or to hold an upright wall of planks, posts or wattle-and-daub. The positions of structural posts are marked by ranging poles held upright by the excavation team. This building stood on the more sheltered eastern slopes of the hillfort; its site can still be seen there today. (Pen Dinas excavation archive, National Monuments Record of Wales, DI2015_0404)

Figure 1.15. Centre of ceremony? Castell Nadolig hillfort, Penbryn, not far from the south Ceredigion coastline, has concentric ramparts that now merge with the more regular field patterns of the present day. There is evidence that the site may have been used as a centre for cult activities and burial during the Iron Age, as further described in Chapter 5. (Crown Copyright RCAHMW, AP_2012_4297)

A handful of other defended enclosures, often in unusual or exceptional topographic settings, may have served different functions, such as the seasonal corralling of stock. Others could perhaps have been ceremonial enclosures reserved for seasonal festivals, rituals or even burial. Only excavation (perhaps on a substantial scale) could provide support for such functions, perhaps by identifying a lack of normal domestic structures and debris or a prevalence, instead, of burials or ritual deposits.

One good example may be provided by Castell Rhyfel, high in the hills above Tregaron. This unusual site occupies a remote hill summit with a prominent spring head but has minimal defences and no sign of houses or other structures in its interior. Perhaps it was a meeting place or sacred enclosure rather than a permanent settlement? Castell Nadolig, near Penbryn in coastal south Ceredigion, also encloses a spring and has produced unusual finds including a pair of 'divination spoons' as well as possibly Iron Age cremation burials. Was it perhaps a sacred enclosure and cemetery rather than a regularly occupied hillfort? Or could domestic and ceremonial roles perhaps have co-existed alongside one another at such a settlement? The location of shrines and temples at the highest points within the great hillforts at Danebury in Hampshire and at Cadbury Castle in Somerset, suggests that this could have been so. Unusual coastal forts such as Castell Bach at Cwmtydu or the Ynyslochtyn promontory fort at Llangrannog, sited in exposed and seemingly dangerous locations, may not have been functional settlements at all. Maybe they were reserved for ceremonies or sacrifice at the spiritual interface between land and sea?

When were Hillforts?

Our dating of Ceredigion hillforts and defended farmsteads has improved considerably in the last decade as a result of new excavation projects and research. Some settlements can be dated, in broad terms, by comparison with similar sites that have a known date range. Others may produce material objects that can be dated on stylistic grounds – distinctive pottery or decorated metalwork, for instance – but such finds are extremely rare in Wales. Nowadays the most secure form of dating comes from the radiocarbon analysis of charcoal, bone or other organic materials found in layers or features which can be directly related to the structural history of the site being explored. Even radiocarbon dating, however, leaves a fair degree of uncertainty, giving no more than a *probable* date range, often with several decades of uncertainty at either end.

To complicate matters even further a settlement may have gone through several phases of development, modification or reoccupation before its final desertion; over this time datable material from an early phase might well have found its way into a later deposit, or vice versa. Without large-scale excavation, as seen at Castell Henllys in Pembrokeshire (see Chapter 4), it is often difficult to collect radiocarbon samples that can be securely linked to structural features or occupation deposits so as to create a clear picture of how many times the settlement was modified or rebuilt, and over what range of time in the past.

Iron Age hillforts and defended farms are among the most visible prehistoric monuments to survive in Wales from the ten centuries or so leading up to the Roman conquest. Early settlements from around 1150-800 BC, in the later Bronze Age, are known from north and east Wales, notable examples being the great hilltop forts of the Breiddin near Welshpool and Llwyn Bryn Dinas in the Tanat Valley. Excavation evidence from hillforts near Lampeter in the central Teifi valley, including Bryn Maen Caerau, along with recently excavated defended enclosures in lowland south Ceredigion and north Pembrokeshire, has suggested initial construction activity in the Late Bronze Age or very early Iron Age.

Most hillforts in Wales date from sometime in the range between about 800 BC and 50 AD. Those of the early Iron Age, built before about 400 BC, were often large and relatively simple enclosures with a single rampart or defensive palisade. As the population grew and society became more complex during the middle and later Iron Age, from about 400 BC to the Roman conquest, so hillfort defences and gateways became progressively more sophisticated and deliberately impressive. Many smaller hillforts and defended settlements flourished in the later parts of the Iron Age and in some cases well into Romano-British times. Even small defended farmsteads with space for only two or three roundhouses sometimes boasted massively ostentatious defences and gateways, no doubt intended to proclaim the wealth and social standing of the occupants within.

Darren Camp in the north of Ceredigion can serve as an instructive example. This strong hilltop fort still displays great banks and ditches facing west towards the sea but the defences around the eastern side are far less strong. Excavations by the Early Mines Research Group in 2005 (Figures 4.12 and 4.16)[15] obtained radiocarbon dates from close to the western entrance which showed that construction of the main rampart took place

Figure 1.16. Reconstructed roundhouses at Castell Henllys, Pembrokeshire.
The raw materials for the Iron Age versions of these large and sturdily built structures must have been drawn from a wide area, requiring careful management of woodland resources as well as access to wetlands for thatch. The reconstructions teach us much about the original abilities of the hillfort's Iron Age occupants and craftsmen. (Iain Wright; Crown Copyright RCAHMW, DS2012_068_002)

between about 400 and 190 BC. The rubble core of a second bank, overlying this first phase, produced dates in the range 380 to 80 BC. The construction of the hillfort is thus firmly dated to the Middle to Late Iron Age, between 400 and 100 years before the Roman conquest of Wales. A similar dating applies to the construction of the six-post gateway at Caer Cadwgan near Lampeter. No doubt the construction and occupation of many other hillforts and enclosed farmsteads would fall broadly within this range. The more extensively excavated hilltop settlement at Castell Henllys in north Pembrokeshire was found to have begun life in around 370 BC, then fallen into disrepair between about 150 BC and the end of the millennium before being briefly refurbished and partially reoccupied in late Roman or post-Roman times.[16]

Ffynnonwen farmstead, a great circular enclosure near Tremain in south Ceredigion with several internal roundhouses, was excavated in August 2006 and is illustrated in Figures 1.5 and 1.10. Radiocarbon dates indicated the early construction of a palisaded settlement some time between the 8th and 4th centuries BC, in the Early to Middle Iron Age. Between the 4th and 2nd centuries BC the palisade was replaced by a more substantial enclosure with a bank and ditch encircling the roundhouses. Occupation in roundhouses continued through the 1st century BC and into the 2nd century AD, spanning Late Iron Age to Romano-British times.[17]

During Romano-British times, until Roman control of Britain began to wane in the later 4th century AD, occupants of many traditional hillforts and farmsteads adopted elements of Roman life, including the use of coinage and fine – as well as – utilitarian pottery. Excavations in 2014 at the Penyrheol defended enclosure south of Bronnant, a typical defended enclosure with at least one internal roundhouse, produced two sherds of 1st-century AD Roman

Figure: 1.17. A mountain fortress. The hillfort known as Pen Dinas at Elerch in the north of the county (SN 677 876) is set high on the eastern edge of an upland plateau. The fort shares its distinctive and prominent gateway bastion (on the right-hand slope of hill) with a similar feature at Castell Grogwynion, in the Ystwyth valley near Pontrhydygroes (see Figures 4.20 and 4.21). The fort at Elerch is approached from the south by way of a natural rock causeway (right) and is bounded on the west by a bog, seen here in the foreground. (T. Driver)

amphora, a type of imported storage vessel perhaps originally containing wine or oil. This came from the uppermost fill of the inner enclosure ditch, which must therefore have been largely filled-in by this stage. In addition a sherd of possible Severn Valley Ware, from the 2nd-4th centuries AD, was discovered in the circular gully of a roundhouse in the interior.[18]

In the coastal farmland of south Ceredigion a scatter of square and rectangular enclosures betrays Roman influence in the construction of local defended farms (Figure 6.5). The Troedyrhiw rectangular defended farmstead, near Y Ferwig, Cardigan, was constructed in the Late Iron Age, with occupation continuing into Romano-British times. The only known Romano-British villa in Ceredigion, showing the true adoption of the Roman way of life by a wealthy local owner, was first discovered from the air at Abermagwr in 2006. It has subsequently been shown by excavation to have begun life in around 230 AD before falling out of use about a hundred years later. It is described more fully in Chapter 6.

Post-Roman hillforts?

An intriguing question, which we cannot yet answer with certainty, is the degree to which hillforts and defended farms continued in occupation in post-Roman times, during the Early Medieval or Early Christian period – often referred to in the past as the Dark Ages. The Abermagwr Roman villa, as noted above, was abandoned in around 330 AD. From

Figure 1.18. The Glan Fred cropmark enclosure near Llandre in north Ceredigion has always looked like a typical Iron Age promontory fort, ever since its discovery from the air during the summer drought of 1975. However, excavations in 2013 confirmed post-Roman dates for one of the infilled ditches and for industrial activity within the interior, raising questions about whether any part of the enclosure dates from prehistoric times. Compare this aerial shot with the ground-based view in Figure 1.8. (Crown Copyright RCAHMW, DI2005_0263)

that time until the arrival of the Normans over 700 years later, very little is known about the homes and daily lives of the inhabitants of west Wales. The unexpected discovery of an Early Medieval cemetery at Plas Gogerddan, south of Bow Street, during excavations in 1986 yielded a single radiocarbon date centred on 370 AD, showing an active late Roman or early post-Roman population in the region. A decorated stone typical of the 9th to 10th centuries, from Cribyn near Lampeter, may originally have stood within the hillfort at Cribyn Gaer (also known as Caer Maesmynach or 'place of the monks' (SN 520 509)). If that were so it might indicate Early Medieval re-use of this large fort. The stone now stands in the porch of Llanilar church.

In 2013 a team from Archaeology Wales under the direction of Iestyn Jones carried out small-scale excavations, as part of the S4C archaeology series *Olion*, at what appeared to be an Iron Age cropmark enclosure called Glan Fred, near Llandre in north Ceredigion (Figure 1.18). The site was chosen for investigation as a small plough-levelled promontory fort. The enclosure ditches were located and sectioned, and rare evidence for industrial activity was discovered from the interior in the form of slag from iron smelting. Only during the post-excavation phase did signs of something very unusual emerge. Charcoal from the iron smelting debris was radiocarbon dated to 688-889 AD, more than two centuries after the Roman abandonment of Britain. In addition, grain samples from one of the lower ditch deposits turned up early post-Roman dates of 418-564 AD. This unassuming site has thus produced quite unexpected dates, raising the potential for post-Roman re-occupation or initial construction of other sites in this part of Ceredigion. It also shows evidence for pre-Roman building traditions surviving on the coastal fringes of Cardigan Bay, possibly linked to the nearby discovery of a timber trackway and smelting evidence at Llangynfelyn to the north.[19]

Chapter 2

BEFORE THE HILLFORTS

Chapter frontispiece: The Llanilar Urn, on display in Amgueddfa Ceredigion Museum, is over 4,000 years old and was discovered during building work at Gwarfelin, close to the modern village. The urn contained the cremated bones of an adolescent, a child and a piglet's foot. It stands nearly 34cms high, is elaborately decorated and would have been extremely fragile even when new. (T. Driver. By kind permission Amgueddfa Ceredigion Museum)

Homeland: from hunter gatherers to the Neolithic farming 'revolution'

Humans have long valued ideas of territory, property, permanence and protection. Such concepts appear to have originated at least 3,000 years before the Iron Age, and in Wales would have followed the Neolithic farming 'revolution' in about 4500 to 4000 BC). Around this time the nomadic hunter-gatherers of post-glacial Europe gradually began to adopt more settled patterns of life, discovering animal husbandry and the cultivation of crops. The life of a hunter-gatherer during the Mesolithic, or Middle Stone Age, was mobile, tracking herds of wild animals and occupying semi-permanent summer and winter camps in rotation. Surface finds of flint implements from Mesolithic times, between about 10000 and 4500 BC, are common in the ploughed fields of Ceredigion, not only on the coastal cliffs of Cardigan Bay but also inland where former valley wetlands frequented by hunters have now become cultivated fields. Excavations on a rocky outcrop overlooking Aberystwyth Harbour in 1922 uncovered a flint-working floor which produced scores of worked flints of this type. Around 9,000 to 7,000 years ago this coastal settlement would have looked out across a broad and heavily wooded plain to the west, before rising sea levels stabilised during the Bronze Age to create the present day outline of Cardigan Bay. The farming 'revolution' was not sudden. Excavations at British Mesolithic hunter camps such as Starr Carr in North Yorkshire have shown that later Mesolithic communities, in this case dated to about 6700 BC, could be semi-permanent. The Starr Carr settlement included a brushwood platform on the edge of a lake as well as several hearths. Some Mesolithic communities had begun to master the domestication of animals as well as experimenting with the small-scale cultivation of crops. At South Street in Wiltshire, a ploughed-out early Neolithic long barrow had once sealed far earlier plough marks made by a wooden 'ard', showing that local people were ploughing well before the great monuments of the early Neolithic farmers were constructed.

In contrast to hunter-gatherers, farmers make a long-term investment in their territory. Wild land was cleared of trees and undergrowth, gradually removing the subsistence base of the hunter-gatherers with whom the farmers may have co-existed. Once people had begun to demarcate and divide the wild land, and territories were extended through exchange, inheritance, conquest and expansion, there would have been little room left for the old ways of life.

Harvesting crops can generate a surplus of food which needs to be suitably stored for the year ahead, requiring a place of permanent and protected storage away from damp and rodents. If livestock is bred it has to be reared, enclosed and controlled. As livestock multiply, they acquire value and create wealth for the owner. All these changes in the farming 'revolution' required land to be owned and populated with buildings and settled homes, and for territory to be demarcated by walls, hedges, fences or other barriers. A consequence of this sedentary lifestyle, with 'slack' periods in the farming year between planting and harvesting, was that communities could develop new crafts which included pottery production, weaving and the sourcing and production of stone tools. Ideas of design and building traditions soon followed. Being tied to land over generations would only have strengthened concepts such as 'ancestry' and a connection to the 'homeland' of the family and community.

Lost monuments from Ceredigion's Neolithic past

> On a common near Blaynport [present-day Blaenporth], lie a great many large stones; among the rest, one standing perpendicularly on one end in the ground, and another large one leaning on it ... these stones they call King Arthur's quoits.[1]

Ceredigion does not have any surviving Neolithic burial monuments to rival the great dolmens, or cromlechs, of Pembrokeshire, Gwynedd and Anglesey. One possible element of such a tomb, however, can be found in the Garreg Fawr stone slab, mounted on a plinth in Llanbadarn Fawr square and reputed to have once stood on four 'legs' or upright stones during the 19th century before being fractured by fire. Following this damage it was reassembled and mounted in its present position (Figure 2.1). Although opinions vary about its age and origins, many still hold to its having been the capstone of a now-vanished chambered tomb, albeit much altered. Topographically the tomb seems to have occupied a river valley backed by rising ground, looking out over a lowland expanse to the south-west, now the present village of Llanbadarn Fawr. A similar burial site was chosen for the Early Bronze Age urn burial unearthed at Penllwyn Chapel, Capel Bangor (described below).

In looking at the evidence for lost, destroyed or reputed Neolithic chambered tombs in the county, it seems that landowners of past centuries were grimly efficient in breaking up what remained of Ceredigion's Neolithic burial monuments.[2] However, a good collection

Figure 2.1: Y Garreg Fawr, Llanbadarn Fawr, Aberystwyth. The flat stone slab mounted on a plinth in the village square is thought to have been part of a Neolithic tomb, although it is much altered today. A plaque below the slab states 'This ancient structure belongs to the Powells of Nanteos as lords of the manor of Llanbadarnfawr'.
(T. Driver)

Figure 2.2. Closer to the gods. Moel y Llyn cairn, on high moorland east of Talybont, (SN 712 916), is one of four stone cairns surrounding a tiny upland lake. Here, it looks out across Cardigan Bay on a clear winter's day. The Early Bronze Age cairn is the low and rounded mound beneath the modern stone cairn and would originally have contained one or more burials in a stone-lined cist. Many upland cairns were explored by early antiquarians and treasure seekers, but some remain relatively undisturbed. (T. Driver)

of polished stone axe finds attests to settlement activity and woodland clearance during this period. Excavated and dated evidence, including a Neolithic pit at Plas Gogerddan near Bow Street, along with sherds of Neolithic 'Peterborough Ware' pottery from a disturbed settlement site at Llanilar, and settlement evidence from excavations before the building of an industrial estate near Llandysul, show that the fertile valleys of the Ystwyth and Teifi attracted early farming settlers.

Metals, monuments and magic: the Bronze Age background

It is possible that Ceredigion was a special place in Bronze Age times. The county is home to some exceptional sites and chance finds from the two millennia before the Iron Age, showing that there was an expanding farming population accruing personal and community wealth along Cardigan Bay from at least the Early Bronze Age, around 2500-1500 BC.[3] Cardigan Bay does have a handful of stone circles in the uplands, including a good example below Moel y Llyn (SN 699 911) in the hills above Talybont. However, the stones are usually so small that they are difficult to spot in tussocky upland grassland. By contrast a series of large stones built into the circular churchyard wall at Ysbyty Cynfyn, north of Devils Bridge, have been interpreted by some to be the remnants of a stone circle; it seems more likely, however, that only a single earthfast standing stone, a huge monolith on the north-east side of the churchyard, is of probable Bronze Age date.

There are many well-preserved upland cairns – some bounded by upright stone 'kerbs' that make them look like miniature stone circles, as at Hirnant north of Ponterwyd (SN 753 839) and Dolgamfa (SN 745 792) east of Ystumtuen) – impressive enough when encountered on a hill walk. Several major Neolithic and Early Bronze Age monument complexes are known but these are almost all plough-levelled, and so invisible in the landscape. They have mostly been discovered through aerial photography and excavation, particularly along the coastal valleys of the Ystwyth and the Rheidol in north Ceredigion. A great complex of cropmark 'ring-ditches' at Pant y Peran on the south side of Llandre (SN 626 861) in the north of the county, for example, represents five large plough-levelled burial mounds sited on a flat valley terrace which must have been a significant place for ceremony and burial over four millennia ago. There is little to match the scale of this site elsewhere along the coastal lowlands of Cardigan Bay.

After about 2200 BC burial rites changed from the interment of complete skeletons or cremations in stone-lined cists, to consist instead of the burial of cremated remains in large pottery urns. Examples from the Cardigan Bay region, including urns from Llanilar and from Penllwyn Chapel at Capel Bangor, are among the largest and most spectacular in Wales. The Penllwyn 'encrusted' urn was revealed during grave digging behind the chapel in 1926 (Figure 2.4). Rather than originating from a hill-top burial, the urn was evidently laid to rest just a few metres above the valley floor on a hillslope.

A further important group of burials was excavated at Gwarfelin, Llanilar, following accidental discovery of a near-complete pottery urn in a builder's trench in 1980.[4] One of the most impressive vessels, an 'Enlarged Food Vessel', was discovered almost complete, placed standing upside down on a flat stone. Today this urn stands in a display cabinet in Ceredigion Museum; it is easy to pass it by, but think back over 4,000 years to when this urn was an important symbol of death and commemoration to the community who made it. Its manufacture would have required the hand of a skilled potter with knowledge of wider prevailing traditions in pottery decoration and symbolism, yet it was almost certainly too fragile once fired to have been carried any great distance. Analysis of the fragments of cremated bone from inside the urn revealed the human story behind the burial. Two individuals, approximately 7 and 14 years old, were represented by the single deposit which also included nine fragments of bone from the foot of a young pig. One can only guess

Figure 2.3. Resting place of the Early Bronze Age dead. A well preserved stone cist within a cairn on the slopes below Castell Rhyfel hillfort, in the Groes Fawr valley (SN 727 598) east of Tregaron. A dry-walled shelter of relatively recent date has been erected around the cist (T. Driver).

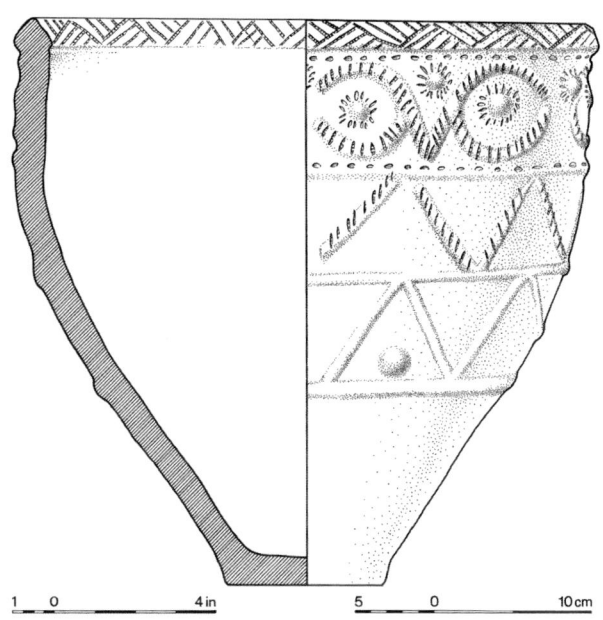

Figure 2.4. The elaborate encrusted urn from Penllwyn Chapel, Capel Bangor, found by chance during grave digging, is one of the finest known from Wales. (Crown Copyright RCAHMW, DI2015_0378.)

1   0   4 in   5   0   10 cm

at the story which lay behind the burial of a young person and a child from a Bronze Age community that once lived somewhere near Llanilar.

Unexpected discoveries continue to come to light. In 2009-10 the excavation of a pair of Early Bronze Age barrows at Pant y Butler, a short distance east of Cardigan, yielded a rare jet necklace[5] consisting of 72 disc-beads and a triangular fastener. These were accompanied by the cremated remains of a young adult or adolescent between 13 and 21 years old, with an associated radiocarbon date of 2180-1950 BC. Jet in Early Bronze Age Britain was derived almost exclusively from the Whitby area in north Yorkshire, meaning that this particular item of jewellery – or the raw material to make it – had travelled by one means or another all the way from there to the west coast of Wales.

Although one cannot be certain, it is possible that north Ceredigion's great mineral wealth was responsible for a local blossoming of innovation and expertise during the Early Bronze Age. The remains of Bronze Age mines in the northern hills of the county are among the earliest in the British Isles. Initial discoveries by the Early Mines Research Group (EMRG) in the early 1990s at the Comet Lode Opencast at Copa Hill (SN 812 752), Cwmystwyth, identified Bronze Age exploitation of mineral ores on a seasonal basis. Other early mines have since been confirmed throughout the north of the county from Twyll y Mwyn (SN 681 833) near Banc-y-Darren to Erglodd (SN 657 904) at Talybont, and further north towards Machynlleth. Simon Timberlake, who has studied and excavated many of these sites with members of the Group, thinks that the Bronze Age farmers worked the mines on a seasonal basis, collecting hammer-stones in the form of large cobbles from the county's beaches before travelling inland to mine the hills. These cobbles were hafted with wooden handles and used to break up ore or smash away the rock. The knowledge acquired in finding metal ores in the hills, and transforming the raw material into finished artefacts through the use of fire and furnaces, was a striking and powerful innovation, likened to the future alchemist's art by Steve Burrow.[6] If these communities were devel-

Figure 2.5. The Banc Tynddol sun disc, photographed shortly after excavation. This is the oldest worked object of gold from Wales.[7] It measures 3.8cms in diameter and weighs 2.5 grams. Only eleven similar discs are known from mainland Britain. (By kind permission of Simon Timberlake)

oping knowledge, expertise and wealth in their regional mining endeavours, perhaps they were also responsible for some of the large burial complexes in the coastal valleys, described above.

The landscapes in which these early metal ores were won clearly seemed significant to prehistoric communities. The hills and moors are dotted with standing stones and burial cairns, but remains of one of the most important burials was discovered in October 2002 at the very foot of Copa Hill's Bronze Age mine. During the excavation of a Roman and early medieval smelting site, on a knoll above the valley floor, archaeologists from the EMRG unearthed a brilliant gold 'sun disc', illustrated in Figure 2.5.[8] Further excavation showed that this came from the site of a shallow Bronze Age grave, disturbed by the later industrial activity. The tiny perforated disc dates to around 2400 BC and is the earliest known evidence for gold being worn as an ornament in Wales. Most sun-discs have been found in Ireland (21) with only 11 known from Scotland and England; the Banc Tynddol disc is the first example from Wales. Metallurgical analysis showed it was composed of 93.5% gold and 6.5% silver, a mix consistent with the use of Irish, Scottish or Welsh alluvial gold. To unearth such a rare and special find at the foot of a hill where Bronze Age mining was just beginning in Britain suggests that the Cwmystwyth valley might have been an important through-route for travellers to and from Cardigan Bay, eastern Wales and perhaps beyond. With these travellers came ideas, inspiration and innovation to enliven and fundamentally change the lives of those living in mid Wales.

Of weapons and walls; changes in the late Bronze Age, 1150-800 BC

The later Bronze Age was a time of considerable change. Burial evidence, previously visible and widespread, became virtually absent. In much of Britain settlement evidence, ephemeral and largely invisible during the Neolithic and Earlier Bronze Ages, became monumental and widespread. Weaponry, hitherto limited to bows and arrows, and heavy tools such as axes and maces which could have been used equally well for farming or for combat, also began to change. After about 2000 BC specialized weapons appear.

Figure 2.6. The two standing stones known as Buwch a'r Llo ('cow and calf') – with a third close by – lie close to the mountain road from Pendam to Ponterwyd in north Ceredigion (SN 723 833). They form part of a loose chain of standing stones which stretch from the coastal plain near Penrhyncoch to the high ground of the Cambrian Mountains. They can be interpreted as the remains of a waymarked Bronze Age trading route. (T. Driver)

Daggers, which could have functioned as effective hand weapons, either with or without long handles, originated first as exquisite flint examples and then developed through early copper types into tougher bronze examples with the addition of tin. Between about 2200 and 1450 BC 'flat axes' of copper make an appearance, the product of casting in one-sided moulds. Several of these are known from Ceredigion; some may have been casual losses although an axe found near Rhydypennau river, the 'Ford of the Heads', may originate from a burial or votive deposit. Weaponry and metal technology developed through the Middle Bronze Age, from around 1450 to 1150 BC, with new forms including 'palstave' axes, which had a built-in flange for hafting onto a handle, as well as spearheads and halberds – a sort of tomahawk. These new types could be both deadly weapons and symbols of the wealth and power of whoever possessed them.

Elsewhere in Wales great hoards of metalwork and weaponry are known from this period, perhaps ostentatiously deposited or disposed of in public ceremonies by leaders keen to show the extent of their wealth. Undoubtedly one of the most splendid prehistoric finds from the entire sweep of Cardigan Bay is the Rhos Rydd Late Bronze Age shield, rightly described as the most exciting piece of metalwork from the county both 'technically and aesthetically, and as a potential indicator of social and political conditions …'.[9] The shield is more fully described in Chapter 5.

Along with the rise in metal technologies, strong defended settlements and early hill-forts emerge in the landscape, serving as the protected homes and villages of a growing elite. Great planned field systems are also evident for the first time, extending beyond the needs of single farming families. The most famous examples are on Dartmoor where the 'reaves'

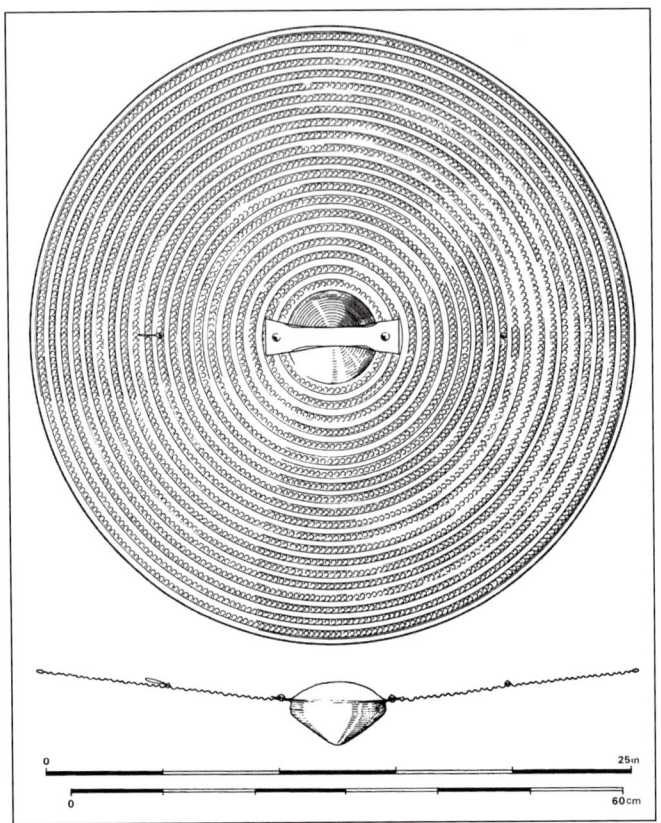

Figure 2.7. Drawing of the remarkable Rhos Rydd Late Bronze Age shield found near Blaenplwyf, north Ceredigion. This is undoubtedly one of the finest prehistoric finds from the Cardigan Bay region (compare with Figure 5.4). (Crown Copyright RCAHMW, DI2015_0379, CCH.01.01.34.)

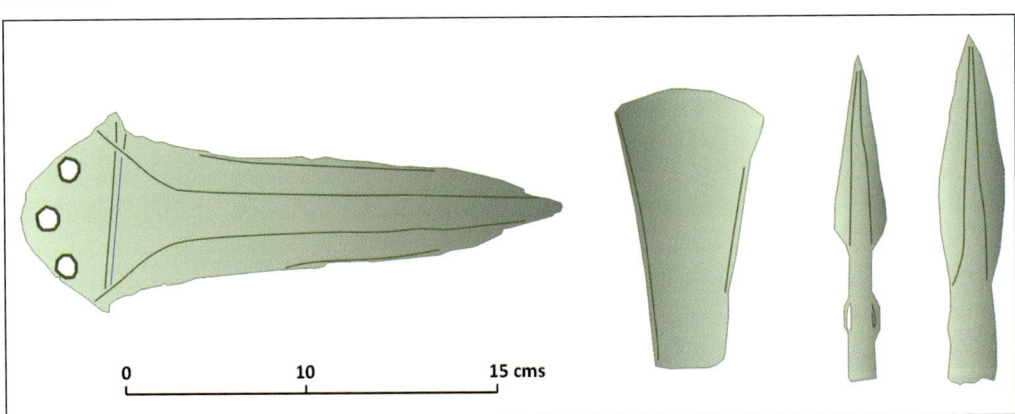

Figure 2.8. Bronze Age weapons from Ceredigion, dating from about 2200 to 1500 BC.
From left to right: halberd 'found near a copper mine' from Ysbyty Ystwyth, Pontrhydygroes;
flat axe from Rhydypennau, near Bow Street; spearheads from near Aber-meurig, Trefilan, and
from Carn Saith Wraig, west of Soar-y-Mynydd. Halberds, a common type of weapon found
across Bronze Age Wales, could be hafted on short handles and used like tomahawks for hand
to hand combat. Whilst flat axes were no doubt functional tools, they may have also had a
votive significance or signified the wealth of their owner.
(Drawing after Cardiganshire County History 1994, Figure 24)

– a system of long parallel fields – stretched for tens of miles to tame or subdivide the open moorland in an apparently planned enterprise of a ruling elite.[10] Similar late Bronze Age 'co-axial' field systems are known in Pembrokeshire, on St Davids Head and Skomer Island; others may have been removed by later cultivation elsewhere in mid and west Wales.

What brought about this dramatic change in settlement and landscape planning? It is thought by many that widespread climatic deterioration after about 1150 BC caused the uplands to become increasingly wet, with acid bogs expanding to engulf formerly productive farmland. This may have forced communities from central Wales to abandon long-established settlements in the uplands and migrate down to the more fertile valleys of the eastern Borderlands or the coastal valleys of west Wales. A consequence of this population movement, away from Bronze Age hill settlements, would have been increased pressure and competition for agricultural land at lower altitudes. New families may have imposed themselves upon established lowland territories and there would have been the need to assert the strength and power of the family, clan or lineage through the construction of more substantial settlements and the clearer demarcation of the fertile lowland by the establishment of organised field systems.

Excavations along the Welsh Borderland have provided a good picture of the early hillforts of the Later Bronze Age which began to dominate the border region at this time. Early hillforts – sometimes with timber-reinforced stone ramparts – include the Breiddin near Welshpool and Llwyn Bryn Dinas in the Tanat Valley, both of them founded in about the 9th to 8th centuries BC.

There is growing evidence for early hillforts being constructed on Cardigan Bay and along the inland valleys of Ceredigion, although far fewer sites in this region have been the focus of modern excavations. As mentioned above, early radiocarbon dates of 1210-810 BC were obtained from an isolated posthole within Pendinaslochdyn fort when it was excavated in the early 1990s, providing tentative evidence for late Bronze Age occupation on this

Figure 2.9. Pendinaslochdyn coastal fort, Llangrannog, seen from Sarnau village. This prominent coastal hill may have been originally fortified, or settled, in the Late Bronze Age. Excavations in the early 1990s produced radiocarbon dates of 1210-810 BC from a single isolated posthole within the hilltop fort. (T. Driver)

prominent coastal hill. Archaeological work in the 1980s in Cellan parish, along the Teifi valley east of Lampeter, examined two hillforts which produced Late Bronze and Early Iron Age dates. Bryn Maen Caerau is a defended enclosure sited on the valley floor and now infilled with housing. The palisaded defences were associated with an occupation layer radiocarbon dated to 830-393 BC. Other potential early hillforts in the north of the county include one at Lluest y Trafle near Llyn Craigypistyll (Figure 2.10), and another at Castell Rhyfel near Tregaron (Chapter 7), both of them enclosing high-domed summits in the hill fringe with fairly rudimentary – apparently early – defences. Perhaps both of these early 'forts' are in fact unusual Late Bronze Age defended enclosures or communal meeting places, sited high in the hills overlooking Cardigan Bay?

Recent excavations on plough-levelled cropmark sites in south Ceredigion and north Pembrokeshire have demonstrated a trend towards Late Bronze or Early Iron Age origins for defended farmsteads, many of which may have continued in occupation through the Late Iron Age or even into Romano-British times.[11] Excavations in 2006 at the Ffynnonwen defended enclosure in south Ceredigion, for instance, revealed a narrow gully, possibly a foundation trench for an upright palisade of timber posts from an early enclosure, along with associated radiocarbon dates of 740-650 BC and a glass bead tentatively dated to the 8th-6th centuries BC (Figure 3.11). In north Pembrokeshire, radiocarbon dates from excavations in 2007 at the inland promontory fort of Berryhill, near Newport, indicated Late Bronze Age construction in about the 10th to 8th centuries BC.

Here the old ways of the Bronze Age are left behind and an exploration of the Iron Age begins.

Figure 2.10. Lluest y Trafle hillfort (SN 703 849) occupies a bare summit on private land in hills to the east of Bontgoch in north Ceredigion. It was first mentioned by Lewis Morris on his manuscript map of the 'mannor of Perveth', drawn in about 1745. The denuded ramparts on the summit are quite eroded although in this photograph they are thrown into clear relief by the combination of low winter sunlight and a thin covering of snow. The earthworks appear rather different from those of Iron Age hillforts in this part of the county, suggesting that the defended settlement may date from the Late Bronze Age. It occupies a very remote setting, which also suggests that it may have been built during the better climatic conditions which prevailed in the period before the Iron Age. (T. Driver)

Chapter 3

Land and Life in Iron Age Ceredigion

Chapter frontispiece: Ancient homes revealed beneath a farmer's field.
Excavations at Ffynnonwen, south Ceredigion, in 2006 uncovered the footings
of three roundhouses. This view looks across to the largest excavated roundhouse.
It has a narrow wall-gully 8.3 metres in diameter, surrounded by wider drainage gully
10.3 metres across. The two closest figures on the right are working to each side of the east-facing
doorway, with door posts set over 2 metres apart. The roundhouse produced radiocarbon
dates in the range 40 BC to 220 AD. (Copyright Dyfed Archaeological Trust)

LAND AND TERRITORY

> From Saint Davids Promontorie the shore, beeing driven backe aslope Eastward, letteth in the sea with a vast and crooked baye, upon which lieth the third region of the Dimetae, in English called Cardiganshire, in British Sire Aber-Tivi, by old Latin writers Ceretica. A plaine and champion Country it is Westward, where it lieth to the sea ... From Tivy mouth the shore gently giveth back, and openeth for itself the passage of many riverets, among which in the upper part of this shire Stuccia [Ystwyth], whereof Ptolomee maketh mention, is most memorable ...
>
> Description of the Cardigan Bay coast in William Camden's *Britannia*.[1]

Ceredigion is an old land. Patterns of land tenure run deep beneath present-day farms and fields. Many present-day farms and great houses have been occupied since the Middle Ages. At Llannon the survival of medieval open fields or 'slangs' show how the fertile coastal lowlands were once farmed by medieval villagers in long parallel strips. Castle ruins and the mounds of earthen mottes within the county reveal the former sites of lordships and seats of political and royal power. Yet before the medieval and pre-medieval lords or even Roman governors and generals extended control across the county, aristocratic and farming families of the Bronze and Iron Ages owned, cleared, farmed and defended great tracts of land along Cardigan Bay.

The character and variety of the Ceredigion landscape, with green pastures, rolling plateaus and fertile valleys linking the high moorlands of the Cambrian Mountains to the clear waters of Cardigan Bay, allowed locally varied settlement patterns to develop during Iron Age and Romano-British times. In 1808, Samuel Rush Meyrick described the land of Cardiganshire, bringing together some of its particular qualities:

> Cardiganshire is a maritime county... It is well supplied with fish from the sea, particularly cod, herrings &c., and its rivers afford the finest salmon and salmon trout. The country is in general mountainous, though there are very extensive plains, which, however, are boggy ... The hills in general are covered with short grass, but the valleys are extremely fertile. The lands consist of wood, chiefly fir ... and pasture and meadow. The commons of heath and small furze.

The Iron Age settlement pattern was truly shaped by the numerous valleys and lowland 'basins' which cut between the plateau areas to form natural routes for communication as

Figure 3.1: Ghosts of Cardigan Bay's Iron Age farming settlements emerge in dry summers as cropmarks. Close to the coast at Treferedd Uchaf (SN 226 499), near Felinwynt, a large concentric defended farmstead occupies the corner of this modern field. Its scale can be judged by the size of the nearby chapel alongside the road junction. Note the enlarged terminal at the wide gap through the outer ditch, possibly to hold tall and impressive posts at the entrance gate. (Crown Copyright RCAHMW AP_2006_2846)

Figure 3.2: Castell Henllys, north Pembrokeshire. The reconstructed roundhouses seen from afar give a fair impression of the likely appearance of many small hillforts in Iron Age times, with a patchwork of managed woodland and small fields close by. (T. Driver)

well as focal points for farming settlement. In the lowlands the quality of the agricultural land improves and the coastal plain offers a largely frost-free agricultural climate. Along the coast itself promontory forts looked out across the international waters of the Irish Sea. Despite frequent lengths of steep cliffs the Cardigan Bay coastline offered numerous landing places, many with welcoming freshwater streams and springs.

The coastal river valleys connect to the uplands, remote today but once good land for hill grazing, metal prospection, hunting, fishing and fowling, and traversed by well-used mountain routes. Lowland Ceredigion was always productive for crops and livestock. One local writer[2] noted that '… in the 1830s the Vales of Ystwyth, Tywi and Teifi were notable for their heavy yields of wheat … But the real wealth of the farmers lay in their livestock. The uplands and mountains were primarily used to pasture cattle and sheep …'. Another,[3] in a study of Tregaron, wrote that 'Cattle-rearing is the basis of farming on the coastal plateau to the west'.

Clearing the land: from Bronze Age forests to Iron Age fields

Ceredigion in the Iron Age was not a dark, forested landscape with hillforts rising above a dense blanket of wild woodland. On the contrary, agriculture and widespread clearance had already transformed the landscape during the Bronze Age or even earlier. Much of what is known about the prehistoric environment of west Wales derives from palaeoenvironmental analysis and research. Pollen in particular is extremely durable and can survive well in damp or oxygen-starved environments such as peat bogs, waterlogged soils or the bottoms of hillfort or other enclosure ditches. Skilled environmental archaeologists can examine pollen grains through a microscope, building a picture of the prehistoric environment. A predominance of cereal pollens may point to arable farming close to a prehistoric settlement, whereas different mixes of weed or tree pollen can indicate different kinds of wooded or open environments.

Palaeoenvironmental evidence in Ceredigion demonstrates the clearance of remaining ancient woodland from the Late Bronze Age onwards, intensifying in lowland clearances during the later Iron Age and Roman period, a trend which can be seen across much of central Wales. A peat core from the Plynlimon ridge sampled in 2012 suggested an unbroken phase of woodland clearance from the end of the Late Bronze Age around 885 BC lasting through to around 465 BC in the earlier part of the Iron Age, with some regeneration thereafter continuing into the Roman period.[4]

Pollen samples from Tregaron Bog showed deforestation in the neighbourhood around 400 BC,[5] suggesting growing population pressure in the Tregaron area at around this time. This matches radiocarbon dates for the start of construction at the complex hillfort of Darren Camp further north in the county. There is also evidence for woodland clearance along the lower slopes of the Ystwyth valley during the 3rd century BC, intensifying into severe deforestation[6] in the late Iron Age/early Roman period, with evidence for burning of woodland and valley slopes in the middle of the 2nd century BC. The presence of arable and grass weeds both before and after clearance shows a mixed farming economy spreading into the region following clearance.

The striking conclusion of experts is that the Iron Age and Roman woodland clearances were so extensive that '… the ratio of tree to non-tree pollen fell to levels resembling those

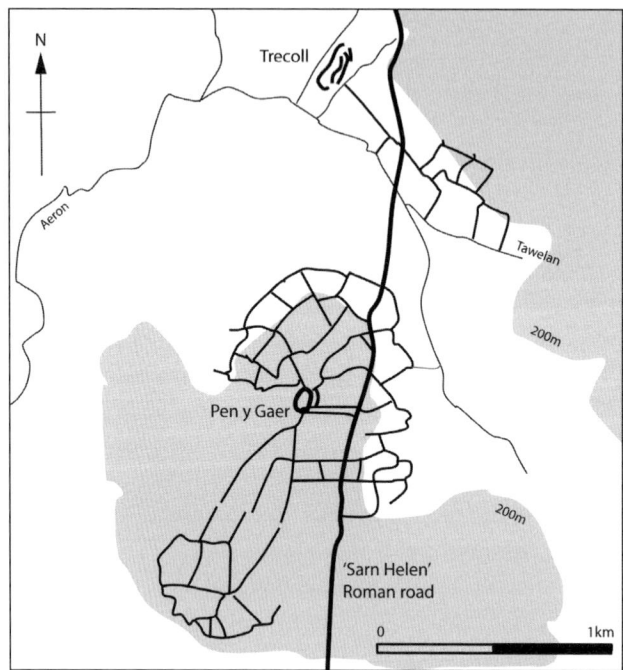

Figure 3.3. Probable remains of a rare Iron Age field system in Ceredigion, south of Bronnant. Field boundaries radiating down-hill from Pen-y-Gaer hillfort, Llanbadarn Odwyn (SN 639 608), are cut on the east (right-hand) side by the north-south line of the Roman road, Sarn Helen. A block of fields to the north, near Trecoll hillfort, is similarly cut by the road. This relationship suggests the fields pre-date the Roman road. Similar techniques of map analysis have been used to discover pre-Roman fields in other parts of Britain. (T. Driver)

of the present day'.[8] This means that anyone who looks out from a hillfort today at the landscapes of the Teifi or Ystwyth valleys may well be seeing a broadly similar density of woodland as met the eyes of our Iron Age predecessors.

The Iron Age farming economy

> What I have seen impresses on my mind the idea that the structure [Cribyn Clota or Cribyn Clottas, SN 536 514] was intended for nothing but peaceful purposes – those of a fold or buarth where the tribesman could place his cattle and other domestic animals for safe keeping over night ... such a provision was highly necessary at a time when the country was open, fenceless and defenceless, and the law, such as it was, did not always protect the weak.[9]

The prehistoric farming regime along Cardigan Bay was likely to have been mainly pastoral, with sheep and cattle predominating and pigs and goats reared in lesser numbers. Arable farming seems to have been practised more at a subsistence level to judge by the small amounts of charred grain found and the few storage structures identified within excavated hillforts and smaller farmstead settlements.

Livestock

The acidic soils of the Cardigan Bay region place us at a disadvantage when seeking preserved bone to identify the species of animals that were common in and around Iron Age settlements. Very few bones have been recovered from the excavation of prehistoric or Roman sites in Ceredigion; indeed, in this acidic area truly exceptional conditions are required for

Figure 3.4. Mudstone spindle-whorl with incised decoration found during excavations at Caerau, Henllan, promontory fort.[10] (By kind permission of the Cambrian Archaeological Association)

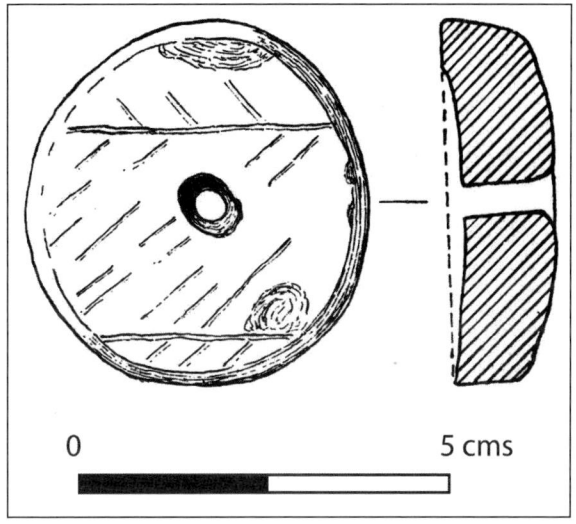

0   5 cms

their good preservation. However, in 1985 during excavations at Caer Cadwgan hillfort near Cellan, animal bones – albeit highly fragmented – were preserved because they had been burnt and calcined and then protected from excess acidity by being incorporated within charcoal-rich occupation deposits. Even so, study of the bones showed that the high degree of fragmentation meant that the species represented by some 80% of the assemblage were unidentifiable. Nevertheless sheep or goats were found to have outnumbered cattle by a ratio of roughly two to one, with pig and dog also present in smaller numbers.[11] Further north in the county similar charcoal-rich occupation deposits allowed the preservation of Roman bronze coins at the Abermagwr villa described in Chapter 6; these would otherwise have long ago corroded to no more than a fugitive green stain in the acidic soils of the site.

In lieu of evidence from preserved bone it is the recovery of associated finds such as spindle-whorls and loom-weights that provide evidence for wool processing from sheep and goats in the region. Spindle-whorls, perforated discs fashioned from local shale, baked clay or even re-used sherds of Roman pottery (as at Ffynnonwen, Tremain) were used to draw out a yarn from wool to prepare it for spinning; as relatively durable objects these are comparatively common finds in Ceredigion. Although stray finds could be of either prehistoric or much later date, the discovery of spindle whorls from Iron Age settlements including Caerau, Henllan; Pen Dinas at Aberystwyth; Caer Cadwgan; Cellan and Ffynnonwen, Tremain, as well as two from the Romano-British villa at Abermagwr, suggest that the majority are Iron Age or Roman in date. A baked clay loom-weight found below occupation layers on the eastern terraces of the south fort of Pen Dinas provides evidence for weaving within this major hillfort.

Cattle were a major source of wealth and prestige in Iron Age society. They are frequently shown in the art and religious symbolism from the period. The later Early Christian sagas from Ireland, which have parallels with the Welsh Iron Age, show that cattle were a major source of wealth for the warrior aristocracy. Professor Barry Cunliffe, writing in 1991, concluded that a lack of field systems around defended settlements in south-west England showed that '... wealth and status may have been measured in terms of cattle'. The historic

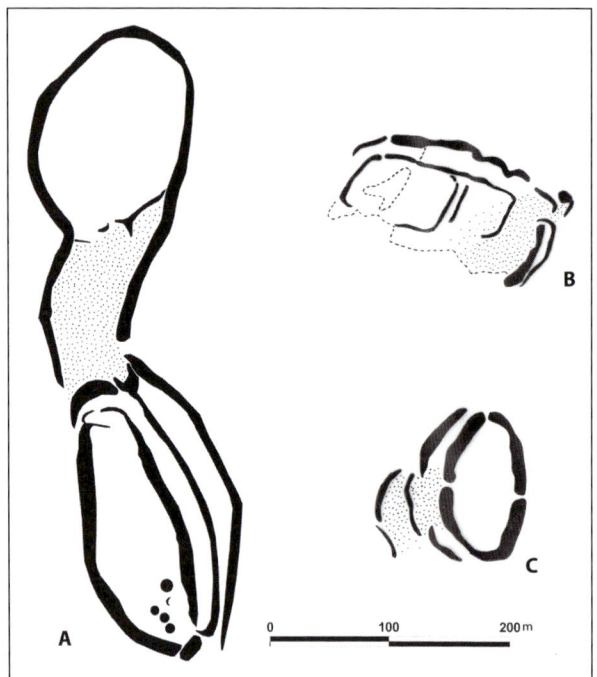

Figure 3.5. A number of the larger and more impressive hillforts in Ceredigion have annexes or public areas (stippled in these three plans) which are enclosed within ramparts or outworks but are clearly demarcated from the hillfort interiors. The demarcation of 'public' and 'private' space at these sites may have maintained the status of the hillfort's leader and inhabitants, as well as providing functional space for penning stock or holding public markets or fairs that would have reinforced the regional role of the fort as a trading centre.
(A) Pen Dinas, Aberystwyth
(B) Castell Grogwynion
(C) Darren Camp.
(T. Driver)

Figure 3.6. Farming the land. An Iron Age farming scene showing small-scale cultivation with a wooden ard and yoked oxen. (Painting by Anne Robinson for the Heather and Hillforts Project; courtesy of Fiona Gale, © Denbighshire County Council)

Scottish highland chieftains in the Western Isles placed great value on the theft and appropriation of cattle through raiding from neighbouring chiefdoms. A cattle-based economy may explain the general lack of relict prehistoric field systems in Ceredigion to match surviving field systems known in the uplands of western Pembrokeshire and Gwynedd.

In Ceredigion several hillforts have annexes which may have been for keeping stock or hosting seasonal fairs and markets. Smaller palisaded enclosures on hillslopes discovered through aerial photography may also be evidence of stock corrals in the lee of larger hillforts. At Cefngwrthafarn Uchaf, inland from Aberarth, a very large (18 hectare) possible cattle enclosure or stockade, perhaps originally only defined by a hedge or palisade, has been preserved in the shape of modern fields. If prehistoric, this site may suggest that this coastal plateau, devoid of larger hillforts, was reserved for cattle grazing, much as in medieval and post-medieval times.

Crops and grain

Modern excavations pay close attention to sampling archaeological deposits for palaeoenvironmental residues that can shed new light onto the details of daily life. Excavations at the Ffynnonwen defended enclosure in south Ceredigion in 2006 by two leading experts in the field, Ken Murphy and Professor Harold Mytum, showed what can be learned through meticulous excavation and recording. Palaeoenvironmental analysis of deposits within the defended settlement showed that plant remains were scarce. Wheat grains were most abundant, both spelt, the main crop used for human consumption during the Iron Age, and bread wheat. Hulled barley was also present, perhaps for use as animal fodder. The presence of chaff and a few weed seeds suggested that crop processing was taking place within the enclosure, and particularly around the largest roundhouse. Based on the available evidence the excavators concluded that the sparse cereal remains suggested a subsistence level of arable cultivation, secondary to animal husbandry. Weed seeds and pollen were also recovered from Ffynnonwen, including knotgrass, nettle, clover and gorse, bracken and heather. Analysis suggested a grassy habitat close to the settlement with scrub ground of bramble and hazel, along with heather and bracken for animal bedding or thatch.[12]

Once again, these findings probably help to account for the lack of evidence for Iron Age field systems around the many isolated enclosures discovered or explored through aerial photography and geophysics across great swathes of lowland Ceredigion.

Across Ceredigion and west Wales more generally, indirect evidence for grain storage is found in the form of 'four-posters', buildings raised on four or occasionally six upright posts, perhaps to store grain and other foodstuffs away from damp and rodents; prominent grain stores inside a hillfort may also have advertised the farming wealth of the settlement. Individual four-posters have been excavated at Pen Dinas at Aberystwyth and at Pendinaslochtyn near Llangrannog.[13] An excavated example from Caer Cadwgan, Cellan, measuring 2.8m square, was built across an earlier building platform. The Ffynnonwen enclosure had a quite substantial four-poster with massive legs almost a metre in diameter, forming a structure 2.6m square. Wheat and barley grains from one of the postholes were interpreted as either the remains of grain stored within the building or as general waste from around the site.

The limited number of four-posters in the hillforts and farmsteads of the Cardigan Bay region suggests a more modest level of grain storage than is inferred from the dense clusters found inside hillforts on the Welsh Borderlands and across southern England. Hillforts with large numbers of these buildings may have provided for the centralized storage of regional grain surpluses required in productive arable landscapes. Along Cardigan Bay the farming wealth seems to have been measured instead in sheep, goats and cattle with cereal cultivation on a subsistence or household level.

PEOPLING THE IRON AGE

'Celtic' west Wales?

Who were the people who inhabited and controlled the land around Cardigan Bay before the Roman conquest? Whether they were 'Celts' is a matter which remains hotly debated even today. The term 'Celtic' is perhaps best paralleled with our modern use of the term 'European'. In modern-day Ceredigion there are many aspects of our life, and particularly our culture, which are in a sense 'European' and would be familiar to people from other European countries. Yet much in the county, from its traditional buildings and local accents to its farming practices and folk customs, would be best described as 'Welsh', or even local to Ceredigion. Regional differences between Ceredigion and the rest of western Britain would have been even more pronounced a century ago. Therefore it seldom seems right to describe the hillforts and defended farms of Ceredigion as 'Celtic' achievements. They belong to the local and regional families, clans and leaders of the late Bronze and Iron Ages who, from time to time, may have reflected or adopted wider 'Celtic' culture in their beliefs, social structures, technologies and decorative arts.

Figure 3.7. Conjectural reconstruction of a wealthy Iron Age warrior from 1st-century BC Wales. He carries a leather-covered wooden La Tène style shield and a fine spear, has a sword at his waist in a plain scabbard and wears a torque around his neck. The boar figurine that crowns his helmet is similar to an actual example found at Guilsfield in Montgomeryshire, in the shadow of the great Gaer Fawr hillfort. Such finery may only have been worn for ceremonial occasions or combat, and would have been beyond the reach of most individuals at that time. Yet this represents a realistic portrayal of an individual from the upper elite in Iron Age Ceredigion. The Roman historian Tacitus, interestingly, noted that: '... Britons make no distinction of sex in their leader'.[14] (Painting by Anne Robinson for the Heather and Hillforts Project; courtesy of Fiona Gale, © Denbighshire County Council.)

The Roman record of Welsh tribes

Early sea voyages by Greek and Roman authors charted the geography and people of Britain. The Roman geographer Ptolemy, for instance, recorded the names of some of the pre-Roman tribes of Wales but left many gaps. The Romans identified six main Iron Age tribes in Wales and along its eastern borderland at the time of the conquest: the Demetae in the south-west, approximating to Pembrokeshire and Carmarthenshire; the Silures in the south and south-east, approximately modern Glamorgan, Monmouthshire and perhaps parts of Brecknock; the Ordovices in the mid and north-west of Wales, broadly Anglesey, Gwynedd and much of Powys although some scholars suggest their territory extended as far south as the Dyfi valley; and the Deceangli in the north-east, modern Denbighshire and the Clwydian Range. The Cornovii occupied the fringe of north-east Wales, the borderlands and the Cheshire and Shropshire plains. Some authorities[15] show the Dobunni occupying parts of Wales east of the Usk, together with the bulk of Avon and Somerset. A pre-Roman tribal name – for the Ordovices – survives, inscribed on the post-Roman 'Corbalengi' stone at Penbryn in south Ceredigion (see below); the phrasing of the inscription from the late 5th century AD suggests that the person referred to was an outsider to the region. Two further minor tribes are recorded by Ptolemy – the Gangani/ganganoi occupying the Lleyn peninsula, a region with distinct stone-built hillforts. Another small tribe, the Octapitae, probably occupied the St David's Head peninsula in Pembrokeshire, also home to a major Iron Age hillfort.

Ptolemy's five or six tribes and their allocated territories are at best a generalized representation of the varied Iron Age people of Wales who no doubt comprised tens or hundreds of smaller groups or clans. His record of the minor tribal names along the west coast, on

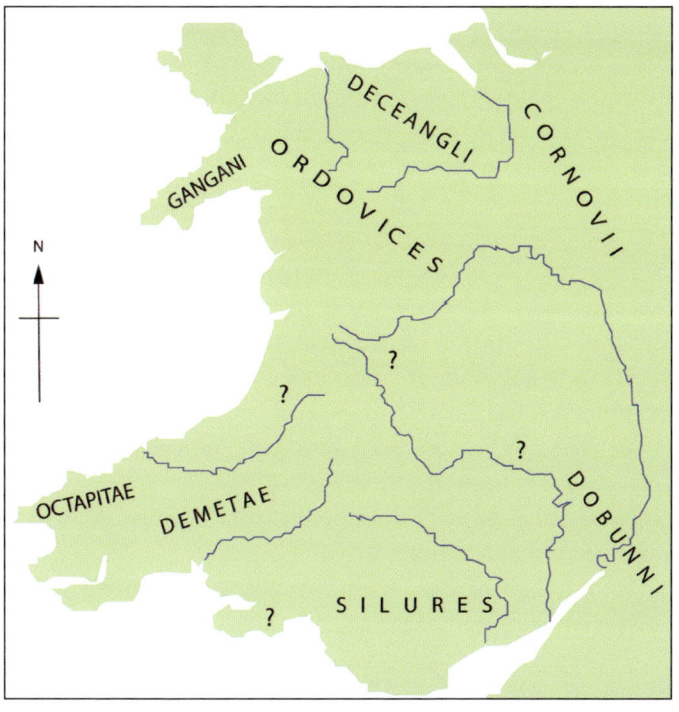

Figure 3.8. Map of Ptolemy's tribes for the western lands that became Wales, including the minor tribes of the Octapitae and the Gangani who occupied discrete territories on the far western peninsulas of north Pembrokeshire and the Lleyn. No tribal names exist for the people who occupied Ceredigion, the upper and middle Wye valley, or other distinct parts of Wales including the Gower peninsula – reflected in this map by question marks.
(T. Driver; sources: various)

47

the Lleyn and in Pembrokeshire, is potentially instructive as regards the true number of smaller tribes that probably existed in Wales, each tied to a distinct area. On the basis of the present writer's study of hillfort groupings in north Ceredigion, each sharing similar architectural styles, it seems probable that the county had a number of smaller tribes clustered along particular river valleys or tracts of countryside, with territories of around 15-30 kilometres across. As such this would provide a plausible comparison with Ptolemy's Gangani and Octapitai on the northern and southern peninsulas of the country. The Demetae, in south-west Wales may have had some influence and identity in southern Ceredigion as well, across the natural border of the river Teifi. Detailed analysis of their tribal name[16] has suggested its meaning as 'the supreme cutters-down', hinting at a special proficiency with swords and the ostentatious use of weaponry.

Personal wealth: bronze, amber, stone and glass

Iron Age finds of any sort from Ceredigion are very rare but there are nevertheless a few fascinating glimpses of the personal wealth of the Iron Age inhabitants of the county. Occasional stray finds, mostly discovered at a time when agricultural practices such as ploughing, quarrying and peat cutting were done by hand, show the type of objects that the very wealthiest members of the Iron Age or Romano-British aristocracy owned and wore. Excavations have also turned up more modest personal items such as glass and amber beads from within hillforts and other settlements, perhaps the 'everyday' jewellery of farming communities.

The Pencoed-y-foel neck-ring

Chance finds such as the Pencoed-y-foel bronze neck-ring can shine a light into the darkness of late prehistory and early history, in this case late Iron Age or Romano-British times in the 1st or early 2nd century AD. This rare piece shows us the delicate beauty and quality of the jewellery of a wealthy hillfort occupant. Appearing bright like glistening gold when new, the Pencoed-y-foel neck-ring (previously referred to as a 'collar'[17]) would have been a showy and expensive piece. The intricately flowing and sinuous design based upon leaves, berries or vines owes its origins to the European La Tène Art style. Wearing it would have proclaimed the owner's vast wealth and international perspective.

Measuring 15 centimetres in diameter, the neck-ring is similar to a handful of others from south Wales and south-west England.[18] All share a rear hinge, worn at the back of the neck, and a larger joint at the front. In 2005 a similar neck-ring was discovered by a metal detectorist in a field in Boverton in the Vale of Glamorgan, in that case with both halves surviving. The Boverton example was fixed with a tongue-and-recess mechanism and shows how the Pencoed-y-foel neck-ring might have been fastened. Archaeologists from the National Museum of Wales returned promptly to the Boverton findspot and were able to excavate a complete and fragmentary bracelet as well as bones from what was clearly a disturbed burial; the interred body was probably female.

Unfortunately we only now have one half of the Pencoed-y-foel ring; Figure 3.9 also shows a digital reconstruction of the missing left side. In the summer of 1896 Eleazer Davies, a farm bailiff of Gellifaharen, reportedly dug up 'two brooches' or 'handles' whilst quarrying on the side of the hillfort, along with some horse teeth.[19] By the time it was

Figure 3.9. The Pencoed-y-foel neck-ring, a highlight of late Iron Age or Romano-British La Tène art from south-western Britain, was discovered at the hillfort near Llandysul in 1896. Comparable neck-rings hang as illustrated, with the narrower part and hinge at the back of the neck and the broader part and clip-fastening at the front. The digital reconstruction of the missing left side allows us to appreciate the symmetry and elegance of the complete piece. (Permission of the National Museum of Wales; image courtesy of Bristol Museums, Galleries & Archives. DH002572_02. Digital reconstruction: T. Driver)

Figure 3.10. Aerial view of Pencoed-y-foel hillfort, Llandysul, findspot of the magnificent neck-ring illustrated in Figure 3.9. The fort is supremely well sited on a locally prominent and domed summit commanding the confluence of two small rivers bordering the Teifi. The hillfort has an interesting plan; its otherwise curving perimeter turns sharply to form a flattened northern side, seen here in the foreground. This appears to be a deliberate design feature. Historic quarrying has disturbed parts of the hillfort and the hillslope in the foreground. (Crown Copyright RCAHMW, AP_2015_0019)

exhibited in 1901 only one half of the neck-ring remained and it can now been seen in the collections of the National Museum of Wales, Cardiff, on loan from Bristol Museum. Its discovery at a hillfort could suggest a loss during some form of catastrophe or conflict, but it is perhaps more likely to have come from a disturbed burial, as was the case at Boverton. Some archaeologists have queried whether conspicuous objects of this kind really represent personal wealth or were instead ceremonial or inherited pieces akin to the mayoral chains of the present day – worn but not owned by elected or appointed officials.

Roundels, brooches and beads

There are glimpses of other personal items. One example is a late 1st- or early 2nd-century AD bronze roundel from Aberporth, decorated with La Tène-inspired petals and S-coils along with 'berried rosettes'. Thought to be a casket ornament, originally mounted on a wooden or leather base for decorative purposes, the roundel was 'retrieved from the sea shore near Aberporth' in the late 1960s and so is entirely without an archaeologically mean-ingful context.[20]

Fragments of two La Tène brooches of similar date were found with late Iron Age burials at Plas Gogerddan, near Bow Street, during excavations by the Dyfed Archaeological Trust in 1986, on the periphery of a prehistoric and later ritual and burial site. These fragmented brooches, which may have been used to fasten a cloak, are on display in the Ceredigion Museum at Aberystwyth. They were assessed as probably having been '… inexpensive and practical necessities [belonging to someone of] relatively low social standing' from late Iron Age or Romano-British times in the 1st or early 2nd century AD.[21] Although this might have been the case in the 'wealthier' parts of Iron Age south Wales and southern England where such brooches were more common, they may have been regarded in this more modest part of west Wales as rare and high-status items. The context here is important. Who was important enough to be laid to rest in this particular burial ground? Were these the burials of successive chieftains, of an elite family or of another group of people altogether? This location remained significant for elite burials in the north Ceredigion landscape, as shown by an Early Medieval cemetery of square barrows and mortuary structures of the late 4th or 5th centuries AD encountered during the same excavations.

More recent excavations by the Dyfed Archaeological Trust on the plough-levelled Iron Age cropmark enclosures of south Ceredigion have not produced quantities of high status

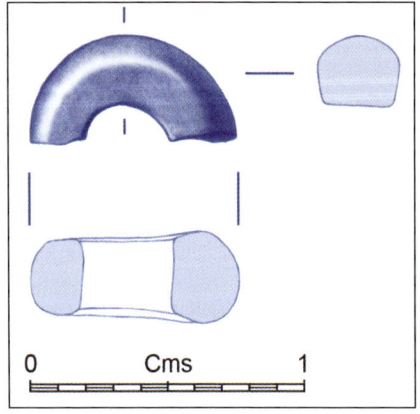

0   Cms   1

Figure 3.11. Half of an early Iron Age blue glass bead excavated at Ffynnonwen defended enclosure, south Ceredigion. It was no doubt once a treasured possession for its owner. (J. Chadwick, by permission of the National Museum of Wales)

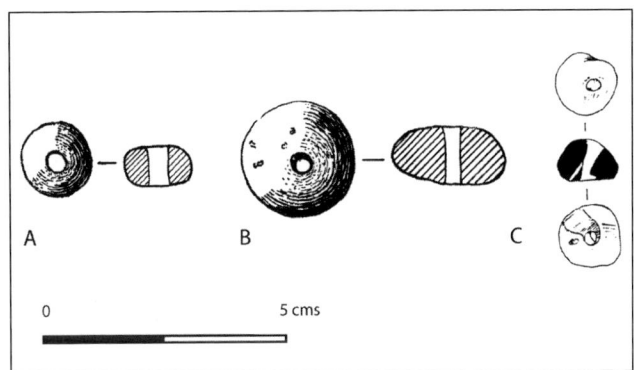

Figure 3.12. Beads from Ceredigion hillforts. A: Broken amber bead, Caerau, Henllan. B: Grey-black clay bead with shell backing, Caerau, Henllan. C: Large bead made from a pebble of amber, Caer Cadwgan. (By kind permission of the Cambrian Archaeological Association and Professor Barry Burnham)

finds. This might tell us that these defended farms, sited in the agriculturally rich coastal lowlands, were not where the aristocratic elite lived.

Excavations at the Ffynnonwen enclosure, which lies east of Penparc near Cardigan, yielded little metalwork or pottery but did produce half a glass bead tentatively dated to the 8th-6th centuries BC from one of the Early Iron Age palisade gullies (Figure 3.11). This translucent dark blue glass bead has close parallels with those manufactured at the Meare lake village in Somerset. It is no match for the Pencoed-y-foel neck-ring but would have been a treasured personal possession, perhaps even after it was broken. Beads of different materials are probably the most common personal item found in Cardigan Bay hillforts and farmstead settlements.

Excavations at Pen Dinas, Aberystwyth, in the 1930s did produce a stone bead and a pale yellow glass bead with spiral decorations, thought to have been made at Meare village, Somerset. Amber and glass beads were excavated at Caer Cadwgan hillfort near Lampeter in the 1980s, while an amber bead and a grey-black clay bead with shell backing were found during wartime excavations at Caerau hillfort, Henllan, in the south of the county (Figure 3.12). Pottery and stone spindle-whorls, some decorated, have been found in excavations on Iron Age and Romano-British sites across the county (Figure 3.4).

House and home

Iron Age roundhouses were remarkable buildings – strong, warm, windproof and large enough to accommodate an extended family. Archaeologists in the early decades of the 20th century, seeking parallels for houses excavated inside British hillforts, often looked to roughly-built round-huts found in hotter, drier climates around the British Empire, particularly in Africa. Early reconstructions of British hillforts, too, usually showed crudely-dressed natives in 'primitive' huts with conical roofs of rough thatch or grass.

Experimental archaeology from the 1960s onwards at sites such as Butser Ancient Farm in Hampshire and, from the 1980s, at Castell Henllys in Pembrokeshire, has transformed our understanding of prehistoric building technology. Crucially, reconstructed roundhouses have shown the strength and durability of buildings designed for British – rather than African – weather and seasons. The Castell Henllys roundhouses have survived hurricane-force winds even when modern buildings close by were damaged; house platforms, too, are found on many highly exposed forts, including Pen Dinas at Aberystwyth (Figure 1.14). The sizes of some of the larger roundhouses compare well with the floor area of houses lived in today. It is worth measuring out an 8-10 metre diameter space alongside your own house to simulate the size of one of these larger Iron Age dwellings. See how much room the whole family would have had for cooking, eating, sleeping and all manner of other daily activities.

Accurate reconstructions of roundhouses at Castell Henllys (Figure 1.16), using their original wall-gullies, have taught archaeologists a great deal about Iron Age life and domestic architecture. The largest roundhouse, with a huge internal diameter of 13 metres, consumed enormous quantities of wood and thatch: 30 oak trees, 90 coppiced hazel bushes, 2,000 bundles of water reed and two miles of hemp rope and twine went into its rafters, posts, ring-beams and wattle-and-daub walls. One cannot simply walk into a nearby wood and gather these materials. Woodland must be managed for generations to produce the correct products for roundhouse building.

Field evidence for Iron Age roundhouses can be seen across Ceredigion. Hillforts surviving as earthworks often contain house-platforms shelved into the original ground surface, or cut into the native bedrock. Geophysical prospection by Archaeophysica Ltd and the Royal Commission at Castell Grogwynion hillfort examined two denuded house-platforms clustered on the uppermost terrace of the interior. Using advanced gradiometry equipment to detect features beneath the soil, the survey showed the positions of hearths inside the roundhouses and even identified where piles of ash or hearth debris had been piled against the outside of the roundhouse walls.[23]

Several other Iron Age houses have been excavated in Ceredigion. At the Ffynnonwen enclosure three houses clustered close together. The largest had an internal diameter of 8.3

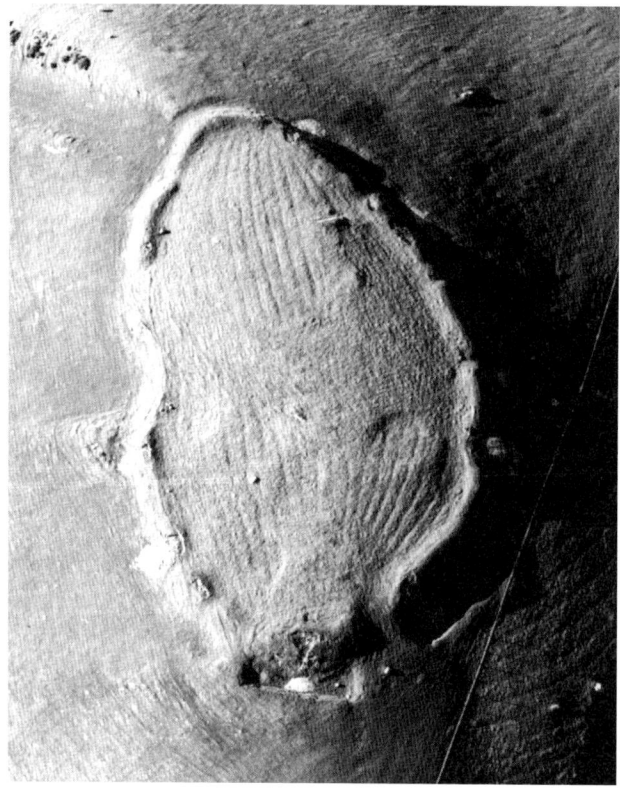

Figure 3.13: Pen y Castell, Bontgoch. Aerial view from the east showing the partial preservation of up to six house platforms within the hillfort, overlain by gently curving ridge and furrow ploughing possibly of medieval date. The main gate lies in the centre foreground, flanked by deeper sections of ditch and better-quality stone walling to heighten its one-time monumentality. The hillfort lies on private land but can be seen reasonably well from a nearby footpath. (Crown Copyright RCAHMW, 2001/5091-51)

metres, comparing well with an example at the Penyrheol enclosure, south of Bronnant, which had a ring-gully measuring 8.9 metres across.

At Caerau, Henllan, in the Teifi Valley, the excavation of a promontory fort in advance of the construction of a Second World War prisoner of war camp nearby uncovered the remains of three roundhouses and other posthole structures in a sheltered position behind the inner rampart. Careful excavation of the best-preserved of the three revealed a number of structural details of a roundhouse 8.2 metres in diameter. A narrow palisade trench defined the circular wall, formerly holding upright planks or logs, with a pair of large postholes flanking the doorway on the south-eastern side. Inside the building there was a rough arrangement of posts, but no central support; some of the postholes had been re-dug, suggesting to the excavator that ongoing renovations had been carried out to shore up the roof. Two hearths had been dug into the floor which appeared to have been surfaced with small stones, with crushed charcoal and bone throughout apart from a clean space about 1.2 metres across at the rear of the house, perhaps reserved for sleeping.[24]

Figure 3.14. Reconstruction of a typical stone-and-timber roundhouse of the 1st century BC, a generously-sized home with the interior segregated for different daily tasks. Here can be seen a quern stone for grinding corn into flour, a hanging cauldron and elaborate iron 'firedogs' beside the hearth to support pans and meat over the fire. The smoky interior was useful for preserving meat and food hung from the ceiling, but perhaps less healthy for the inhabitants' eyesight and breathing. Larger roundhouses may have had partial upper floors or storage lofts. Not all roundhouses had stone walls at their base; many in Ceredigion were defined by circular 'ring gullies' which supported a perimeter wall of upright planks, posts or wattle-and-daub. (Painting by Anne Robinson for the Heather and Hillforts Project; courtesy of Fiona Gale, © Denbighshire County Council)

Trade and Contact: Hillforts and the coastline of Cardigan Bay

> The regular succession and great number of these Celtic defences, occurring, as is the case, at almost every mile along this road, and commanding the heads of streams, or ravines, leading from sea-creeks to the hill country, at once designate their use to repel invasion.
>
> John Fenton describing hillforts from Cardigan common
> to Blaenporth, Aberporth, Castell Nadolig and onwards.[25]

Although prestige items such as the Pencoed-y-foel neck-ring may have been made by highly skilled local bronze-smiths in Ceredigion, distinctive imports such as the glass beads show that there was a healthy trade in exotics. Undoubtedly much contact with north and south Wales, and possibly even the south-west of England and the wider world, took place by sea in light seagoing vessels which drew on a long history of native shipbuilding and seafaring.

There are relatively few deep natural harbours or sheltered inlets along the predominantly steep, rocky coastline of Ceredigion. Where there are good inlets, gravel beaches or river mouths suitable for pulling up small seagoing craft, then there are often found hillforts nearby: Pen Dinas at Aberystwyth at the confluence of the rivers Rheidol and Ystwyth, a concentration of hillforts near Llanrhystud, Pendinaslochdyn high above Llangrannog, or the promontory fort above the little beach at Mwnt, to name only some of the examples.

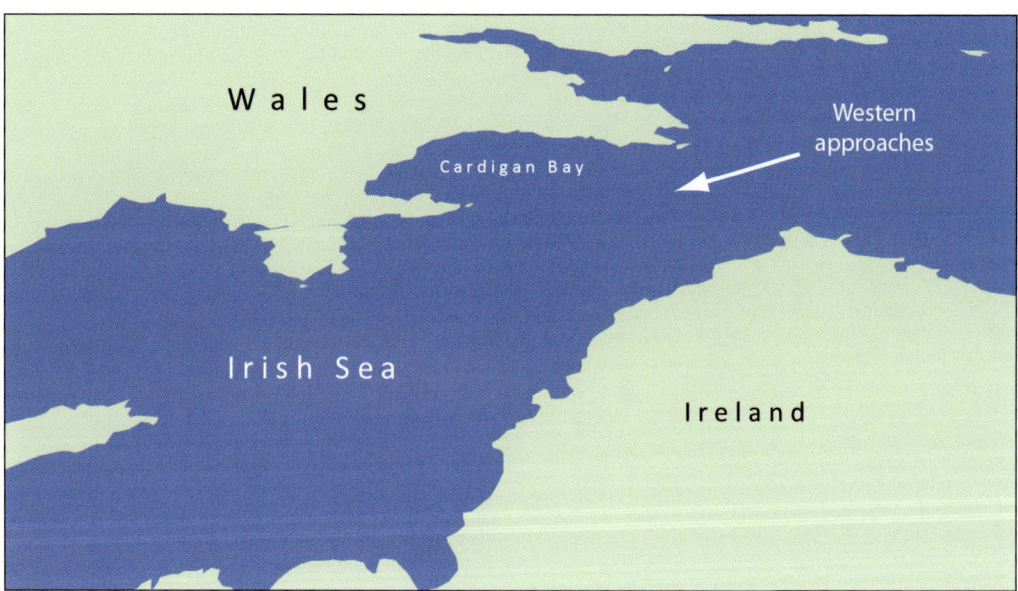

Figure 3.15. Altering the perspective of modern maps can help us to appreciate the world view of prehistoric mariners approaching the western seas of Britain. In a normal map, with north at the top, Wales can appear remote from the English Channel and mainland Europe. In this view looking south-east across the Irish Sea, one instead sees Wales as a sheltered and inviting coastline dotted with headlands and estuaries, with each nation – and the Isle of Man on the left – easily reached by ship and accessible from the wider Atlantic coastline of Europe.
(T. Driver)

Yet there are anomalies. No coastal forts are known on either of the very prominent rocky headlands of Newquay or Aberporth, although both have modern development which may have obscured prehistoric settlements. Nor are there any coastal forts north of Aberystwyth, where it may be that larger forts exerted a degree of territorial control over the excellent grazing and maritime resources along this part of the coast, precluding the development of other large forts within their particular territories. Similar examples can be seen in Pembrokeshire where prominent 'empty' headlands are found near very large coastal promontory forts.

Iron Age boats and ships of the western seaways

> Britain yields gold, silver and other metals, to make it worth conquering.
>
> Roman historian and senator, Publius Cornelius Tacitus[26]

> The … ships were built and rigged in a different way from ours. Their keels were some-what flatter, so they could cope more easily with the shoals and shallows when the tide was ebbing. Their prows were unusually high and so were their sterns, designed to stand up to great waves and violent storms. They used sails made of hides or soft leather …
>
> Caesar describing the ships of the Veneti tribe encountered along the Amorican coast.[27]

A Roman lead anchor stock from the 2nd or 1st century BC, discovered in 1974 at Porth Felen off the Lleyn Peninsula, is a telling reminder of the international shipping which would have been a familiar sight along the coast of Cardigan Bay. The anchor may have come from a relatively small Mediterranean ship travelling to and from Anglesey, where copper was being mined.[28] Alternatively the ship may have been scouting north Wales for the promise of gold-bearing ore. Whatever its destination and business, the inhabitants of coastal Iron Age forts along Cardigan Bay would have been well aware of foreign vessels appearing on their distant horizons, or coming closer inshore to establish contact, exchange traded goods and swap local information, or indeed to take on fresh food and water. In stormy weather, like that which may have sunk the Porth Felen vessel, ships of all nations

Figure 3.16. From the sea the great hill occupied by Pen Dinas hillfort at Aberystwyth remains an obvious presence which may well have attracted opportunistic overseas visitors for trade or shelter in the Late Iron Age. (T. Driver)

would have been forced to shelter at coastal landing points in Ceredigion, owned or over-looked by local tribes. What sort of meeting of cultures, and languages, might have ensued?

There are a few examples of prehistoric boats from the British Isles, as well as the descriptions of Roman writers. Boats can be conventionally divided into three building traditions – log boats, hide boats and plank boats. Log boats have a long tradition in Britain and had become quite advanced by the Iron Age. The Hasholme log boat was found in 1984 in a coastal tributary of the Humber in the north of England. More sophisticated than a simple hollowed-out trunk, it measured 12.8 metres (41 feet 11 inches) in length and was 1.4 metres (4 feet) wide. It was suited to river transport and was perhaps of a type once used on some of the deeper rivers and estuaries of Ceredigion. A shallow boat like this, lacking a keel or outriggers, would not have fared well out on the open sea.

For seagoing transport it is thought that Iron Age sailors relied on larger hide boats, similar to the currachs in used until quite recently around the western isles of Ireland, or a larger version of the Ceredigion coracle. Some idea of the type can be seen in a remarkable gold model of a 1st-century BC hide boat, part of the Broighter hoard from County Derry, Ireland (Figure 3.17). This unique model gives us a rare glimpse of the sophisticated type of ocean-going vessel which may have been a familiar sight off the coast of Cardigan Bay.

Penbryn: a centre for trade and contact?

Penbryn parish, midway along the Cardigan Bay coast, seems to have had an unusual density of monuments and finds spanning the Iron Age, Roman and early medieval periods. The concentration here, in a coastal parish looking out across the Irish Sea, suggests a long history of trade and contact. The parish is home to a number of Iron Age or Romano-British defended enclosures and hillforts. The most notable is Castell Nadolig which crowns

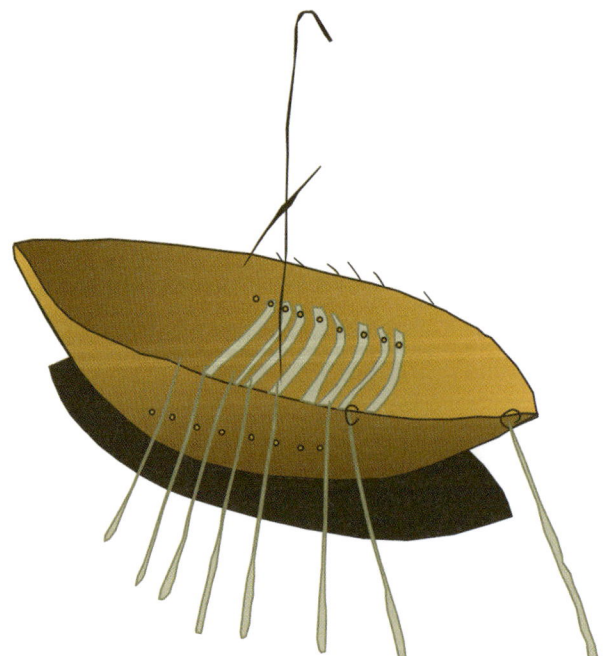

Figure 3.17. Gold model of a 1st-century BC hide boat found at Broighter, County Derry. This was a sea-going craft of the type which no doubt traded on the Atlantic seaways. It had nine rowing thwarts or benches, a stepped mast amidships and a steering oar to the stern. (T. Driver)

a gentle but prominent hill summit to the south, lying alongside a long-lived north-east to south-west ridge route fossilized in the present-day A487 coast road. Overlooking Penbryn hamlet and the beach is Gaer Lwyd hillfort. Four plough-levelled cropmark settlements are also known nearby including a large rectangular enclosure, possibly a Romano-British farm, lying between Castell Nadolig and the early medieval *Corbalengi* stone (SN 289 514).

It seems that special or unusual events may have been happening in Penbryn in Late Iron Age and Roman times. The gold-inlaid Penbryn divination spoons found in Castell Nadolig are described in Chapter 5. Another significant find was one of only seventeen Iron Age gold coins or 'staters' known from Wales, a 'Corieltauvian Type A' coin dating from *c.*70-55 BC from Penbryn. The Corieltauvi or Coritani tribe occupied what is now the English east Midlands including Lincolnshire, Leicestershire and Northamptonshire. The Type A is the earliest type of Corieltauvian coin and remains rare even in central England. For Wales it is exceedingly rare, most of the known Iron Age coins coming from south-east Wales, far closer to the currency-using societies of southern and south-west England.

That this east Midlands coin found its way to the Cardigan Bay coast could imply long distance communication with far-off peoples. One theory of distant finds of English Iron Age gold coins on south-western shores is linked to the invasion of Julius Caesar in south-east Britain in 55-54 BC. It is possible that the Penbryn coin might be a remnant from a 'hoard of flight', carried for safety far from the Roman incursions. However, one can only wonder at the occasion which brought this coin (or coins) to Ceredigion shores. Who stepped off the boat on Penbryn beach with such a precious cargo? Was it just another over-land trader making a fair purchase with a coastal community? Or perhaps the coin's arrival suggests a long-distance tribal, family or kinship link to Penbryn parish? Was Penbryn, with a potential ceremonial centre at Castell Nadolig, important enough to warrant a significant journey to bring the gold coin to this place?

Another unusual feature at Penbryn is the discovery there of one of the very few early Roman cremation burials known from mid or west Wales, in a region devoid – as yet – of any known Roman forts or coastal installations. The burial was discovered in the first decade of the 19th century at the foot of the *Corbalengi* stone, thought to be an early medi-eval inscribed funerary or memorial stone re-using an earlier prehistoric standing stone. The Latin inscription 'CORBALENGI IACIT / ORDOVS', translates as '(The body) of Corbalengus lies here, an Ordovician'. The stone stands on top of a probable Bronze Age barrow, into which there had been inserted Roman cremation burials dating from about

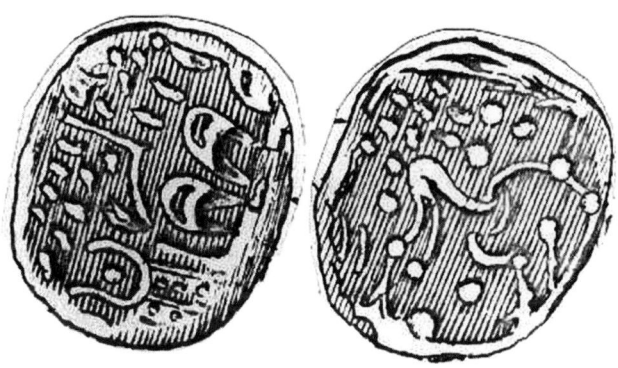

Figure 3.18: Iron Age gold coin or 'stater' of 70-55 BC found some time before 1722 in the parish of Penbryn on the Cardigan Bay coast. It once belonged to 'John Williams of Aber Nant bychan'. It is one of only seventeen such coins known from Wales.

150 to 120 AD. These were discovered about two years before Meyrick's history of the county was published in 1810.

This burial in question is very early indeed; a small black-burnished cooking-pot is dated to about 120-50 AD while an accompanying Roman gold coin, an *aureus* of Titus, was minted in 74 AD. There is no doubt that this was a genuine burial of the early to mid 2nd century AD. Given the lack of known Roman forts, settlements or other installations in this part of central-southern Ceredigion, the conclusion must be that some particular significance was attached to the stone or to the parish, encouraging someone to inter a cremation burial and gold coin at this particular point.[29]

Taken together, the hillforts, the advantageous coastal setting, the gold-inlaid divination spoons, an Iron Age gold coin from the east Midlands, an early Roman burial with a high-value gold coin, and the inscribed stone incorporating a pre-Roman tribal name, suggest some kind of special importance attached in Iron Age, Roman and Early Medieval times to the area around the present-day parish of Penbryn. This may have been a focal point for ceremony, trade and overseas contact, difficult to parallel anywhere else along the west-facing sweep of Cardigan Bay.

Salt, metal and trade routes across the hills

Although sea transport has long been accepted as a vital part of prehistoric trade and contact within the Irish Sea zone, the practicality of overland contact has often been questioned. Historically, the Cambrian Mountains have long been seen as a significant barrier to east-west movement between the west coast and inland areas on the eastern side of Wales and beyond. In 1922 the coastal plain of Cardiganshire was described as lying '… along the western flank of Plynlymon, which ever lifts its mighty shoulders to retard the westward advance of the ways of the eastern plain', and elsewhere as a 'formidable barrier'.[30] It can now be appreciated that the central mountains were very much a permeable barrier, breached by many valleys and overland passes. Undoubtedly later prehistoric communities in Ceredigion drew many of their cultural influences, traded goods and contacts from east-west movement across the Cambrian Mountains and the uplands of central Wales to and from the communities of the Severn, Wye and Usk valleys, and even beyond that to the plains of Shropshire, Herefordshire and Cheshire and south Wales.

Well-used cross-mountain routes, marked by standing stones, have been suggested[31] in the north of the county to explain trade in the products of Ceredigion's early Bronze Age metal mines (for which see Chapter 2). These routes would probably have remained in use during Iron Age and Roman times, since Iron Age and Roman exploitation of metal mines is known around Erglodd at Talybont and Frongoch at Trawsgoed. Roman camps and forts of the early conquest period, sited along the obvious mountain routes, show how Roman generals probably combined their own military expertise with the use of local knowledge, or even local guides, to direct their journeys from central and eastern Wales across the hills toward Cardigan Bay and north Wales.

Exotic overland trading contacts are further demonstrated by the single, but important, discovery of an imported Malvernian 'duck-stamped' pottery jar at Pen Dinas, Aberystwyth (Figure 3.21). The transport of this vessel a hundred miles or so from the Herefordshire/Worcestershire boundary implies that Pen Dinas had a role in long distance trade during

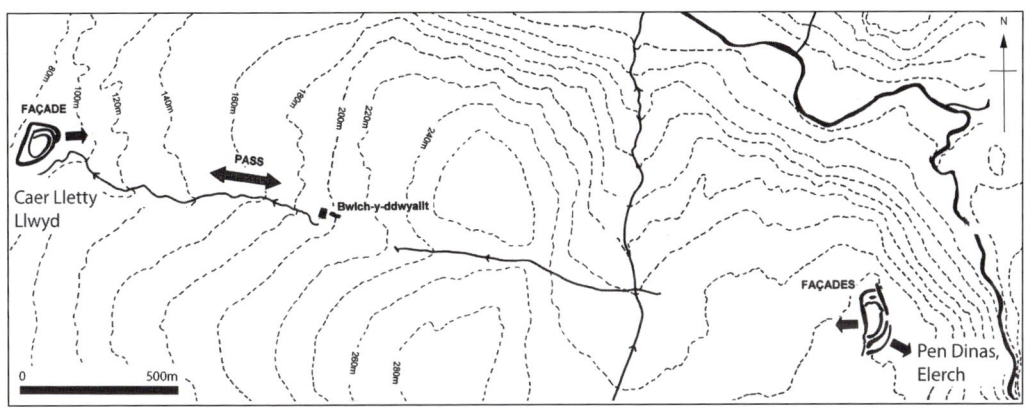

Figure 3.19. Tracing human movement between hillforts south of Talybont in north Ceredigion. Why do the enormous defences of Caer Lletty Llwyd fort near Talybont (left) face a 'blind' hillslope to its east? The answer may lie in the route of the old mountain track up the pass – 'bwlch' in Welsh – that climbs to the mountain plateau above Bontgoch reaching another great hillfort, Pen Dinas Elerch, (right) high above the Leri Valley. The walled western side and blocked gate at Pen Dinas suggest that it once expected to receive visitors from the lowlands to the west. Perhaps for a time both hillforts saw contemporary occupation, reflected in shared architectural expression that is further discussed in Chapter 4. (T. Driver)

Figure 3.20. Caer Lletty Llwyd fort. A view of the impressive terraced ramparts of this low-lying fort, which face east to a mountain track descending from the hills above. The hillfort lies on private land but can be viewed from an adjacent footpath. (T. Driver)

the 2nd or 1st centuries BC and that the physical journey across Wales was secure enough for travellers and traders not to be excessively impeded by thieves or the like. The surviving fragments of the vessel show no signs of repair and the jar is assumed to have reached its destination intact. It is highly likely that future excavations in the region would reveal further evidence for traded salt and ceramics which would place the Pen Dinas find in a more realistic context. This rich tradition was continued in the remarkable drovers' journeys of recent centuries which saw people and livestock travelling on a regular basis a hundred miles and more from west Wales to markets in south Wales and the Borderlands.

Iron Age metalworking

Indirect evidence for Iron Age metal working has been known for some years in the form of iron slag at five hillforts from various parts of Ceredigion.[32] A recent discovery of iron slag during excavations at Glan Fred promontory fort near Llandre in the north of the county was dated to the early medieval period (see Chapter 1). Where were metals ores being mined and worked in the Iron Age in the Cardigan Bay region?

In 2011-2013 an ambitious programme of surface sampling in three Ceredigion hillforts – Darren Camp, Pen-bont Rhydybeddau, Pen Dinas, Elerch and Castell Grogwynion, Llanafan – was carried out by Keith Haylock from Aberystwyth University in partnership with the present author at the Royal Commission. Despite thorough sampling of the hillforts no *in-situ* evidence of prehistoric metal-working or ore processing was found.[33] So far the best evidence for such activity in a Ceredigion hillfort or similar settlement was discovered in a spread of charcoal and occupation material behind the rampart at Caer Cadwgan, Cellan in 1988. Finds included the remains of small triangular crucibles of Iron Age type together with slag, furnace lining and fired clay.

Building on the ground-breaking discoveries of Early Bronze Age mining in the north of the county by Simon Timberlake and the Early Mines Research Group over the last two decades, excavation in 2005 on a timber trackway and associated industrial deposits at Llangynfelyn, on the edge of Borth Bog below Erglodd, revealed evidence for late Iron Age and 1st- to 2nd-century Roman lead smelting on an industrial scale.[34] The site was overseen by the nearby Roman fort at Erglodd, just north of Talybont. Excavations in the same year at Darren Camp showed that a mineral vein had been cut by the hillfort builders while digging one of the defensive ditches on the north-west side of the hillfort (Figure 1.6). It is not clear, however, whether this lucky chance prompted the start of opencast mining on or near the site during the Middle Iron Age.[35] It is interesting to note that there is a gap in the opencast workings west of the hillfort, corresponding with the main approach to the

Figure 3.21 (opposite). A visitor from distant lands. Numerous fragments of a 'duck-stamped' jar from Herefordshire were excavated at Pen Dinas hillfort, Aberystwyth, in 1934. The jar was evidently transported from the Malvern Hills, arriving safely on the west Wales coast after a long overland journey, or alternatively an even longer voyage by sea. This tells us a great deal about the relative safety of Late Iron Age Wales for travellers and traders, or of intrepid sailors in the centuries before the arrival of the Romans. The original is held at the National Museum of Wales in Cardiff, while a copy is on display in the Ceredigion Museum at Aberystwyth. (By kind permission of the National Museum of Wales. DH000419)

west gate, suggesting that this path was kept clear during any Iron Age exploitation of the mineral vein.

Clearly, by the time the Romans arrived in west Wales they could draw upon existing local knowledge about available metal ores. Excavations at the Abermagwr Romano-British villa near Trawsgoed in 2011 uncovered a perforated lead sheet, found through isotope analysis by Keith Haylock at Aberystwyth University to be of local Frongoch lead. This confirms mid to late Roman exploitation of local metal resources which, as perhaps at Erglodd, may have built on local knowledge from the preceding Iron Age.

Chapter 4

HILLFORTS: CONSTRUCTION, CONFLICT AND COMMAND

*Chapter frontispiece: Power of place. The summit crowned by Darren Camp above
Pen-bont Rhydybeddau is seen here from the north-west, with 'notches' on the skyline
showing gates through its ramparts. The hilltop was already crowned by an Early Bronze Age
burial mound when construction began on the hillfort defences around 400 BC.
The flat-topped hill was made more obvious and commanding by the addition of massive
defences raised against the horizon. The forward-facing natural escarpments and ridges
of outcropping rock below the fort, caught by shadow on the right, may have been interpreted
as ancient man-made walls which could be seen as part of the monumental approach
to the summit of the hill. (T. Driver)*

Command of the Landscape

> The purpose, then, of a hill camp was defence rather than offence, command of a good view of valleys below and a place where the population ... could feel secure. It follows from this that prime regard was given to the water supply ... Great regard, too, was given to fertile patches, suitable grazing lands and regions of game ... That is to say, hill camps were permanent homes about which and within which members of the community lived.[1]

Scouting the hilltop

Visiting a hillfort, one should take a moment to imagine the summit before construction began. Who first selected the site? Who stood at the hilltop and surveyed the land in all directions, taking account of the territory they controlled, the natural routes of communication and access to resources such as fresh water, agricultural land, hill pasture and woodland? Perhaps the leader had grown up nearby and had always considered this particular location as a future home? Perhaps ownership of prominent hills, like those now crowned by Pendinaslochdyn at Llangrannog or Pen Dinas at Aberystwyth, had been hard won by the leader now standing there to cast his or her eye over the land below?

In 1975 the hillfort scholar A.H.A. Hogg envisaged a 'council of elders' making decisions on the siting and form of a new hillfort. A chieftain and his or her retainers can be imagined riding to the hilltop, dismounting and pacing over the ground, discussing and planning the lead-up to the first days of construction. There would have been real issues of labour, tools and food supply but also a sense of anticipation. If nearby woodland was not controlled by the hillfort builders, deals would have to be struck about timber supply and labour. Wagons and carts would be needed in numbers; were these to be acquired from other farms and forts, or built for the task? Surveyors may already have been hard at work marking out rampart lines. Perhaps Druids or priests had been consulted to divine an auspicious day or month on which to start. Messengers or senior elders may have been despatched on horseback to other parts of Wales to meet with reputed hillfort 'architects', or specialist fort builders known through kinship ties, to procure services or to seek advice for the new building project. Closer to home, word may already have gone out to local communities about the plans, with debts and outstanding obligations called in from minor chiefs and farming families.

Figure 4.1. Although now partly infilled, the rock-cut lip of the outer ditch of Gaer Fawr hillfort, Lledrod, testifies to the brutal hard work required to construct defences at such a large fort. The site lies on private land. (T. Driver. Crown Copyright, RCAHMW, CD2005_620_018).

Figure 4.2. Great feats of engineering, including this 3-4 metre high rampart and rock-cut ditch at Hen Gaer, near Bow Street, show the ability of charismatic or powerful local leaders to galvanise and organize labour towards a common goal. The hillfort lies on private land. (T. Driver)

Hillfort siting and landscape control

Where were hillforts positioned? What lands did they command? How good was their local and regional visibility? What routes might be taken by people approaching them with good or evil intent? These were all critical factors to those choosing the building site and planning the defences. It is recorded that the historic Highland chiefdoms of Scotland 'secured themselves', both as controllers of: '… social networks of kinship and alliance and … as controllers of land and its resources'.[2] The chiefdoms were: '… cultivating men as well as land …'. Clans drew 'meaning' and 'relevance' from being rooted in particular areas, and became 'broken clans' when without land.[3] This understanding sheds important light back to the Welsh Iron Age. Used with caution it shows us how important the concepts of land and territory may have been to the early aristocracies of Cardigan Bay.

There was an obsession with reshaping the natural landscape in the Iron Age, and with making a hillfort highly visible and conspicuous. Sometimes natural outcrops or iconic hills were harnessed to increase the 'power of place', such as the upland outcrops enclosed by hillforts at Pen Dinas, Elerch, at Bontgoch or Pen y Bannau at Strata Florida. Yet it appears that it was the *transformation* of natural locations through the building of boldly artificial ('man-made') walls, ramparts and ditches which was of key importance to hillfort builders, rather than any attempt to *respect* the natural terrain. So it is that at Darren Camp and Pen Dinas, Aberystwyth, great effort was put into forming striking horizontal lines with the main ramparts – completely at odds with the local terrain – so that the hillfort, when seen from far or near, would appear striking, new and modern in the landscape (Figure 7.1). This may also have demonstrated man's power over rock and earth, the ability to reshape the very form of the land. Existing natural rock escarpments below the summit may have been seen as ancient lines of early defence, as at Darren Camp in the chapter frontispiece.

For some hillforts high visibility was the key. Both Castell Moeddyn and Darren Camp can be seen from great distances as you approach, dominating the view. In many respects they 'own' the land around them through this visibility. Castell Perthi-mawr in the Aeron valley and Caer Cadwgan at Cellan both occupy lofty local summits commanding wide vistas. But other factors may also have been important. The scree-covered summit at Caer Cadwgan – offering a regionally unusual source of building stone – was no doubt a factor in the choice of the site, just as the command of an inland pass or 'bwlch' was important at Castell Perthi-mawr.

Valley junctions were critical points of control since these were where lowland valley territories met and where people, livestock and traders moved through the landscape. Many Cardigan Bay hillforts control valley junctions, as at Caer Pwll Glas at Llandre, Caer Penrhos at Llanrhystud, Castell above Tregaron, and Dinas Cerdin at Ffostrasol. Powerful hillforts were often sited at key junctions or promontories above or along great river valleys, heightening their regional visibility and their control over valley resources and movement. Such nodal sites can be seen at Pen y Castell, Llanilar, controlling a key change of direction in the Ystwyth Valley, or at Caerau, Henllan, in the valley of the Teifi.

The control of major passes is suggested by the siting of a number of hillforts bordering high ground. Tan-y-ffordd hillfort, a terraced 'miniature' version of Pen Dinas at

Aberystwyth, sits on an elevated spur above the floor of the Rheidol Valley just above the modern Cwm Rheidol reservoir (Figure 4.7). Its impressively high ramparts were built on the opposite side of the fort from the main entrance, apparently to face people descending along a well-used trackway from higher ground to the north-east. The same situation can be seen at Caer Lletty Llwyd near Talybont (Figure 3.20), where the terraced ramparts seem to face a blind hillslope; in fact they watch over a mountain track descending from high ground above and to the east (Figure 3.19). The impressive ramparts at Pen y Bannau, near Strata Florida, have a very restricted inland view and are best seen as one descends from the mountainous ground around Teifi Pools to the north-east (Figure 7.14). The hillfort's

Figure 4.3. Castell Perthi-mawr dominates the middle Aeron Valley from a high knoll, but also commands a narrow pass seen at the base of this picture. Roundhouse footings survive within the fort while the inner and outer gate terminals (upper right) overlap, forcing visitors to follow a zig-zag course into the hillfort. Note the line of the original sunken hollow way entering the hillfort from the right. The site lies on private land.
(Crown Copyright RCAHMW, AP_2015_3928)

striking 'triple façade' seems to have been designed to greet – or intimidate – overland visitors approaching from the higher land. Similarly Pen y Castell at Bontgoch occupies a knoll at the head of a great valley. Its main gateway is not turned towards the west coast but instead faces inland towards the mountain and moorland of Plynlimon, an area long traversed by Bronze Age and later trading routes. Castell Nadolig, on the coastal plain near Penbryn, occupies a locally prominent summit skirted by an ancient ridgeway, now fossilised in the modern coast road. Perhaps it was purposely sited along the ancient ridgeway to command this longstanding communication route.

Some forts are surprisingly hidden. Pencoed-y-Foel, on the River Teifi, can barely be seen within the local landscape (Figure 3.10). In prehistory, perhaps, knowledge of the *territory* commanded by a hillfort was just as important as its *visibility* from the valley below.

Iron Age territories: resourcing the 'chiefly feast'

The varied landscape of Ceredigion probably helped to shape distinctive Iron Age territories in a way that may be more difficult to recognise in less hilly parts of Britain. North Ceredigion is dominated by the great rivers of the Ystwyth and Rheidol, which converge on modern Aberystwyth. In the south it is the Teifi headwaters and Aeron Valley which define the landscape. Feeding into these principal river valleys is a network of minor rivers and lowland 'basins', sheltered side valleys which are well-watered and offer a mix of productive grassland and wooded hillslopes. Within these basins around Talybont, Goginan, Llanfihangel y Creuddyn, Ciliau Aeron and Cribyn there are clustered groups of small defended farmsteads, many known today only from aerial photography. These concentrations of defended farms are often overlooked by one or two larger hillforts which look out over the lowland basins, commanding wider vistas.

Programmes of excavation in other parts of Wales, some lasting a number of years, have shown that close groups of hillforts were not necessarily contemporary. A number of excavated small hillforts and defended farms at Llawhaden in Pembrokeshire were found to have been occupied at various times from the Early Bronze Age to Romano-British and post-Roman centuries, in the passage of time being abandoned and rebuilt many times over.[4]

A major study by the present writer[5] has shown how the Iron Age hillforts in the 'ridge and valley' landscape to the north of the River Rheidol may have coexisted. Hillforts built around the lowland basins of the Leri and the northern valley sides of the Rheidol were closely spaced. In contrast, larger hillforts occupying the central belt of narrow east-west ridges and valleys connecting mountain to coastal lowland may have exerted control over long linear territories defined by rivers or watersheds and stretching from the coastal valleys to the mountain hinterland, as illustrated in Figure 4.4.

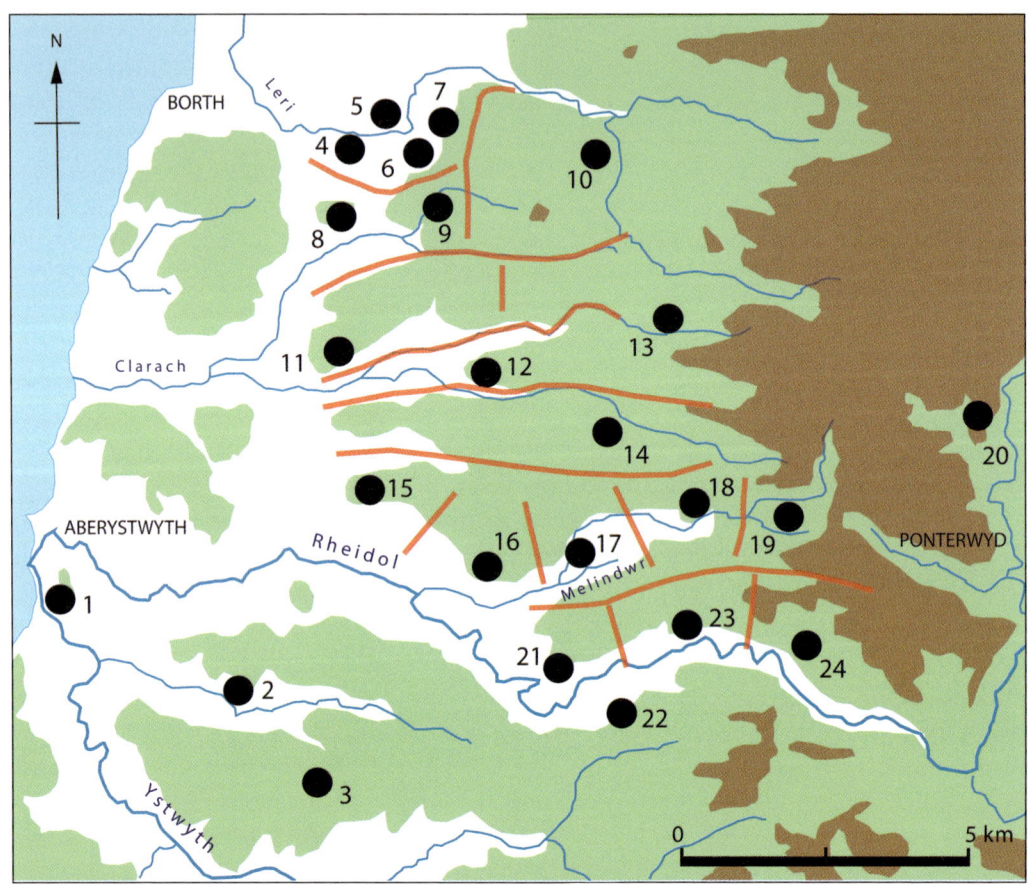

Figure 4.4. The spacing of major hillforts and defended farmsteads (black circles) north of the River Rheidol in north Ceredigion invites speculation as to the way land was managed in the Iron Age. Although not all settlements were necessarily contemporary with one another, the regular or close spacing of some sites, in contrast to the isolation of others, suggests differential patterns of land-holding. The notional boundaries of potential 'hillfort territories' are shown by red lines. Larger hillforts sited on east-west ridges linking the coast to the mountains (sites 11, 12, 13 and 14) were able to exploit a variety of differing zones for food and other resources. Noteworthy is the regular positioning of hillforts along the Melindwr valley between Capel Bangor and Goginan (sites 15, 16, 17, 18 and 19) and the isolation of Pen Dinas, Aberystwyth (1) on the coast.
Key: (1) Pen Dinas, Aberystwyth, (2) Old Warren Hill, (3) New Cross, (4) Glan Fred, (5) Caer Allt-goch, (6) Odyn Fach, (7) Caer Lletty Llwyd, (8) Caer Pwll Glas, (9) Bryngwyn-mawr, (10) Pen Dinas, Elerch, (11) Hen Gaer, (12) Penrhyncoch Camp, (13) Pen y Castell, (14) Darren Camp, (15) Banc-y-Gwmryn, (16) Caerau or Capel Bangor Camp, (17) Cyncoed, (18) Banc y Castell, (19) Esgair Nant yr Arian, (20) Dinas, Ponterwyd, (21) Pant Da Wood, (22) Pen-y-Felin Wynt, (23) Tan-y-ffordd, (24) Castell Bwa-drain.
Contours at 100m and 300m above sea level.
(T. Driver)

In Figure 4.4 the positioning of the principal hillforts in the hill fringe zone, Pen Dinas, Elerch (10), (SN 677 876), Pen y Castell (13) (SN 689 848) and Darren Camp (14) (SN 678 830), suggests that the three forts commanded particular ridges and valleys so as to exploit a variety of resources. This would compare well with other studies, including that of the Brecknock hillforts which were sited '… on hilltops … all within easy reach of good or medium-quality land and adequate water' while 'Enclosures … on hill-slopes, appear to be sited at the transition between the open uplands and the more wooded valley slopes, indicating a mixed economic strategy'.[6]

Access to these mixed resource zones was important, not just for providing daily food but also for the value of owning and regulating varied lands for the supply of a range of lavish foodstuffs, including game and conceivably seafood. These staple foods and delicacies would be used to supply chiefly feasts and reinforce the position of the local leader. The range and scale of the chief's feast reflected the extent of his or her landholdings. To put on the table wildfowl from the hills, bread and beef from the lowlands, and fish and shellfish from the coast would have indicated a landowner of great power and influence.

Noteworthy in Figure 4.4 is the isolation of Pen Dinas, Aberystwyth (1), on the west coast. There is also a lack of coastal promontory forts between Aberystwyth and the Dyfi Estuary. The ability of Pen Dinas to control access to unique coastal resources would perhaps have strengthened the power of its inhabitants and may have excluded the construction of other forts nearby.

Blueprints for the Iron Age: hillfort design and shared traditions

Hillfort 'architecture' seems to be infinitely varied, but in fact dominant cultural traditions appear to have influenced the construction and design of at least some of the larger hillforts flanking Cardigan Bay. Several of the more complex and later hillforts were built in very similar ways, with repeating structural elements employed despite issues of local terrain. 'Branding' the hillfort with the design elements of a regional tradition may well have proclaimed allegiance to, or membership of, a wider cultural group, in turn helping to develop or reinforce regional identities between groups of people. In a sense these were cultural 'blueprints', influential enough to guide and inspire the builders of hillforts within the local area.

Pen Dinas, at Aberystwyth, stands out as different from most other hillforts in mid Wales but shares architectural characteristics with a small group of forts in the north of the county. These include Gaer Fawr at Lledrod and Tan-y-ffordd in the Rheidol Valley, but also Pen Dinas, Elerch, and Castell Grogwynion at Llanafan. These hillforts are all set against a precipitous slope or cliff edge along one long side, using the steep natural scarp for defence. They all have one or more wide-spaced terraces on the opposing side, running the full length of the fort. There is no direct access *through* these terraces, making it possible to enter the forts only through gateways positioned at the narrow ends of the ridge. The gateways sited at these narrow ends are 'open', meaning that access was not blocked by outworks or overlapping banks and ditches. The gateways are 'exotic' regionally, with stone-lined passageways, bastions or command posts, and bridges crossing the entrances.

Figure 4.5. The hillfort of Gaer Fawr sits on a high ridge overlooking Lledrod in north Ceredigion. The great terrace on the north (right-hand) side is a distinctive feature found at a handful of other north Ceredigion forts, suggesting a broadly contemporary group sharing the same architectural style. The terrace is unbroken by original gates; these are instead positioned at each end of the fort on the line of the ridge. Gaer Fawr lies on private land.
(Crown Copyright RCAHMW, DI2006_2003)

Hillforts sharing this 'Pen Dinas design scheme' contrast with those within the 'Cors Caron design scheme', whose distinctive architecture is exemplified by Pen y Bannau hillfort above Strata Florida, but is also found at the hillforts of Trecoll, south of Tyncelyn, and Castell, Tregaron.

These three 'Cors Caron' hillforts (Figure 4.8) are all sited around prominent outcrops or ridges, but with meagre defences along the sides of the forts. Instead, the main ramparts were built at the narrow end of the promontory or ridge, are steep and close-set, and block direct access to the gateway. They do vary, however, as do their topographical settings, but the visual characteristics of the defences remain similar. Trecoll is sited on a river-promontory overlooked on most sides but its pronounced ramparts are nevertheless steep and impressive. Castell, Tregaron does not have short lengths of rampart defining its façade; on the contrary, the façade here is long and sweeping, but still serves the purpose of providing a physically and visually impenetrable barrier to all those approaching (Figure 4.15). The façade of Pen y Bannau is most impressive, and appears to mimic the multiple ramparts of larger hillforts on the Welsh borderland but on a small scale (Figure 7.12). Also of considerable interest is a 'hybrid' fort, Pen-y-ffrwd Llwyd (Figure 4.10), which shares characteristics of both hillfort groups. This fort occupies a spectacular liminal position on crags on the northern watershed of the Cors Caron landscape, where the land to the north falls away to the catchment of the Ystwyth.

Figure 4.6. Pen Dinas at Aberystwyth spans two summits. The marked difference between the earlier and simple north fort (right) and the later terraced south fort (left) is clear in this view taken from the National Library of Wales. The upper terrace of the south fort creates a functional, sheltered space for settlement and craft activities. The lower terrace was apparently built purely for symbolic effect and completeness; it slopes too much to be a usable space. The builders thus created a hillfort with enormous monumental symbolism. (T. Driver)

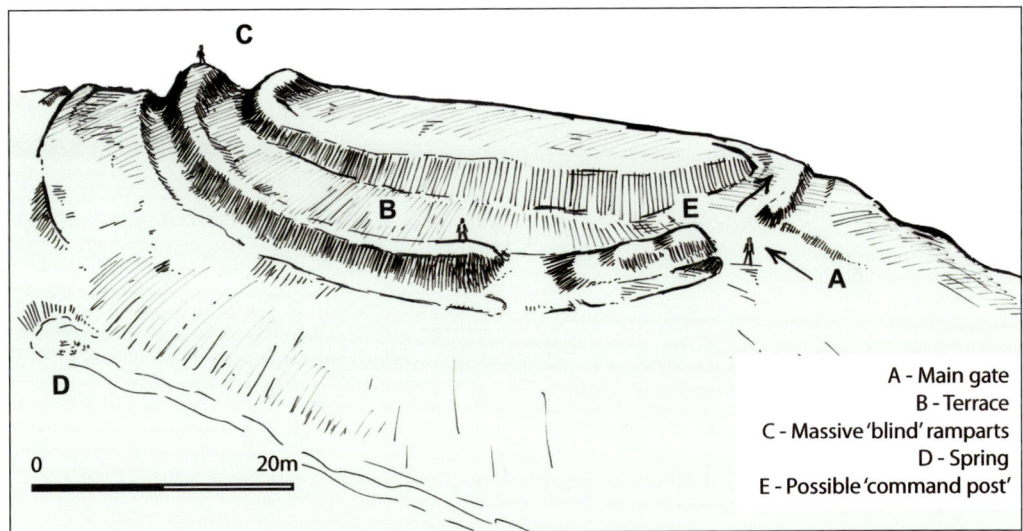

A - Main gate
B - Terrace
C - Massive 'blind' ramparts
D - Spring
E - Possible 'command post'

Figure 4.7. Sketch view of Tan-y-ffordd hillfort, an inconspicuous and heavily wooded site above the Rheidol Valley for which an overall photograph is at present impossible.
It is virtually a copy of the south fort at Pen Dinas, Aberystwyth, albeit on a reduced scale. This fort seems to have been built with a clear design from the outset, mirroring the architecture of Pen Dinas and Gaer Fawr, Lledrod. There are differences, however: the massive 'blind' ramparts, unbroken by any gateways, at the rear (left) of the hillfort, present a symbol of strength to those descending a mountain trackway from the north-east, mirroring the situation seen at Caer Llety Llwyd, Talybont. (T. Driver)

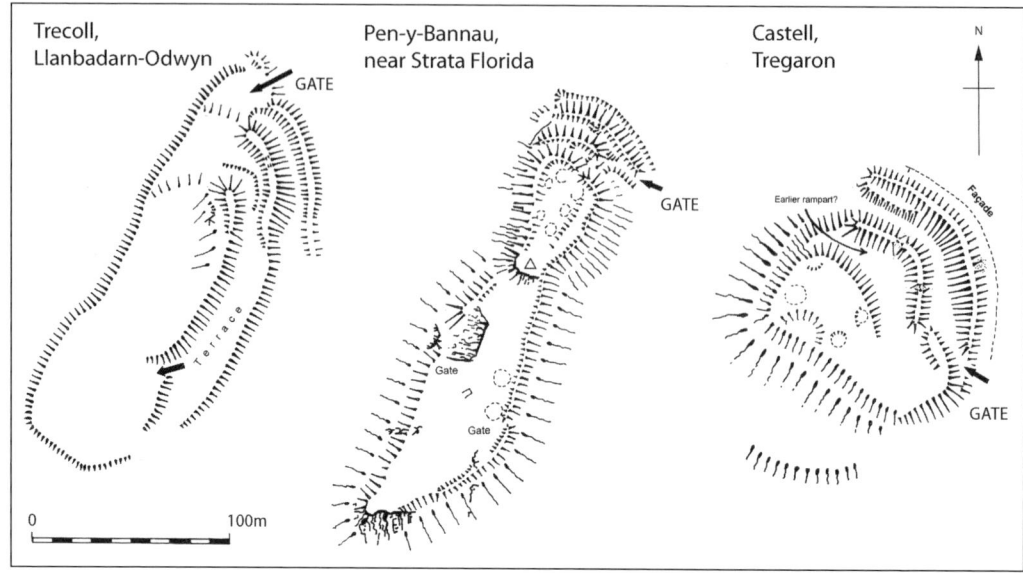

Figure 4.8. Elements of shared architecture. Designs quite different from Pen Dinas and Gaer Fawr hillforts link a handful of hillforts built on the fringes of Cors Caron/Tregaron Bog. Short, steep lengths of ramparts defend the narrow ends of Trecoll and Pen y Bannau while at Castell, Tregaron the steep ramparts block direct access to an inland rocky promontory. (T. Driver; sources: various)

In the final decades of the Iron Age the hillforts which shared recognisable design schemes stood as monumental ideological symbols in the landscape, built so that the main ramparts commanded particular vistas. The terraces of the south fort at Pen Dinas, Aberystwyth, were a radical departure from an earlier and much simpler enclosure on the north summit. These terraces still stand as a striking symbol to those arriving at the west coast from the interior of Wales. The symbolism of Pen Dinas was repeated at other forts around the Rheidol and Ystwyth Valleys, seen by prehistoric visitors when descending mountains passes from the east. Further to the south, crossing from the Wye Valley above Rhayader, visitors would have encountered the impressive defences of the Cors Caron forts which gazed out towards the eastern hills.

BUILDING THE HILLFORTS

The size of the camp varies ... They may be of different ages within a given period of time, built for different purposes, or they may have been built by groups of tribesmen differing in strength of numbers.[7]

Building a new hillfort was not purely an engineering task. There is force in the argument that ritual and ceremony had their place in bringing good luck, or good magic, to the start of building work.

74

The chosen hill may already have had its own myths and legends. Early Bronze Age burial mounds within many Welsh hillforts, including Darren Camp and Pen Dinas, Aberystwyth, were respected during their construction and subsequent lifetime. These ancient mounds were probably recognised as places of deep ancestral power that could be harnessed or appropriated through the construction of a new settlement around them. Pre-Iron Age enclosures are hinted at inside Pen Dinas, Aberystwyth, and within multi-phase enclosures such as Pen Dinas, Elerch, or Castell Grogwynion, Llanafan. Perhaps the Iron Age communities had strong myths and legends describing the origins of kings, queens and powerful lineages, or the ways in which the landscape around them came into being. If so, these would no doubt have included explanations for earlier monuments from the Neolithic and Bronze Ages. 'Watery places' also had a strong resonance in Iron Age society and it is perhaps not a coincidence that Castell Nadolig at Penbryn has a prominent spring close to the summit of the hill. This may well have helped in the choice of location, suitable for the religious or cult activities within or around the hillfort. Similarly, Castell Bach at Cwmtydu seems to have deliberately enclosed three cliff-top springs.

Unusually large or 'exotic' boulders were built into the gateways of some hillforts. A quartz boulder at Darren Camp, and large boulders incorporated into the latest phase of the Isthmus Gate at Pen Dinas, Aberystwyth, may have been 'guardians' at the entrances to these settlements (Figures 4.16 & 4.17). The gateways at Troedyrhiw (Figure 4.11) in south Ceredigion and Cnwc y Bugail (Figure 7.18), near Trawsgoed, were revetted with quartz blocks. 'Foundation deposits' of burials, including those of children, are sometimes found in ditch terminals close to gateways. Before construction began at Castell Henllys in north Pembrokeshire sacrificial offerings were placed in a pit dug at the foot of a wooden post near the main gateway, though the nature of the deposit, whether human or animal, was impossible to ascertain.

Figure 4.9. The grand scale of the defences of a great European hillfort can be seen here in this modern reconstruction of the Porte du Rebout gateway at the Mont Beuvray oppidum in Burgundy, France. The rampart is 'timber-laced', being reinforced with an internal frame-work of massive posts and horizontal beams, some of the latter protruding through the front face of the wall. The wall itself stands nearly three times the height of a person and was flanked by a rock-cut external ditch. The size of this hilltop settlement, in reality a prehistoric 'town', is excep-tional, enclosing some 135 hectares.[8] (T. Driver)

Assembling a workforce: debt and obligation

How were the hillforts of Wales – and the rest of Britain – built? Did powerful chieftains draw in labour from their own people or use force or influence to enslave others? It has been suggested[9] that monumental architecture implies '… the ability of some members of the society to control and organise others'. Iron gang-chains recovered from the Llyn Cerrig Bach hoard on Anglesey, were designed to link five people together by their necks – a clear indication that enslavement was a feature of Iron Age life.

However, there are other ways in which leaders and their communities could come together to help in the construction of a new hillfort. It is generally agreed that the act of building and enclosure was a reflection of status in itself. Building a hillfort confirmed that one was 'allowed' to take control of a section of land or a prominent hilltop, and to enclose it with a bank and ditch. This indicates the power of the leader, able to call on a network of social debts and obligations in order to carry out the building of a new settlement or power base. Neighbours or family groups may alternatively have freely contributed their own time, keen to be involved in a prestige project of this kind. In return they would expect to receive help when the time came to build their own farm or fort, as well as to benefit from the protection offered by belonging to a wider social group. Such communal

Figure 4.10. Pen-y-ffrwd Llwyd hillfort above Ystradmeurig (SN 709 687) commands a cliff-edge position, its ramparts breaking the skyline when seen from afar. The fort ditches were cut through the bedrock, with two or perhaps three distinct phases of enlargement suggested by the variable character of the ramparts and the numerous breaks in the defences. The interior is pock-marked with house platforms shelved into the hillslope. The site lies on private land. (Crown Copyright RCAHMW, AP_2012_1350)

approaches are common in developing countries where a 'potlatch' system of gift, debt and repayment allows work to be exchanged between individuals and communities without financial payment.

There may have been other incentives. It is likely that the chieftain who could offer better feasts, and perhaps even better beer, at the rampart-raising would draw in a bigger crowd of helpers. Some archaeologists have even suggested that it may have been the act of building which was important, not the finished fort. A hillfort which was a constant scene of activity and change showed a vigorous and well-connected leader at work, commanding the allegiance of many people and extending his or her hold over a wide territory.

Sons or daughters taking over the fort from elders may have wished to stamp their own mark by renewing its defences, perhaps explaining why many Welsh hillforts have evidence for different phases of work. Gateways were a particular focus for change. Evidence from excavations at Pen Dinas, Aberystwyth, suggests frequent renewal, change and narrowing at the main gates, often as a response to subsidence or collapse of sections of rampart walling. The main gate at the smaller fort of Castell Henllys in Pembrokeshire underwent several phases of change, yet by contrast the ramparts around the other parts of the circuit were not altered or even refurbished during the lifetime of the hillfort.

The Iron Age building site

The construction of a medium-sized or large hillfort required the organisation of labour, materials and food over several months, in a period free from conflict or disruption and ideally at a quiet time in the farming year when a good supply of manpower was available. Hillforts consumed vast quantities of timber and stone and archaeologists have made calculations of the resources required to build some of Britain's largest hillforts. Construction of the rampart at Danebury hillfort in Hampshire, for instance, would have consumed 1,700 five-metre lengths of timber for upright posts and an equivalent number for cross-bracing, in addition to manpower required for the digging, carting and dumping of over 20,000 cubic metres of soil and rubble. This represented a vast amount of woodland felling, clearing and transportation for the construction of a large and wealthy hillfort.[10] Another estimation[11] of the resources needed for a 'timber-laced' hillfort rampart, essentially a box-like framing of timber to stabilise a core of rubble and soil between dry-stone walls at front and rear, suggested the need for 4,680 trees from 76 hectares of land to provide sufficient timber for vertical posts and tie beams within a rampart enclosing a 4-hectare hillfort – roughly the internal area of Pen Dinas at Aberystwyth.

Fire, rock and hard labour

When visiting the construction site of a new hillfort, what would have been seen? Perhaps something along the lines of a rural 18th-century Cardiganshire mine, vividly described by W.J. Lewis in 1951:

> The conveyance of the ore out of the trenches was in wicker baskets carried by men and women on their heads or strapped to their backs. Many of the trenches had steps at one end, these being faced with wood and filled with waste material … When the workings were deep and wide, wooden ladders were used.

Ditch-digging would have required a level of skill as well as strong arms. The process has been described for the construction of Castell Henllys in Pembrokeshire: 'The ditch was begun with requisitioned labour, supervised by the inhabitants as they awaited the arrival of the specialist fort and entrance builders.'[12]

What methods were used to dig through the rock? The Iron Age people of mid Wales were unlikely to have had iron picks and shovels before the arrival of the Romans. Socketed antler picks, originally fitted with wooden handles, were found during excavations at the large north Wales hillforts of Dinorben at Abergele and Bwrdd Arthur on Anglesey, suggesting effective but nonetheless 'primitive' tools for excavating rock. Although not certain, fire-setting of the kind employed in later mining enterprises may have been one of the methods used to break up difficult bedrock:

> When confronted with very hard rock, a preliminary process of 'softening' occurred. A fire was built against the rock face or in a convenient crack. It was started with thin shavings of dry wood which could be set on fire ... then larger wood would be added and finally, cordwood ... These fires were left to burn for periods of 3 to 14 hours and then, while the rock was still hot, water was thrown on it causing it to crack and crumble. Wedges were then driven into these cracks to complete the loosening. Such a method was extremely uncomfortable to the miners on account of the dense clouds of smoke which filled the workings ...[13]

Figure 4.11. Troedyrhiw defended enclosure in south Ceredigion, under excavation in 2005. The view shows the gap for the main gateway between the terminals of the rock-cut ditch, each measuring up to 3.4 metres deep. Tumbled blocks of the original boulder and quartz gateway revetment can be seen in the base of the right-hand ditch. Note how thin the topsoil is over this plough-levelled site, first discovered during aerial survey some years earlier. (Crown Copyright RCAHMW, DS2005_109_004)

Impressive rock-cut ditches can still be seen at some of Ceredigion's hillforts, including Caer Pwll Glas north of Bow Street, Pen-y-ffrwd Llwyd at Ystradmeurig (Figure 4.10) and Gaer Fawr above Lledrod (Figure 4.1).[14] Recent excavations in south Ceredigion have shown the monumental nature of the defended enclosures built on or near the coastal plain. The Troedyrhiw enclosure, Y Ferwig, mostly dated to Romano-British times, was enclosed by deep rock-cut ditches about 3.4 metres wide and between 2.6 to 3.4 metres deep, calculated by the excavators[15] as having required the quarrying of 700 square metres of hard bedrock. Assuming that one person could dig and move one cubic metre of rock a week and build it into the rampart, the bank and ditch alone would have taken 13 people over one year to build; it could have been built faster, of course, with a larger number of people. This would undoubtedly have been beyond the resources that the inhabitants of such an enclosure could muster alone and therefore a wider network of help is implied, probably provided seasonally and at slack times of the farming year.

At times the shale bedrock of south Ceredigion seems to have defeated the construction gangs. On the north side of the Ffynnonwen enclosure the bedrock was far harder and more tightly bedded than elsewhere on the site. Rather than matching the main rock-cut ditch, which measured up to 4.2 metres wide and 2.2 metres deep (Figure 1.5), the ditch on the north side of the enclosure averaged only 30 centimetres deep. There were also 'pockmarks from percussion tools ... visible on the ditch floor'.[16] Clearly the rock here had defeated the builders who had then resigned themselves to leaving an irregular ditch which was barely begun in places, despite the interior of the enclosure showing clear evidence for settled occupation.

With these descriptions in mind, a visit to a hillfort today becomes less of a quiet ramble in the countryside. We must imagine the fervour of activity during construction, with shouts and perhaps smoke rising from the deepening ditches as fire-setting got underway, punctuated by the crack of broken rock. Carts would arrive continuously, loaded with tree trunks or prepared timbers, with crowds of labourers carrying baskets of earth or rock, setting the foundations for stone rampart walls or repairing tools. Somewhere would be key engineers or specialists in charge, checking horizontal and vertical timbers for position, stability and jointing, inspecting walling and defences for quality and strength and instructing foremen and parties working at distance from the fort about future requirements, deliveries and tasks with the aid of messengers. A regular supply of food and water for the workforce would have been essential, with cooking and food preparation no doubt occupying a good number of people on site throughout each day.

HILLFORT DEFENCES: WALLS FOR WAR OR FOR DISPLAY?

> ... though warfare between different tribes was imminent, it was chiefly in the nature of raids soon spent.[17]

Were the west Wales hillforts military strongholds, with defences designed to repel frontal attacks? Or were the ramparts and ditches primarily symbolic, intended to frighten and intimidate potential enemies or raiders? Or were they built simply to impress rival communities and leaders? There are no easy answers to such questions.

Figure 4.12. Erosion by sheep or excavation by archaeologists on any steep-faced hillfort rampart in Ceredigion is likely to reveal vestiges of stone walling, confirming that the hillforts once looked radically different from the grassy earthworks which stand today. This view shows small-scale archaeological excavation at Darren Camp, Trefeurig, in 2005. It also illustrates the enormous scale of the defensive outworks. In the 19th century it was recorded that 'Darren camp was pronounced ..., by an Indian officer, equal in defensive capability to any of the hill forts of the present time that he had seen in India'.[18] (Crown Copyright RCAHMW, DS2005_108_012)

Hillfort ramparts took a number of forms. 'Dump' ramparts were formed when material from upslope was thrown forward to form a great bank of rubble on the hillside. Alternatively upstanding rampart walls were built. It seems likely, on the basis of the limited amount of excavation available, that in Ceredigion the ramparts mostly took the form of inner and outer walls of stone retaining a core of soil and rubble. Taller ramparts may have required elements of timber-lacing to reinforce and hold the structure together; such timbering will of course have long since rotted away though traces within the core of the rampart can be detected if excavation is undertaken on a large enough scale.

Quite how ramparts were topped is a matter of some debate. Although it is known for certain that the rampart walk at Pen Dinas, Aberystwyth, was floored with clay it is uncertain what form any 'parapet' wall or fence would have taken. A palisade of upright timber posts – perhaps sharpened – is suggested in one of the present writer's early reconstruction drawings of the fort (Figure 4.18). However, such a heavy wall of upright timbers would have required a deep foundation within the body of the rampart, or bracing of some other kind. An alternative might have been a lighter fence, or perhaps a crenelated wattle or post-and-plank barrier as shown in more recent reconstructions (Figure 4.19). Whatever the arrangement, it is reasonably certain that a prestigious finished appearance would have been aspired to by the Iron Age builders, with carefully sawn or planed squared timbers or wattle fencing above well-finished wall faces, and perhaps even painted symbols or flags at the gateways.

'Warfare' or conflict can take many different forms, from bloody pitched battles to small-scale skirmishes or highly symbolic raiding or confrontations linked to rivalry, inter-clan competition and status-raising. In this context hillforts have been considered by one specialist as having been strategic 'machines' built to repel attack, with the 'hillfort

Figure 4.13. A vigorously depicted scene of Iron Age mounted warriors, with spears and rectangular shields, carved on a rock face at Tegneby in Sweden. The horses in the carving measure about 40 centimetres from head to tail. The style of the shields dates the scene to around 300 BC and it is one of the world's oldest known illustrations of shield-bearing horsemen. It is not clear from the surviving evidence whether anything similar would have been witnessed around the hillforts of Cardigan Bay. (T. Driver)

engineer' judging his tactical aims against the type of attack he expected, whether close combat or missile warfare.[19] As will be shown below, many Ceredigion hillforts were heavily defended, with well-designed gateway systems and 'command posts' or 'slinging platforms' overlooking the field of approach. In this sense the hillforts and their occupants were ready-armed – sling-stones have been recovered from many forts both in west Wales and other parts of Britain. The role of slingshot in the defence of a hillfort is described at the end of this chapter.

Even so, the hillforts of Cardigan Bay do not for the most part appear to have been robust military strongholds. Instead, they often seem to have been built 'on a budget', with the biggest defences flanking the 'front doors' while the 'back doors' and rear parts of the hillfort are only lightly defended, or not defended at all. A situation of this kind was also seen at Castell Henllys in Pembrokeshire where, despite a strong towered entrance gateway on the north-west, there were many other minor breaks in the rampart which seem never to have been blocked or controlled by gates. This implies that the hillfort was never actually impregnable to intruders, yet the main gateway remained outwardly a defensible and impenetrable structure which went through many episodes of rebuilding and reorganisation. The main purpose of the gate at Castell Henllys was therefore to control access and stand as a show of strength to visitors, whether friend or foe.[20]

The ideology of warfare, and the ability to launch a counter-attack from a hillfort, would have served as a strong deterrent in itself. The point was well made by one expert on the hillforts of Wales when he wrote that these (locally, but not entirely) terrifying defences could easily have fulfilled a military role, for '… ideally a fortress should be so strong as to make any thought of attack appear hopeless'.[21] This is a crucial point. The front-facing defences of a hillfort could be strong enough to dismiss the thought of an attack in the minds of hostile neighbours or raiders whilst at the same time serving to impress and humble any friendly visitors approaching the front gate.

It is likely that hillfort defences in Ceredigion were more suited to repelling frequent feuding and competitive raiding by rivals than to surviving a determined attack or siege. It is well documented that among the historic chiefdoms of the Scottish highlands and

Figure 4.14. Castell Moeddyn, near Lampeter, is a small but perfectly-built hillfort in a highly visible position. The rampart stands 4-5 metres high in places and is neat and steep-faced, suggesting that the original stone revetment walling must still stand below the present-day covering of turf. This is a good example of a prestigious residence of a minor leader on the southern flank of Cardigan Bay. The fort lies on private land but can be viewed from a nearby footpath. (T. Driver)

islands feuding and feasting were the two principal forms of display behaviour practised by the chieftains: '… feuding itself was food-focused. Raids on rival clans routinely involved … destruction of standing corn, and the theft of cattle.'[22] The Plains Indians of the United States also carried out raids and shows of bravery which were quite different from violent acts of conflict. These included horse-stealing and 'counting coup', where the rival was touched with a warrior's hand or weapon during a daring raid, but not killed, in the ultimate show of daring and bravado.

It is perhaps against this backdrop of irregular, low-level aggression, inter-clan rivalry and raiding that one should understand the piecemeal defences of most west Wales hillforts. Rather than standing as impregnable fortresses facing the threat of direct military attack, the hillforts served as a permanent symbol of wealth, status and power over the rural population, in much the same way as grand country houses did in more recent times.

Hillfort Gateways: impressing the neighbours

The hillfort gateway was the point where all the defensive and architectural ingenuity of the hillfort was focussed. This was more than a front door. It was the culmination of every visitor's journey to the fort. Here was the chance to intimidate and overawe new arrivals, impressing them with your status and clearly demarcating *their* public world from *your* private residence and power base. The approaches to a number of Ceredigion hillfort gateways, such as those at Darren Camp and Castell Allt-goch, were designed with a series of outworks – banks and ditches – to impress friendly visitors but to confuse, hinder, baffle or delay enemies before their arrival at the gate.

Gates have long been seen as one of the most informative parts of any hillfort, as evidenced by the following quotations: 'Hill-fort entrances tend to be elaborate and interesting. Further, since a gateway where the timber has rotted is worse than useless, they are more likely to retain evidence of repair and reconstruction than other parts of the defences …'.[23] Or … 'More complex entrances use a variety of devices to detain an attacking party in a cramped and vulnerable position, where defenders would have the advantage of height and freedom of action. [They] … are often remarkably complex and sophisticated structures: they reflect the concentration of defensive ingenuity in an area where attack also would be concentrated.'[24]

Castell Henllys: learning lessons from long-term hillfort excavation

More than two decades of excavation and research at Castell Henllys, Pembrokeshire, including the total excavation of the main gate, have resulted in one of the best-understood Iron Age defensive systems anywhere in Britain.[25] By example and inference the results have taught us much about hillfort gateways in west Wales. It was found, for example, that the gate at Castell Henllys was probably built by a 'hillfort architect', or a team of specialist builders, rather than by the community who lived in the hillfort. Excavators first discovered that the great ditch flanking the gateway had been accidentally over-dug along its southern edge, creating a void where the future gateway should stand. Before the gate was built, therefore, this mistaken over-digging had to be backfilled so that the new entrance could be constructed on top. The implication is that an error in the relatively unskilled preparatory work had to be put right when the specialist gate-building team arrived.

The main gate was then developed and modified through five main phases from the early 4th century BC onwards, initially taking the form of a narrow gateway passage flanked by two sets of concave guard chambers or recesses. Guard chambers are currently unknown in Ceredigion but were hinted at by the partial discovery of a concave recess at the gateway of Darren Camp during excavations in 2005. In its final phase the Castell Henllys gate was a dilapidated structure, with old structural timbers leaning in at such an angle that there was barely a passage through; despite this the gateway was still being used. Why was it not repaired, instead of being allowed to decay while the hillfort was still occupied? The excavators suggest that, just as in earlier phases, the specialist architectural or carpentry skills needed to repair this complex structure did not exist within the local community.

The meticulous excavations at Castell Henllys allow us to date the construction of the main earthwork defences and towered gateway to around 370 BC. The excavators thought that the gateway might subsequently have required rebuilding every 30 years or so. This means that any gate passage lined with stone walling and integral upright timbers, exactly the type of gate recorded at Pen Dinas, Aberystwyth, might have needed renovation every generation or two before rotting timbers and collapsing masonry necessitated a complete rebuild. This might explain why the south and north gates at Pen Dinas were each rebuilt at least once on different plans.

Figure 4.15. Very steep forward-facing ramparts, preserving in places a 70° angle of slope, front the hillfort at Castell, Tregaron, seen here in profile. Such ramparts attest to very careful methods of rampart construction, especially for the most important parts of the defences. Castell, Tregaron has perhaps the most extraordinary defensive façade of any hillfort in mid Wales, with a great sweeping outer rampart (left) forming an impenetrable curving wall at the front of the fort. The site lies on private land. (T. Driver)

Fieldwork in north Ceredigion by the author has shown that ramparts at the 'front' of forts were not only more impressive but were actually better built than other parts of the ramparts. Well-preserved and steep rampart faces with little erosion, for instance, survive on forward-facing or 'entrance' defences at Pen y Bannau and Castell, Tregaron, together with Darren Camp and other hillforts, implying that these parts of the banks were carefully structured and revetted during building. Whereas the oft-cited formidable defences at Maiden Castle, Dorset, have only a 40° slope to the ramparts, the steep face of the outer rampart at Castell, Tregaron preserves a 70° slope, and at Darren Camp 60°, attesting to a desire on the part of the Ceredigion builders to impress by ensuring a steep-faced, robust and long-lasting rampart build.

Quartz and defences

There is good evidence that quartz was used at Ceredigion hillforts and farmstead settlements to enhance the showy, prestigious appearance of gateways and ramparts. The name Castell Grogwynion means 'Stronghold (of) pebbles white' – *gro*, 'pebbles', plus the plural of *gwyn*.[26] All across the site are small squarish quartz blocks of a suitable size for dry-stone walling, while excavations on the north terrace in 2013[27] revealed blocks of quartz tumbled from the eroded rampart face.

Figure 4.16. Darren Camp during excavations in 2005. An improbable foundation for the prestigious dry-stone walling was provided by an enormous quartz boulder. It seems this was an important 'guardian' at the gateway. Similar stones were encountered at Pen Dinas, as illustrated in Figure 4.17. (Crown Copyright RCAHMW, DS2005_108_001)

The Troedyrhiw Romano-British defended enclosure in south Ceredigion, excavated in 2005, had a quartz-revetted main gate. The excavators described the significance of this as follows: 'The brightly coloured white and orange quartz would have made the approach visible, even at dusk ... Large blocks of other rock also lie across the landscape, so the selection of quartz would seem to be deliberate ... Associating the quartz with the entrance of the enclosure may have held some symbolic significance at this liminal area, such as some form of protective function, or as a sign of a certain status.'[28] Quartz blocks are known from the gateways of a number of hillforts including Darren Camp, Cnwc y Bugail near Trawsgoed and Castell Moeddyn near Lampeter, while quartz was used to embellish hillfort ramparts at Castell Allt-goch and Castell Goetre near Lampeter as well as at Trecoll and Castell Flemish between Bronnant and Tregaron. Early photographs of the 1934 excavations of the Isthmus Gate at Pen Dinas, Aberystwyth, show two large boulders and one flat slab (of uncertain stone type) incorporated in the latest walling of the since reburied south gate of the south fort (Figure 4.17). Did these curious, bulky additions to the gateway walling perhaps have some symbolic significance?

Entering Pen Dinas, Aberystwyth

The most sophisticated gateways yet recorded in Ceredigion were found at Pen Dinas, Aberystwyth in the 1930s, as described in Chapter 7. The gateways of the second to fourth phases of the south fort were elaborate but all conformed to the general principle of a

Figure 4.17. Excavations at Pen Dinas, Aberystwyth, in 1934. The outermost and latest wall of the Isthmus gate incorporated this set of large boulders where it joined the southern terminal of the flanking rampart, something not observed anywhere else on the site. This was dismissed in the final report of the Pen Dinas excavations[29] as a 'poorly-built face', but the similarity to the large quartz boulder revealed at Darren Camp (Figure 4.16) is striking. The boulders would have been an unusual and prominent sight to those approaching either of these forts and may indeed have served some kind of ceremonial or symbolic role. (Pen Dinas excavation archive, National Monuments Record of Wales, DI2015_0402)

stone-lined gateway passage through the rampart, with a well-surfaced roadway crossed by a bridge continuing the rampart walk and supported on strong timber posts. The bridges would have had great display potential and could no doubt have been lined by armed warriors, banners or the heads of enemies. Bridges of this kind were a late feature in the west of Britain, recorded on the Welsh Borderlands from around 100 BC.

The main gates into the south fort at Pen Dinas, both at the south (Figures 1.4 and 4.19) and at the north (Figure 4.18), were asymmetric structures, featuring prominent right-hand bastions (from the intruder's or visitor's perspective). These provided superior fields of view, exposing the traditionally unshielded right arms of any approaching attackers, making them vulnerable to missiles from above. The north gate had a sharply-angled entrance passage, turning almost 90° to the left as one approached uphill from the Isthmus. In the third phase, the south-facing wall of the entrance passage was enlarged with a massive projecting bastion, increasing the passage wall on this side to some 12 metres in length, with a bridge set at the inner point. From the vantage of the bastion, rampart walk and crossing bridge the entrance passage would have formed a closely guarded 'killing ground'. Despite the relative sophistication of the gateway plan there is evidence for instability and collapse of the many wall-lines revealed during the excavations: buttresses, rebuilds and the bolstering of old walls by encasing them in new ramparts, show some of the ways in which the Iron Age builders tackled the recurring problem of maintaining high walls built with the rather poor shale slabs available on the hilltop.

Evidence for a similarly complex gateway on a smaller scale, dating to the Middle Iron Age, was uncovered at Caer Cadwgan, Cellan in the 1980s. The 2m-wide stone-lined passage through the rampart was a two-phase structure, culminating in a six-posted gateway sufficient for supporting a timber superstructure or crossing-bridge. There were hints of structural instability here, too, in the narrowing of the gateway passage in the second phase of construction, with the addition of a strong boulder revetment lining each side.[30] This may well have been a response to outward pressure from the loose rampart material pushing into the gateway passage, just as appears to have been the case at Castell Henllys.

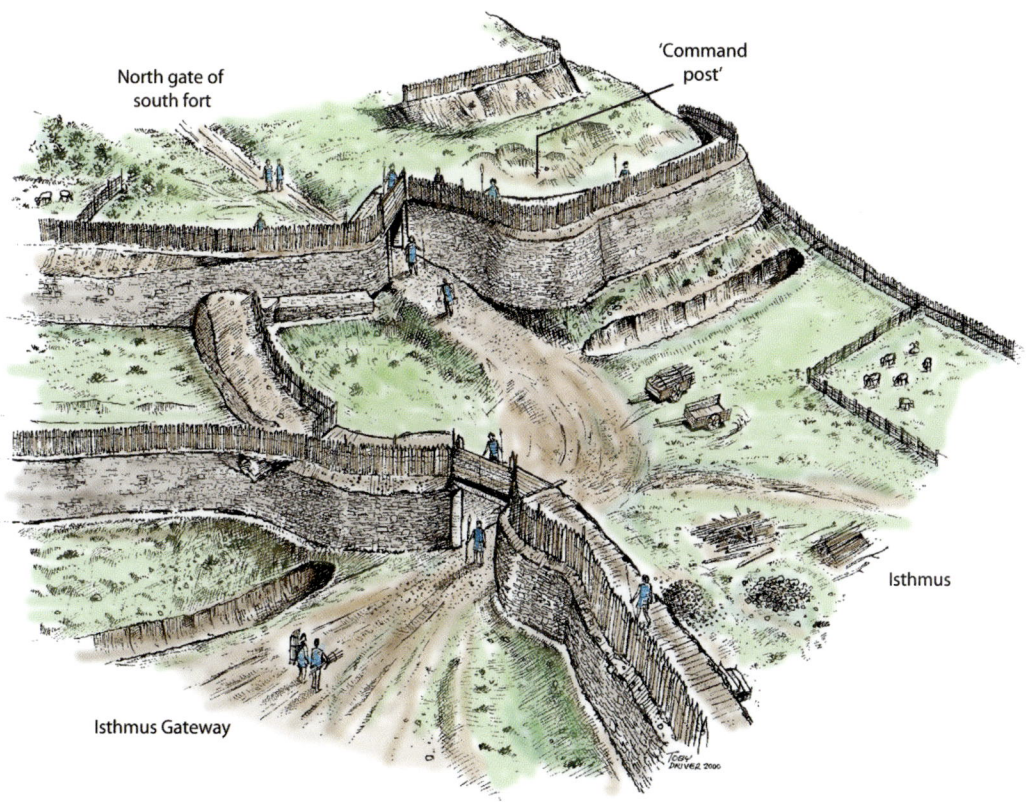

Figure 4.18. Pen Dinas, Aberystwyth. Reconstruction of the north gate of the south fort (background) and the Isthmus gate (foreground) in the last form of the hillfort defences. The north gate is shown with reinforcing buttresses at the base of the left-hand wall, shoring up a collapsing rampart face. The outward face of the Isthmus gate stood over 4 metres high, almost as high as a modest two-storey domestic building of the present day. Warriors atop the tallest rampart (upper right) would have towered 5 metres above the heads of any attackers who had already penetrated the Isthmus gate. Compare with Figure 7.6. (T. Driver)

There is potentially relevant surface evidence at several other Ceredigion forts which display close-set, massive rampart terminals and a narrow entrance passage-way lurking beneath the modern turf. These features suggest that gateways with a through-passage, bastions and a crossing bridge may once have existed at forts such as Hen Gaer near Bow Street, Pen y Bannau above Strata Florida, Caer Penrhos at Llanrhystud, Pen y Castell at Llanilar, Gaer Fawr at Lledrod, and perhaps Craig y Gwbert promontory fort near Cardigan, as well as at many other hillforts as yet untouched by excavation.

Figure 4.19. Controlling access at Pen Dinas, Aberystwyth. Reconstruction of the Phase III south gate of the south fort as it might have appeared at around 100 BC. The gateway looked out over steep approaches with a dramatic asymmetric design, its northern (right-hand) wall jutting far out to form a sort of command post. This right-hand bastion would probably have towered more than 3 metres above the heads of those approaching the gateway.
The reconstruction shows an alternative form of rampart 'parapet' compared with those shown in Figure 4.18, in this case the equally authentic possibility of a wattle fence atop the wall.
Note the prestigious squared posts supporting the bridge across the entrance-way.
(T. Driver)

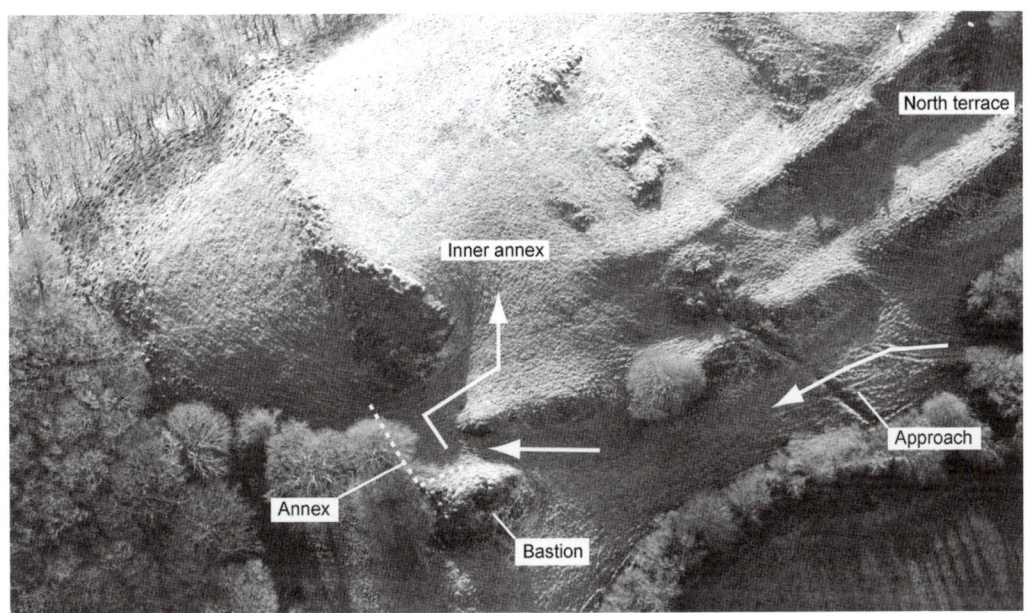

Figure 4.20. The elaborate entrance-way into Castell Grogwynion hillfort above Llanafan. Visitors approaching from below the fort may have had to walk the full length of the main rampart before gaining access at the lowest point of the hillfort, the design delaying their entrance but showing off the fort's impressive defences. A freestanding bastion flanked the left-hand side of the entrance where visitors entered a small annex, then turned through 90° into the lower public area of the hillfort. Other minor gateways around the hillfort attest to centuries of change and development at this complex site.
(Crown Copyright RCAHMW, detail of AP_2012_1378)

Figure 4.21. The main gateway bastion at Castell Grogwynion. The mound on which the figure stands would probably have resembled a free-standing bastion or low stone-walled tower, with the entrance passage into the hillfort on the right in this view. A timber gate was probably hung from the bastion, with timber palisades completing the defences.
The hillfort lies on private farmland. (Crown Copyright RCAHMW)

> [Hillforts] are the products of peace and not of war and I would disabuse the minds of those prone to imagine scenes of battle and strife ... I, however, do not want anyone to believe that the old Celt was remarkable for his peace-loving character; no one loved a scrap more than he.[31]

There are no surviving Iron Age weapons from Ceredigion, apart from numerous slingshot – small rounded beach or river pebbles, recovered from a number of hillforts. The arrival of iron seems to have upset the balance between manufacture and trade of any bronze or iron objects during the first few centuries of the Iron Age, as metal finds from this period remain rare. This shows a contrast to the Late Bronze Age when experienced metalworkers with high social status produced the Rhos Rydd shield, one of the finest Late Bronze Age shields in Wales.

There are two major differences between bronze and iron technology. The iron ore (sometimes found as bog ore in Wales) was differently distributed compared with those for copper and tin, and also required entirely new methods of manufacture involving hammering and welding rather than casting.[32] Despite a well documented Early Bronze Age mining industry in north Ceredigion, principally sourcing copper, the nature and location of Iron Age ores and metalworking in the region remain obscure. As noted in Chapter 3, a recent study[33] using a portable x-ray fluorescence scanner to look for metal deposits in three hillfort interiors in Ceredigion failed to reveal any evidence of prehistoric metalworking inside the forts. Perhaps the smoky and antisocial business of smelting metal was confined to sites outside the ramparts?

It can safely be assumed that the later Iron Age chieftains and warriors on Cardigan Bay had swords and shields in their possession – perhaps to compare to those from Llyn Cerrig Bach (Figure 4.22) – but to date they have not been found. Fragments of two shields from

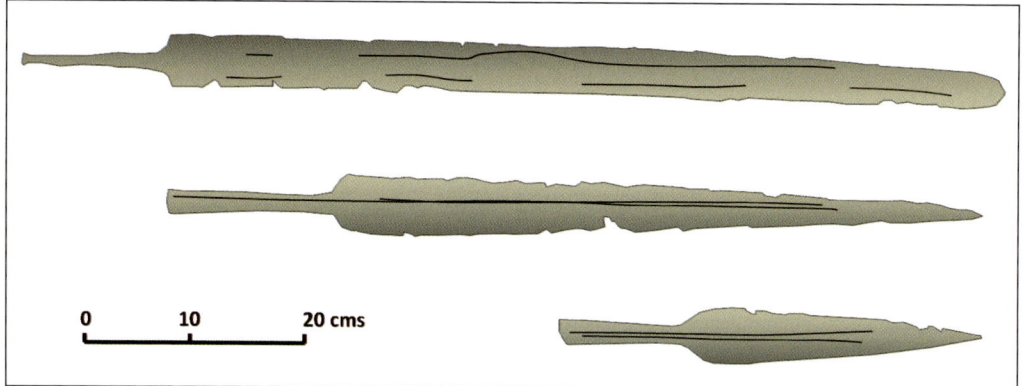

Figure 4.22. Iron narrow sword (top) and spearheads from the Llyn Cerrig Bach late Iron Age votive deposit in Anglesey. Sword hilts and scabbard fittings were also found.
The sword measures nearly a metre long, while the largest spearhead is 74 centimetres long. Similar weapons would have been known amongst the Iron Age aristocracy on Cardigan Bay, but were probably rarely seen on the region's many farms. (T. Driver[34])

a neighbouring area, the slopes of Cadair Idris above Tal-y-llyn lake in Gwynedd, are the best indication that we have so far for the kind of shields that might have been in use at Ceredigion's hillforts during the Late Iron Age or early Romano-British period (see box feature below).

A shield from the Cardigan Bay Iron Age

0   10 cms

A symbol of late Iron Age power from a neighbouring region, the reconstruction[35] alongside is of one of a pair of La Tène-style late Iron Age or Romano-British shields, found on the slopes of Cadair Idris in southern Gwynedd, by picnickers:

> The find was made in June 1963 ... Mr and Mrs Arthur Jones of Llanbadarn Fawr, Aberystwyth, who were picnicking alongside the path ... happened to notice some pieces of sheet-bronze which were only half-buried in a shallow deposit of silt in a small cavity beneath a large boulder which projects from the mountainside, propped up by two small boulders.[36]

The wooden or leather shield (Figure 4.23 alongside) would have stood 88 centimetres tall. Although probably made by local metalworkers, the Tal-y-llyn metalwork also included part of a Roman lock, suggesting that the hoard was deposited after the Roman conquest of Britain in the 1st century AD.

Dr Adam Gwilt[37] of the National Museum of Wales suggests the Tal-y-llyn shields, probably manufactured between 50 and 80 AD, 'capture a world at the cusp of change, when native Iron Age societies were resisting the advances of the Roman army'. The three Celtic 'triskele' designs on the shield, one either side and another on the central boss, are all differently depicted and positioned: 'The repeated three-limbed triskele design may have given wearers spiritual protection and power.' A decorated bronze plaque from the same hoard can be seen as the frontispiece for Chapter 5.

Death from above: slingers and slingshots

> ... fortifications were very cleverly engineered so that there should be no 'dead ground' down the slopes, and so that the defenders upon the rampart could effectively sweep the hillsides below with their slingstones and javelins and arrows.[38]

The ordinary weapon of the masses was the sling, firing rounded stones or 'shot' slightly smaller than a hen's egg. This was a simple combination, but brutally effective. The power of the sling is exemplified in the biblical tale of David and Goliath, in which an exceptionally strong warrior was killed by a blow to the head from a boy wielding a sling. Trials by archaeologists have shown what a devastating weapon the slingshot could be.

Figure 4.24. An Iron Age defender takes aim with his leather sling over the top of a hillfort rampart, posing a deadly threat to any enemy within 60-100 metres. Close by on the clay-topped rampart walk a basket holds hundreds of rounded pebbles gathered from local beaches, fuelling an almost endless lethal barrage. Men, women and children would all have been proficient with the sling. (T. Driver)

Slingshots are a ubiquitous and cheap weapon across many parts of the world. Rawhide slings were an essential element in the Apache Indian's war-kit. In Peruvian societies, where the sling remains in use even today for managing livestock, a well-aimed shot can be used to encourage a stubborn animal to move, or aimed ahead of a flock so as to encourage sheep or goats to turn in one direction or another.[39] Shot can be also used to scare or kill predators which may threaten livestock. For those growing up in a hillfort the use of a slingshot would have been learnt at a young age, with warriors becoming proficient and deadly into their teenage years. It is likely that Iron Age youngsters honed their skills of range and accuracy whilst out on shepherding duties in tranquil times.

Slingshots were the common, readily available weapon of the Iron Age regardless of wealth or status. A trip to a pebble beach or the gravels of inland rivers yielded as much free ammunition as a community could carry. Excavations at hillforts as diverse as Maiden

Figure 4.25. Iron Age slingshot. Collected from Pen Dinas, Aberystwyth, after a bracken fire (the five on the left and centre) and from Pen Dinas, Elerch (the three on the right). Both hillforts are scheduled ancient monuments so the finds were reported to the landowner and the officers of Cadw before being placed in the Ceredigion Museum. (T. Driver)

Castle in Dorset and Castell Henllys in Pembrokeshire have produced caches of thousands of slingshot placed behind the ramparts or near gateways. They are also a common find from Ceredigion hillforts. A cache of twelve stones from Pendinaslochdyn, and others from Pen Dinas, at Aberystwyth, can be seen on display in the Ceredigion Museum. The ubiquity of slingshot use among the hillfort population, and the ready supply of caches around a fort, no doubt meant that in an emergency all could respond quickly to the threat; shouts would go up from the guards on the rampart walks and gateway towers, and men and women, children and teenagers would grab personal slings and baskets of stones and run to the rampart walks to mount a deadly defence of their homes and possessions.

How deadly and accurate was a small stone in the right hands? Modern experiments have shown that a slingshot would fly at around 25 metres per second and could fracture a human skull at 60 metres. It would have been even more effective when used from above by guards on the rampart walk. The defenders always had the advantage.

Chapter 5

RITUAL, DEATH AND SACRED PLACES

Chapter frontispiece: A prehistoric face from the Cardigan Bay region.
The immaculately combed hair of a Late Iron Age or Romano-British Celt gazes out from
a bronze plaque, a La Tène-style decorative shield mounting. Featuring two opposing heads
(only the upper is shown here) the mounting was found as part of the Tal-y-llyn hoard on the
southern slopes of Cadair Idris, south Gwynedd (see Box Feature, page 91).
The heads portray a simple face with an ambivalent – perhaps menacing – expression
and a fixed gaze. The spot chosen for deposition, beneath a prominent boulder alongside
the present-day path, suggests both a deep antiquity to this mountain track and the likelihood
that the path's destination – the isolated corrie lake of Llyn Cau – may have been a
sacred place in the Iron Age and a locale for votive deposition or sacrifice.
(By permission of the National Museum of Wales. DH000260_02)

Iron Age religion and ritual

> Isolated places of natural beauty such as mountains, lakes, rivers and bogs were often chosen as places to communicate with the pagan gods.[1]

Ritual, belief and ceremony were intrinsic parts of daily life in Iron Age Wales and permeated all things, just as they did in rural communities into recent centuries. Society was underpinned by a complex set of beliefs and superstitions with myriad gods attested both from classical Greek and Roman writings and from archaeological finds. There was no clear separation between secular and religious life as there is today. Many aspects of daily life were guided by long-held rituals and ceremonies, from the orientation of roundhouse doorways towards the rising sun to how and where rubbish should be disposed of.

There was a belief that potent gods and deities inhabited certain natural places such as springs, pools and mountain lakes, as well as 'liminal' or remote points of the landscape such as mist-shrouded mountain tops or dangerous coastal promontories. A recent survey[2] of some of the Iron Age coastal promontory forts of south Pembrokeshire examined several of these tiny coastal enclosures too small for practical settlement and suggested that they may instead have served ceremonial functions. In Ceredigion, a small coastal promontory at Ynyslochtyn, facing an offshore island, and a 'hidden' coastal fort at Castell Bach, Cwmtydu (see Chapter 7), may both have incorporated ceremonial roles in their wider functions.

Two Welsh lakes, Llyn Cerrig Bach on Anglesey and Llyn Fawr in south Wales (described below), have produced votive hoards of exceptional importance, dating from the Late Bronze Age or from the Iron Age and early Roman period. Closer to Cardigan Bay, on the slopes of Cadair Idris in south Gwynedd, two decorative roundels and the central metal bosses from fine bronze shields (Figure 4.23) had been deposited with other metalwork – including the plaque shown in the chapter frontispiece – beneath a prominent naturally-propped boulder on a mountain path above Tal-y-llyn lake. This dryland hoard of metalwork, discovered by chance, shows what may yet be found elsewhere by perceptive eyes searching well-trodden routes, particularly up to mountain lakes.

Iron Age cemeteries and shrines are rare in Wales. Roman temples, known from crop-mark evidence in the Vale of Clwyd near Ruthin and at Llancayo near Usk, may potentially mark the earlier sites of Iron Age shrines. When the Romans conquered Britain they were shrewd in appropriating significant existing shrines and native gods. The major sacred bath complex of *Sulis Minerva* in Bath, Somerset, began life as an Iron Age sanctuary based upon

Figure 5.1. The freestanding stack which dominates the view from Castell Bach fort, looking towards Craig Caerllan headland, Cwmtydu, may have formed part of the coastal promontory fort before being cut off by coastal erosion. Alternatively it may already have been an offshore stack in Iron Age times. Distinct platforms to each side of its summit may be the work of prehistoric builders. The vertical grooves in its peak, undoubtedly of natural geological origin, are nonetheless striking features that may have held significance for the prehistoric inhabitants of the hillfort. (T. Driver)

remarkable natural hot springs. The Roman complex was presided over by a hybrid goddess blending Sulis, the Celtic goddess of healing and sacred waters, with Minerva, the Roman goddess of wisdom.

It is known that Iron Age communities in Ceredigion revered earlier ritual monuments and burial grounds, particularly Early Bronze Age barrows dotted throughout the uplands and along river valleys. Summit barrows survive within hillforts at Darren Camp and Pen Dinas, Aberystwyth, undisturbed during the later construction and occupation of the hillforts despite being readily available sources of building material.

There are two sites of known or probable Iron Age burials in the county. At Castell Nadolig urns and cremated bone, presumed to be from the Iron Age, were dug up shortly before 1859 (see below). In the north of the county at Plas Gogerddan a multiperiod ritual and burial complex was excavated in 1986. Here the locally prominent ridge of gravel, extending into wetter lowlands, first saw human activity in the Neolithic period about 6,000 years ago. In the succeeding Early Bronze Age a standing stone was erected alongside a round barrow, both of which still stand today. Excavations also revealed three linked circular ditches which once surrounded plough-levelled barrows, with Iron Age cremations inserted into them. A number of other pits contained evidence for human burials, one of them accompanied by a pair of bronze 'fibulae' brooches dating from some time in the 1st century BC or 1st century AD. Two other burials were found close by, one of them accompanied by a further brooch. The fragments of the brooches can be seen on display in Ceredigion Museum.

And what of Druids, the archetypal figures of the Iron Age priesthood? Roman historian Tacitus vividly documented the appearance of the Druids of Anglesey during the Roman assault on the island in the mid-1st century AD:

> Close by stood Druids, raising their hands to heaven and screaming dreadful curses …
> it was their religion to drench their altars in the blood of prisoners and consult their
> gods by means of human entrails.[3]

Druids are mentioned in the writings of Pliny,[4] who described a priest 'clad in a white robe' who 'cut the mistletoe with a golden sickle', providing a durable romantic image of the Druid and his work. The real functions of the Druids have been described more prosaically as follows:[5]

> … a consistent picture is painted by the earlier 2nd to 1st century BC writers. They
> portray Druids as religious specialists, effectively a priesthood. Julius Caesar described
> three main roles for the Druids as (i) being in charge of religion, (ii) judges and arbi-
> trators in disputes, and (iii) teachers and keepers of Knowledge.

Figure 5.2. Rare and special treasures from the Cardigan Bay Iron Age. The Castell Nadolig or Penbryn spoons from south Ceredigion were made in the 1st century BC and are thought to be specialist 'tools' for use in religious ceremonies (see also pages 105-106). Of those known from Britain, the Penbryn spoons are the only ones to be inlaid with gold. This view shows exact replicas of the spoons, on display in Amgueddfa Ceredigion Museum, Aberystwyth, held here to give a sense of their size and how they may have been used in prehistoric rituals. The original spoons are on display in the Ashmolean Museum, Oxford. (T. Driver. By kind permission Amgueddfa Ceredigion Museum, Aberystwyth)

The most significant evidence for Iron Age ritual in Ceredigion is a pair of Iron Age 'divination spoons' from Castell Nadolig, Penbryn, in the south of the county (Figures 5.2, 5.6 and 5.7). Such rare and special articles would only have been used by a Druid or high priest. The spoons from Castell Nadolig seem to provide good circumstantial evidence for a practising Druid in a Ceredigion hillfort, perhaps a century before the Romans arrived in west Wales.

Lakes, bogs and votive deposition

> The repeated deposition of prestigious goods in watery contexts undoubtedly reflects ... the episodic renewal of allegiance to the spirit-powers perceived as residing in remote, liminal, dangerous and inaccessible places such as pools and bogs.[6]

At the edge of watery places such as lakes, rivers and bogs, Iron Age people believed that they could commune with the other world. Such beliefs were no doubt only strengthened by the dangerous, remote and inaccessible nature of most bogs and wetlands, and the mysteriously clear and dark waters of mountain lakes and pools. Legends of water monsters still cling to some Welsh lakes, as with Llyn Tegid (Bala Lake) at Bala, while tales of the Lady of the Lake are well known elsewhere. Holy wells in Wales are still visited by pilgrims. Votive deposits of prehistoric metalwork are also known from dryland locations, but are less likely to have been preserved against corrosion and theft into the present day. The Tal-y-llyn hoard, discovered on the slopes of Cadair Idris, was positioned alongside a prominent route up to the remote mountain lake of Llyn Cau, very possibly a focus for Iron Age ritual. The deep, clear waters of this quiet lake drop away sharply from a shallow perimeter and still appear dark and mysterious today.

There is good evidence for the conspicuous deposition of valuable metalwork in Welsh lakes and bogs. Sometime after 800-600 BC, at the end of the Late Bronze Age and the beginning of the Iron Age, two cauldrons, along with tools, weapons and horse-gear, were cast into Llyn Fawr lake near Rhigos in south Wales: '... perhaps as a contract with the gods in return for good harvest and the continued wellbeing of the community'.[7] This isolated lake nestles between high outcrops in a 'cauldron-like setting', occupying a spectacular escarpment-edge position overlooking the rolling moorlands of the Brecon Beacons. The Llyn Fawr cauldrons were already old when deposited; they have been described as belonging '... to a class of ceremonial equipment related to feasting and hospitality, central to the cohesion of the chief and his [or her] warband'.[8] Cauldrons also had a central importance in the Iron Age home, and were often the focus of social gatherings and feasting. Perhaps this lake sat at an important cultural or tribal boundary, or was thought to be at the very edge of the known world for a group of people?

A further famous lake hoard was recovered from Llyn Cerrig Bach on Anglesey. This consisted of an astonishing array of metalwork dating from the 3rd century BC to the 1st century AD, showing use of this watery shrine from the Iron Age into the Roman period. The hoard contained weaponry, including several long swords,[9] a shield boss and decorative plaques along with two 'gang chains' for the control of slaves and evidence for twenty-two chariot wheels. This hoard shines fascinating light on the aristocratic metalwork which may have graced chieftains' homes. Weapons, tools and other artefacts cast as votive offerings into the dark waters of lakes or rivers across Britain were sometimes ritually 'killed', being broken, bent or pierced so as to place them beyond normal use.

The hoards at both Llyn Cerrig Bach and Llyn Fawr were found only through modern, accidental, interventions. At Llyn Cerrig Bach the hoard was found during construction of a Second World War airfield, the intact deposit being disturbed by machinery during draining operations. The hoard at Llyn Fawr was found when the lake was being drained for the construction of a reservoir. Without similar lucky finds at other mountain lakes our wider knowledge of sacred places in Wales will remain limited.

The Rhos Rydd, Aberllolwyn, Late Bronze Age shield

> It is generally agreed that these shields served more of a ritual or symbolic, rather than a bellicose function... The society which made such shields was probably one in which chieftains exercised some control and highly skilled smiths played an important role.[10]

Votive offerings of just three glorious Late Bronze Age shields are known from Wales, two from Snowdonia and one from the coastal belt of Cardigan Bay. Largely forgotten today, the Rhos Rydd or Glan-rhos shield was discovered in 1804 in a bog near Blaenplwyf, between Aberystwyth and Llanrhystud (Figure 5.3). It is considered to be one of the finest

Figure 5.3. Rhos Rydd bog today, inland of Blaenplwyf village to the south of Aberystwyth, is the findspot of one of the finest Late Bronze Age shields from Wales. (T. Driver)

Figure 5.4. A national treasure from a Cardigan Bay bog. Nowhere in west Wales is the power of the Late Bronze Age aristocracy more clearly seen than in the glorious Rhos Rydd shield from Blaenplwyf. Every year thousands of visitors to the British Museum gaze upon its near-perfect form, set alongside some of the greatest archaeological treasures from around the world. It was created by a highly skilled artisan yet its thin metal form was only ever intended for ceremonial use. (British Museum 1168428001)

Late Bronze Age shields yet recovered from Wales (Figures 2.7 & 5.4). Dating to 1100-900 BC, not long before the earliest Iron Age forts began to be erected in Ceredigion, this glorious and finely-made shield was too thin to have provided any practical protection in battle. It was probably reserved for ceremonial use before being cast into the bog as a votive offering. True war-shields would have had a backing of wood or leather. The Rhos Rydd shield measures 66 centimetres in diameter, is perfectly preserved and was beaten out from a single disc of bronze. It is flat with twenty concentric ribs decorated with 3,700 singly punched bosses. The shield currently resides in the British Museum, where its exceptionally thin and delicate form can be admired 'edge-on', as can the breath-taking perfection of its concentric ribs and punched bosses. One wonders who last held the metal grip on the rear of the shield before it was confined to its watery grave in prehistory? A life-size photograph of the shield can be seen in the Ceredigion Museum.

Rhos Rydd bog (SN 573 740) is a half-concealed location set back slightly from the coastal plain. It is unlikely that such a fine and valuable shield was a casual or accidental loss and it is entirely possible that the bog was a focus for ritual deposition of high status metalwork in the Late Bronze Age. It may be significant that the bog is 'tucked away' in an area virtually devoid of recorded prehistoric settlements save for a single cropmarked enclosure at Banc y Gaer, overlooking the bog from the west. One can only guess whether Rhos Rydd continued to be of sacred importance during the Iron Age.

Moel y Llyn: Ceredigion's sacred lake?

There are no known deposits of Iron Age metalwork from a Ceredigion lake or upland pool to match those recorded from Llyn Cerrig Bach. However, it is interesting to consider a possible candidate for a sacred lake, at Llyn Moel y Llyn in the far north of the county. This is a tiny, hidden, upland lake on the summit of a prominent ridge at over 500 metres above sea level, on the fringes of the Plynlimon uplands. The summit dominates the head of the Cletwr Valley, home to one of Ceredigion's few stone circles and many Early Bronze Age cairns. The lake overlooks the foothills of the Dyfi Estuary to the north, with pano-ramic views towards Cadair Idris. At only 80 metres across it is little more than a pool, but it has two notable features. Firstly it is surrounded by an arc of four prominently-sited Early Bronze Age burial cairns, set on high summits to the north, east and south to create a true Early Bronze Age 'cemetery'. Some compelling reason must have encouraged several generations of Bronze Age families to return to the high pool of Llyn Moel y Llyn to bury their dead.

A second notable feature is that the lake has a strong legend – or folk tale – attached to it of a Lady of the Lake – *Arglwyddes y Llyn* – and her pure white cattle. A nearly identical legend is associated with the more famous lake of Llyn y Fan Fach in the Black Mountain of Carmarthenshire. One version of the Llyn Moel y Llyn story relates how the lady married a local farmer and brought with her a dowry of pure white cattle (a farm in the Cletwr Valley still bears the name Cae'r Arglwyddes). During the marriage ceremony the farmer acciden-tally struck his wife with iron for a third time, and the lady called to her cattle and returned beneath the waters of the lake. One calf was left behind and turned black with fright, this being the origin of the Welsh Black cattle breed.[11]

Figure 5.5. Winter sunlight on the small summit lake of Llyn Moel y Llyn, encircled by Early Bronze Age burial cairns. (T. Driver)

Many associate this type of tale with a folk memory of the Celtic festival of *Lughnasa* at the beginning of August when cattle were made to swim or were washed in a river or lake. The reference to being struck with iron may relate to a time when iron was novel, or when its creation and forging by skilled smiths was deemed to be a strange and magical process. Llyn Moel y Llyn clearly had a heightened significance as a burial location in the Early Bronze Age. The association of an unusual folk tale with possible 'Celtic' origins suggests a continuing importance in Iron Age and Roman times.

Centre of ceremony, divination and death? Castell Nadolig, Penbryn

> Castell yn Do'ig [Nadolig] about two miles farther on [from New Inn]: it is evidently the remains of a British Encampment of very large size. The exact form can not, at this time, be ascertained, the embankments having been destroyed in several places ...[12]

Antiquarian discoveries at one south Ceredigion hillfort suggest it may have been a focus for ceremony and burial. Castell Nadolig, at Penbryn, is a great hilltop enclosure marked today by monumental concentric ramparts, fossilised in hedgebanks on the coastal plain alongside a busy modern road (Figures 1.15 and 5.6). The name Castell Nadolig, literally 'Christmas Castle', is unique in Wales and was noted in the 19th century as 'a remarkable appellation for such a work' (by the antiquarian Reverend Edward Lowry Barnwell writing in *Archaeologia Cambrensis* in 1862); in the 16th century it was recorded as Kastell Yn Dolig. It has been suggested that the name originates from a now-forgotten folk memory of ceremonial or ritual gatherings at certain times or seasons of the year.

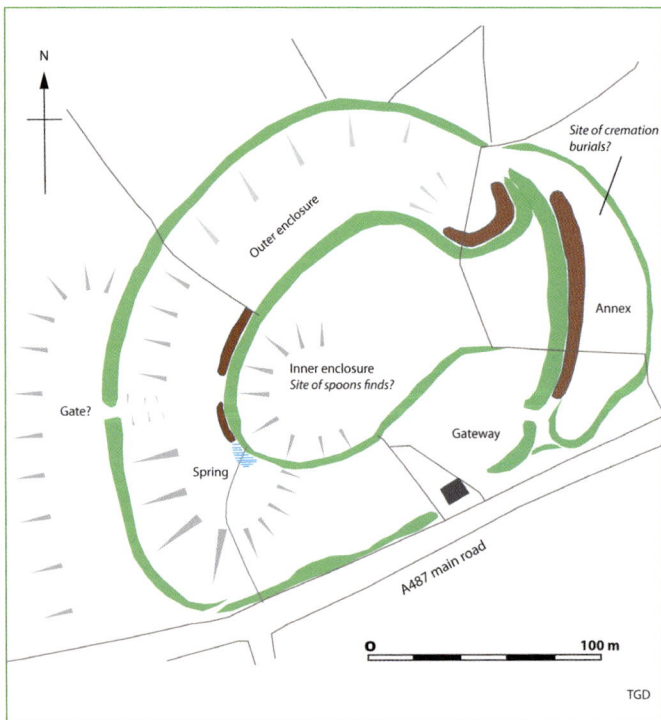

Figure 5.6. Castell Nadolig. New plan of the hillfort showing sketched detail of previously unmapped low earthworks and other topographic features. Note the position of the spring, and the way the earthworks and gateway are respected by the line of the present-day (and probably ancient) road. Ramparts are shown in green, surviving ditches in brown. There is no public access to the fort which lies on private farmland. (T. Driver; based on the Ordnance Survey 1973 with additions)

The fort is deceptively well sited on a prominent but gently rounded summit, commanding wide views. Below and to the west are advantageous coastal inlets between Aberporth and Ynys Lochtyn. The inhabitants of the fort would have felt themselves at the nodal point of the regional landscape, looking out across the sea and inward towards the hills. The busy modern road passing the fort almost certainly fossilizes a prehistoric ridge route running along the watershed so as to skirt a number of deep valleys. The original entrance to the fort lies in the field adjacent to the modern road, which respects the line of the ramparts rather than cutting into them, suggesting that this line of communication might have been in use before the fort was built.

Castell Nadolig is famous, and unusual, for finds made there in the 19th century. A pair of bronze 'spoons', differing in design, almost flat and as large as an adult's palm, were stumbled upon in the collection of the Ashmolean Museum, Oxford (where they are still displayed) by Augustus Wallaston Franks, just as Reverend Barnwell was about to publish his 1862 paper on 'Bronze Articles Supposed to be Spoons' from England and Wales. The spoons had been unearthed by the tenant at Castell Nadolig from beneath 'a heap of stones' in around 1829 in what was regarded as the '*praetorium*', perhaps referring to the inner enclosure of the fort. No other details of the findspot, nor any other associated finds, survive.

Later, shortly before 1859, three urns containing cremated ashes and burnt bones were unearthed from beneath a large stone in what was described as 'another camp' joining onto Castell Nadolig, probably the distinct annex on the south-east side. Members of the Cambrian Archaeological Association visited the fort on 16 August 1859 (before knowledge of the 1829 spoon discovery had been published) to see the site of the burials. Mr Malet described the scene: 'Near the ... spot may be also seen a considerable number of bones, on the surface of the ground, which have undergone the action of fire'. It was later noted[13] that 'Those members who were fortunate enough in sharing in that most agreeable excursion, will remember seeing in a part of the work a large stone slab, under which, a short time before, three urns containing bones had been found...'. The 'large stone' marking the burials has long gone.

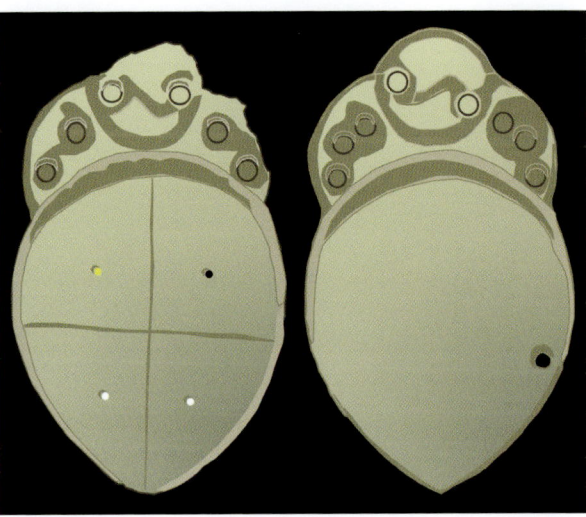

Figure 5.7. The Castell Nadolig spoons, also called the Penbryn spoons, were discovered by a Ceredigion tenant farmer around 1829. New research has identified four, rather than two, perforations in the left-hand spoon, one in each quadrant. These were inlaid with different metals as follows: top left, gold (yellow spot); top right, uncertain; lower right, site of inlay filled with corrosion from spoon; lower left, bronze inlay of different composition from the spoons. (T. Driver[14])

These remarkable spoons are very special in a British context. They date to the 1st century BC and only fifteen other pairs (or single) spoons of similar character, with slightly differing handle designs, are known from Britain and Ireland, of which the Castell Nadolig pair were the earliest to be found. Two of the British pairs come from burials, from Burnmouth in the Scottish Borders and Deal in Kent. The Penbryn spoons may have accompanied a burial, disturbed when the tenant dug away the heap of stones. One of the spoons bears a cross incision and is perforated by four holes (these have only recently all been identified, and do not appear in earlier illustrations). The holes were inlaid with differing metals. The other spoon has no marks except a single larger hole, offset towards the right-hand edge of the spoon.

Divination – and the glint of gold

It has long been suspected that the spoons were used for magical purposes and a new study has suggested that they were likely to have been used by high priests, or perhaps even Druids, in the act of divination. Liquid or another substance would be passed through the upper spoon with the larger hole, with the quadrant spoon held beneath. The quadrant into which the liquid fell might then 'indicate which quarter of the lunar month or year was auspicious … it is possible that the Penbryn spoons, and perhaps all the others, were used in divination, the act or practice of divining which seeks to know the future or hidden things by magical means … The ability to predict events is a powerful knowledge.'[15]

Figure 5.8. Rock cut spring inside Castell Nadolig, sited against – but lying outside – the inner rampart (rear fence line in this view). Although probably altered in size and shape in later times, it is possible that this large and still active spring was a focal point within the hillfort during the Iron Age. (T. Driver)

It is interesting that the larger hole on the 'upper' spoon is too small for water to drip through because of the effect of surface tension. It has been suggested, alternatively, in a discussion of various aspects of the spoons, that a granulated substance such as sand, or perhaps oil, may have passed through the hole in the simpler spoon, with fortunes or future events being foretold by the way it landed within the quadrants of the cross on the other spoon.[16] Or perhaps warm blood, as from a sacrifice, might have flowed better through the hole than cold liquids which can be more viscous.[17] Recent reanalysis has found that at least one of the small holes on the cross-incised spoon was originally inlaid with gold. While gold torques and coins are known from Iron Age Britain, gold inlay is rare, if not unparalleled.[18] In this respect the Penbryn spoons may well be unique.

An interesting 'rediscovery' within Castell Nadolig, not noted by previous writers, is the presence of a prominent rock cut spring or small pond sited against the outer face of the inner rampart, close to the hill summit. It measures 12 metres by 6 metres today but its original form is unclear. Enclosed within a low earthwork mound, possibly once marking a surrounding bank or fence, the spring is one of several dotted around the hilltop but the most prominent one within the hillfort defences. It is clearly old since it is crossed by a hedge bank. 'Watery' places feature prominently in prehistoric ritual and we can perhaps imagine that this spring at Castell Nadolig may once have once played a part in the rituals implied by the presence of the spoons and cremations within this strange and fascinating site.

Ritual heads from prehistory

> If the heads [of Wales] are of Iron Age or Roman date they belong within a very widespread tradition of human-head representation that can be traced over a large area, from Ireland to Europe ... The heads are likely to have represented local divinities ...[19]

> ... the human head was a sacred symbol. It was regarded as the essence of the person or the god, and some tribes made a habit of decapitating and treasuring the heads of their enemies ... the human head held a talismanic function, perhaps giving protection and good luck ...[20]

The Celts considered the human head to be the dwelling place of the immortal soul. Accordingly, classical writers record Celts taking human heads as battle trophies and displaying them on their houses. Such tales may of course have been embellished so as to portray an image of a 'barbarous native', yet impaled human skulls have been found outside a roundhouse during excavations at Bredon Hill in Worcestershire.[21]

Attention has also been drawn[22] to the longevity of 'head' references in Welsh place names, a local example being 'Rhydypennau', the *Ford of the Heads* north of Bow Street in Ceredigion. This fording point correlates well with an area of intense prehistoric activity including one of the largest plough-levelled Early Bronze Age barrow cemeteries on the west coast of Wales, at Llandre, and the findspot of a Bronze Age flat axe from Rhydypennau bridge.[23] One of the most striking representations of a human head from Iron Age Wales was found in the foothills of Cadair Idris, on the decorative bronze shield mounting that forms part of the Tal-y-llyn hoard (see chapter frontispiece). The heads have immaculately combed hair, showing that the late Iron Age peoples of southern Gwynedd – and by extension north Ceredigion – aspired to combed hair and a well-groomed appearance.

Currently two carved stone heads are known from Ceredigion, both probably from the Iron Age although it is impossible to date them accurately. A third head, a carved Romano-British wooden example, is also known from a watery or bog context, again showing a veneration of such places. All three are described below. They may once have been revered cult objects in households, hillforts or outdoor shrines alongside rivers or springs. More could be expected from this county. Around Wales stone heads and figures large and small have been recovered from streams, rivers, back gardens and stone walls or even built into Christian churches.

The Llandysul head

... a most important Celtic Head ... having a remarkably disturbing aspect.[24]

What was presumably intended by the sculptor as a powerful, grim expression is still apparent to modern eyes.[25]

This Celtic stone head, shown in Figure 5.9, is believed to have been dug up on farmland in the vicinity of Llandysul before the Second World War. It came to light in 1978 after being included in a London auction and was briefly exhibited in the Carmarthen Museum before being returned to its private owner. It is made of a coarse-grained sandstone common in the Llandysul/Pencader area and shows weathering consistent with long burial. It bears all the hallmarks of a western British Celtic head: 'flat features, the dominant eyes and nose, the small thick-lipped mouth with its somewhat sombre expression and the "spectacle eyes" which may have been designed to hold stones or beads as eyes'.[26]

Subtle features, such as the springing of the eye ridges from the bridge of the nose, are best paralleled in Ireland and show careful craftsmanship. The nature of this freestanding, three-dimensional head can be closely matched by an example excavated from a household shrine in the Roman town at Caerwent in south-east Wales. The lack of a known findspot for the Llandysul head is frustrating, as it therefore remains unknown if this splendid head perhaps originated from a defended enclosure, from a bog or watery place or even from the site of a lost shrine. Llandysul is dominated by two hillforts, Pencoed-y-Foel (Chapter 3) and Craig Gwrtheyrn to the south across the Teifi valley, so there was clearly a nearby population and social context for such a find.

Figure 5.9. A disturbing gaze from prehistory. This striking stone head, nearly 30 centimetres high, was found near Llandysul in south Ceredigion and is thought to be of Iron Age date. The head is held in a private collection. (Michael Freeman. By kind permission of Amgueddfa Ceredigion Museum)

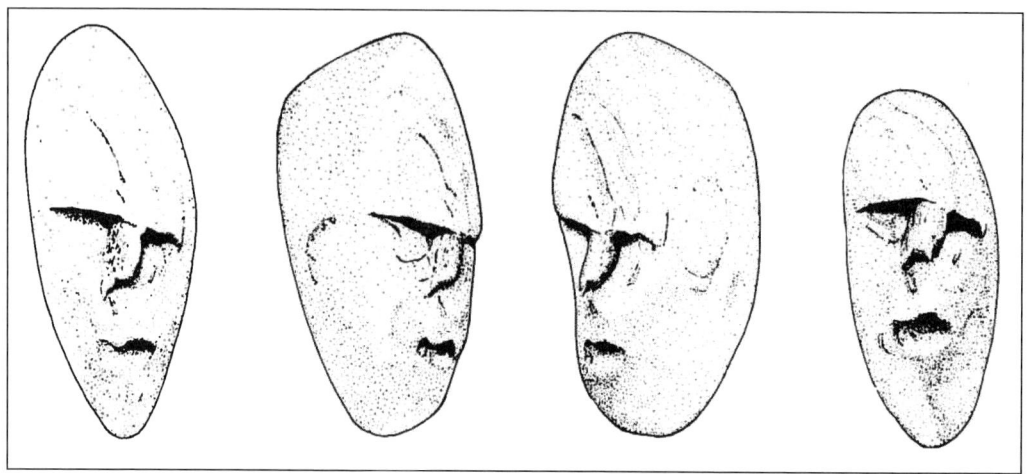

Figure 5.10. Four views of the small Llanfarian pebble head.
(Copyright Dyfed Archaeological Trust)

The Llanfarian Head

A much smaller stone head, fashioned from a water-worn pebble only 5 centimetres in length, was discovered in the bank of the River Ystwyth between Llanfarian and Llanilar in the early 1980s, in the vicinity of the river meander north of Abermad (SN 60 76). The head, which remains in private ownership, does not seem to include '... any particularly "Celtic" features'[27] but its slightly menacing appearance is comparable to a carved head found in a river at Pont Dolgadfan in Merionethshire. Although impossible to date with any certainty it is can reasonably be seen as a further example of a cult or votive head.

Cae Gwerful and the Llanio head: the site of a lost shrine?

> The eyes of the Llanio head were inlaid, but not with the slips of glass or metal generally employed: the carefully worked sockets are unusually deep (8 to 9 mm.), and probably held thorn-like pieces of bone or some other substance, exactly fitting or perhaps driven in.[28]

This remarkable wooden head was first documented by members of the Cambrian Archaeological Association when they visited Llanio Roman fort, near Tregaron, in 1878. It had been found about 50 years previously during peat-digging in Cae Gwerful, a small bog to the north of the Roman fort. The scene in 1878 was described as follows: 'Mr Samuel Evans Jones of Pont Llanio, called attention to a female head carved in wood ... Valuing the head as a family relic, Mr Jones declined to part with it otherwise than as a loan ... Mr Jones said there were "hands with part of an arm" belonging to the head, but they had been lost many years.'[29]

The head measures 17.6 centimetres high, or as long as an adult hand. It has plain features but elaborately carved hair in a 'melon-style coiffure', which stylistically dates it to around 200 AD, in Romano-British times. The head is socketed at its base, suggesting that it had originally been fixed to a larger object.

Figure 5.11. The Llanio head, drawn by 'W.G.S.' in Archaeologia Cambrensis *1879, 81-5. (By kind permission of the Cambrian Archaeological Association)*

The entry for the head in the *Cardiganshire County History* suggests that this remarkable object was part of '… a small cult statue or ex-voto from a shrine situated in or close to a spring or pool in the previously marshy Cae Gwerful'.[30] An ex-voto is a votive offering to a divinity given in thanks for treatment received, taking the form of a gift or statue or even a model of a healed body part – perhaps explaining the find of the hand and arm in this case.

Figure 5.12. Findspot of the Llanio head: Cae Gwerful today. The area is still a wetland, but is cut through by the line of the disused Aberystwyth-Carmarthen railway, the fence-posts of which can be seen in the foreground. (T. Driver)

Such offerings would be placed in a shrine to demonstrate to other visitors the kind of help that had been received. Thus: '… there is no reason why there should not have been a sacred pool or spring in Cae Gwerful, and that its real or fancied therapeutic properties should not have resulted in the offering of carvings of [wooden] limbs, or the like …'.[31]

The Roman fort at Llanio, like that at Trawsgoed Roman fort to the north, is thought to have been occupied from the Roman conquest in the 70s AD up about 130 AD, and thereafter largely abandoned. The probability that a Romano-British shrine, containing a votive statue or statues, may still have stood close by nearly a hundred years later, alongside a sacred spring or pool, is tantalising for our understanding of Ceredigion in Romano-British times. A lowland shrine in this wetland area may well have appropriated a pre-Roman religious site in the shadow of nearby hillforts. If a shrine stood at Cae Gwerful it may have comprised a small wooden building and perhaps a raised timber causeway or jetty over the boggy ground. Perhaps some day more may be learned about this tantalising site and its remarkable wooden head.

Chapter frontispiece: The Abermagwr Romano-British villa. Towards the middle of the 3rd century AD work began on a thoroughly 'Romanised' home for a wealthy local landowner who possessed the financial means to commission surveyors, architects, builders and roofers in the heart of the mid Wales countryside. The new home demonstrated his adoption of Roman ways of life; his ancestors, however, may well have lived in a nearby hillfort or defended farmstead. This view shows excavations in 2011 on the main villa building or domus, *looking south, with the dark-coloured floor-deposits of the principal room in the centre and the verandah and cobbled courtyard in front of the villa at the top of the photograph. The small room in the foreground, Room 6, was a later addition and produced evidence for the finer aspects of Romano-British life including glass beads, a bronze furniture fitting and pieces of a rare cut-glass tableware vessel. (T. Driver; Crown Copyright RCAHMW, DS2014_076_001)*

The following glimpse of the Romans' knowledge of Cardigan Bay, its headlands and rivers, comes from Ptolemy's *Geographia*, dating to the 2nd Century AD but derived from earlier conquest-era sources: '... the promontory of the Ganganoi [Lleyn Peninusla]; the mouth of the river Stuccia [The Ystwyth]; the mouth of the river Tuerobis [The Teifi]; the Octapitarum Promontory [St David's Head]'.

The Iron Age people of Wales left no written documents, but descriptions of their history and even the fictitious paraphrased speeches of key leaders are preserved thanks to a particular Roman historian who sought to document the conquest of *Britannia*. Through the writings of Senator Publius Cornelius Tacitus (56-117 AD) we have a few tangible glimpses of the running battles, family histories and changing political strategies which marked the long years of the conquest of Britain, including the western lands which would later become Wales. These military actions began with the invasion at Richborough in Kent by Emperor Claudius in 43 AD, but were not concluded until nearly thirty years later with the decisive campaigns of Governor Sextus Julius Frontinus between 74 and 77 AD. Frontinus was succeeded in 77 AD by the skilled tactician Gnaeus Julius Agricola, the father-in-law of Tacitus and Governor of Britannia, who swiftly defeated the Ordovices in mid and north Wales, conquered Anglesey and went on to oversee the construction of a network of Roman forts in Wales and beyond. It is perhaps no coincidence that the Welsh words for bridge ('*pont*') and window ('*ffenest*)', both symbols of structural modernity brought by the Romans, are Latin in origin.

Tacitus's book *Agricola*, a history of the life and career of Agricola including his campaigns in Britain, was written in 97-98 AD.[1] Caution must be applied when reading and using this source as a window into Iron Age Britain as the writing is coloured by its author's obvious veneration of the political and military exploits of his father-in-law. The text was also written many years after the events which are described, third-hand, from the viewpoint of a conquering force. Yet this is the closest thing we have to a contemporary account of prehistoric Wales, its land and its peoples, albeit on the eve of transformation. The text still makes engaging reading.

The long path to Roman conquest in west Wales

Much of the work aimed at understanding the dates of forts, temporary camps and strategies for the attack on Cardiganshire/Ceredigion has been undertaken by Jeffrey Davies,[2] formerly of Aberystwyth University. In the years after 47 AD Ostorious Scapula took control of the territory of the Silures, with the wars culminating in the defeat of Caratacus in 51 AD somewhere in central Wales. These first campaigns, chiefly against the Silures in the south and east, and the Ordovices in mid and north-west Wales, may have been consolidated by Scapula's successor, Gallus, in mid Wales with the construction of a timber fort at Llwyn-y-Brain, near Caersws in the Upper Severn Basin. The Severn Valley provided a key route for military penetration into the interior, but the Llwyn-y-Brain fort itself remains undated apart from a few undistinctive scraps of pottery.

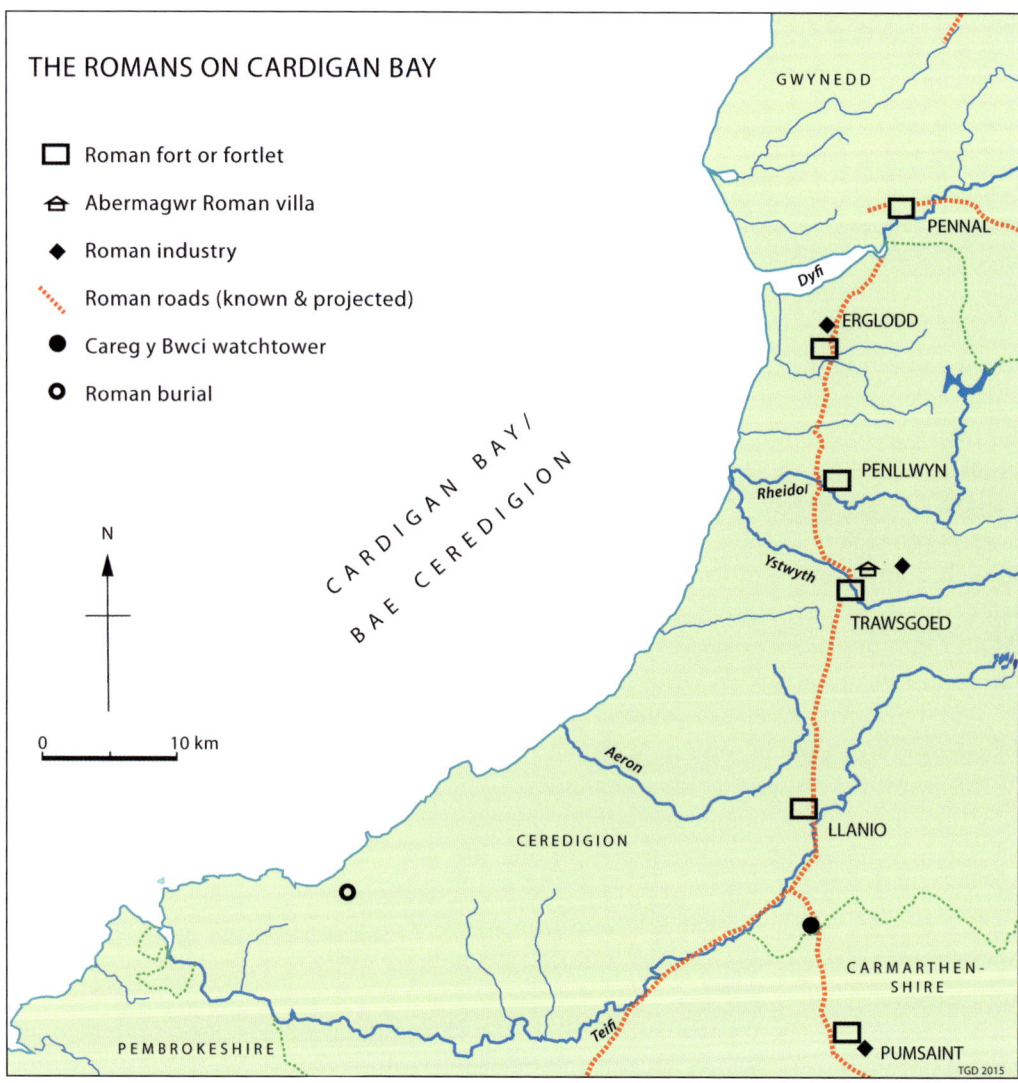

Figure 6.1. Roman forts, industrial sites and roads in the Cardigan Bay region. Stray Roman finds and dated or possible Romano-British 'native' settlements have been omitted for reasons of clarity. Areas of known Roman industry are shown as follows: gold mining at Pumsaint in Carmarthenshire; exploitation of local lead ores near Trawsgoed (as indicated by analysis of lead finds from Trawsgoed Roman fort and the Abermagwr villa); and Late Iron Age and early Roman lead smelting close to the Roman fortlet at Erglodd. (T. Driver)

Davies notes that the establishment of the Flavian (post 69 AD) fort at Pennal, west of Machynlleth on the northern bank of the Dyfi, shows the presence and dominance of the Roman navy in west Wales, scouting the coast and ultimately supplying military installations by sea. It is notable that the Ystwyth, or STVCTIA, is one of the few river valleys to be named by Ptolemy along the western seaboard of Wales. The broad Dyfi estuary to the north remained unnamed in the Roman itineraries. This might be because the Ystwyth was one of the few main rivers on the west coast marked by a large hillfort at its mouth, Pen Dinas, highly visible to seafarers as a useful navigational marker.

Raids as far west as Cardigan Bay could have been launched from the auxiliary fort at Llwyn-y-Brain, in central Wales, if it had already been established by the early/mid 70s AD. Occasional raids and incursions into unconquered territory would have begun to disrupt normal 'Iron Age' life, or what remained of it, on the west coast. Any trade or communication which relied upon eastward contact to the Borderlands would certainly have been disrupted by the Romans and, if so, this would have begun to create severe consequences. In addition, local chieftains and leaders in Ceredigion who travelled through the Cambrian Mountains on horseback would often have encountered Roman bases and troops on manoeuvres, confirming the imminent and inevitable end to their Iron Age way of life.

Figure 6.2. Roman forts in Ceredigion are largely hidden from view by centuries of plough-levelling, stone robbing and landscape change. Yet, in drought summers they occasionally reappear as 'cropmarks'. This view of Trawsgoed Roman fort in 2006 shows the parched grid of streets inside the fort, itself cut from top to bottom of the picture by a modern road. To the upper-right, partly underlying the ornamental gardens of Trawsgoed mansion, a further grid of streets represents the 'vicus' or small village inhabited by traders, camp-followers, locals and retired soldiers who settled alongside the fort.
(Crown Copyright RCAHMW, AP_2006_3817)

Writing in 1994 Jeffrey Davies[3] found that there remained no conclusive evidence to suggest that south-west Wales, and the land between the Dyfi and the Teifi in particular, had been penetrated by the Roman army prior to 70 AD. This was over twenty years after the attacks on the Silures of south-east Wales and the Deceangli of north-east Wales by Ostorius Scapula in 47-52 AD. The Cardigan Bay region effectively enjoyed a twenty-year respite from the Roman military penetration seen in other parts of Wales to the east and south.

Britain through Roman eyes

Tacitus records many pertinent facts about Britain as it emerged from the Iron Age and entered Roman rule. Certain passages, in their English translation, are worth quoting at length:

> … one must remember we are dealing with barbarians … the swarthy faces of the Silures, the tendency of their hair to curl and the fact that Spain lies opposite, all lead one to believe that Spaniards crossed in ancient times and occupied the land.
>
> Their strength is in their infantry. Some tribes also fight from chariots. The nobleman drives, his dependants fight in his defence. Once they owed obedience to kings; now they are distracted between the jarring factions of rival chiefs … The climate is objectionable, with its frequent rains and mists, but there is no extreme cold … The soil can bear all produce, except the olive, the vine, and other natives of warmer climes, and it is fertile. Crops are slow to ripen, but quick to grow – both facts due to one and the same cause, the extreme moistness of land and sky.[4]

West Wales falls under the campaigns of Frontinus

With the accession of the Emperor Vespasian in 69 AD, renewed campaigns to bring Roman Britain under control were launched through Bolanus (69-71 AD), Cerealis (71-74 AD) and most importantly Frontinus (74-77 AD), to whom the final conquest of Wales was entrusted. The Iron Age communities in Ceredigion and Carmarthenshire must still have represented a significant population and threat to the Romans at the time of these campaigns.

The Severn Valley was heavily defended by the Romans as a major strategic route into the heart of Wales,[5] as was the upper Wye east of Plynlimon. This is shown by the construction of the small fort at Cae Gaer (SN 823 818) and a possible fortlet in the form of an undated square earthwork known as Llys Arthur, on the valley floor near Ponterwyd.

Under Frontinus the Silures of south-east Wales were conquered but the Ordovices of mid and north-west Wales remained a thorn in the Roman side. Tacitus documents the brutal suppression of this tribe as follows:

> Shortly before [Agricola's] arrival [in 77 AD] … the tribe of the Ordovices had almost wiped out a squadron of cavalry stationed in their territory, and this initial stroke had excited the province …
>
> In spite of all, Agricola decided to go and meet the threat. He drew together detachments of the legions and a small force of auxiliaries. As the Ordovices did not venture to meet him in the plain, he marched his men into the hills, himself in the

van, to lend his own courage to the rest by sharing their peril. Thus he cut to pieces almost the whole fighting force of the nation.[6]

Agricola followed this swift suppression of the Ordovices with the decisive conquest of Anglesey.

It is possible that a Roman marching camp at Esgair Perfedd (SN 923 699), on the high moorland west of Rhayader, dates from the campaigns of Frontinus, indicating the grim massing of troops prior to the invasion of the west coast. Large and ephemeral rectangular earthworks of this kind in the uplands, and on the valley floors of central and eastern Wales, were rapidly constructed for an overnight stop or for a short pause in the forward progress. They were defended with a low rampart and palisade fronted by a shallow external ditch. Our knowledge of marching camps along the spine of the Cambrian Mountains and facing down onto Cardigan Bay is woefully incomplete as these slight constructions can be easily destroyed or obscured by afforestation, upland ploughing or pasture improvement. It is likely that Roman marching camps await discovery through the Wye valley gap between Llangurig and Ponterwyd to the north, and also from the south-east along the Teifi valley.

The size of the camp at Esgair Perfedd, enclosing 6.5 hectares, suggests that a force of some 5,000 men was involved in this west coast campaign, with a '… large expeditionary force moving west from the upper Wye probably towards the headwaters of the Ystwyth'.[7] Although it cannot be decisively proven that this particular camp was linked to a campaign into Ceredigion along the Ystwyth headwaters, one can imagine the devastating impact of 5,000 highly trained troops descending into Cwmystwyth or the lowland plains of Trawsgoed as they surely must have done. Whether linked to this camp, or others yet to be located, such an event would have taken place with the purpose of completing the conquest of the Cardigan Bay region.

Perhaps local scouts, however, had already got wind of the imminent arrival of crack troops and had spread word to local villages and hillforts. Perhaps a battle, now long forgotten, then ensued somewhere along the reaches of the middle Ystwyth. Tacitus, in *Agricola* 29, vividly records the later battle of Mons Graupius in which Agricola fought north of the Forth-Clyde line in 83/84 AD. The description of the tribal build-up may help us to imagine something of the kind of event which may have befallen the inhabitants of Ceredigion in the face of the Roman advance:

> The Britons were, in fact, undaunted by the loss of the previous battle, and welcomed the choice between revenge and enslavement. They … had sent round embassies and drawn up treaties to rally the full force of their states … they came flocking to the colours – all the young men and those whose 'old age was fresh and green', famous warriors with their battle honours thick upon them. At that point one of the many leaders, named Calgacus, a man of outstanding valour and nobility, summoned the masses who were already thirsting for battle and addressed them.[8]

An alternative view is that the local population may have been resigned to Roman rule in the face of the unassailable force of the Roman army. Tribal leaders and chieftains may have been well aware that their way of life was about to change forever, and may have been willing to enter into negotiations (of sorts) with the Romans over land ownership, power and access to key resources. High-level meetings may have taken place between regional chieftains from Ceredigion and from those parts of Wales already conquered. Indeed, the process of 'Romanisation' was one way in which the Romans won over local populations, achieving peace through the offer of a new and attractive way of life. Tacitus, probably writing about the larger centres of urban population in Roman Britain, describes the process thus:

> To induce a people hitherto scattered, uncivilized and therefore prone to fight, to grow pleasurably inured to peace and ease, Agricola gave private encouragement and official assistance to the building of temples, public squares and private mansions … The result was that in place of distaste for the Latin language came a passion to command it. In the same way, our national dress came into favour and the toga was everywhere to be seen. And so the Britons were gradually led on to the amenities that make vice agreeable – arcades, baths and sumptuous banquets. They spoke of such novelties as 'civilisation', when really they were only a feature of enslavement.[9]

By these means the local population was encouraged to accept Roman rule.

Co-existence and change: Cardigan Bay under Roman rule

> These garrisoned posts [Ceredigion's Roman forts], eventually linked by an all-weather road-system… were normally placed a day's march (12-15 miles) apart; they were mutually supportive and capable of rapid reinforcement or concentration should rebellion be in the offing. The whole system was probably complete by the close of the 70s AD.[10]

Excavation evidence from the Troedyrhiw enclosure near Cardigan, and elsewhere, suggests that many defended farmsteads in the region, and even some hillforts, remained occupied or were newly constructed in Romano-British times. Finds of Roman pottery and coins in the latest occupation layers at these sites show the assimilation of Roman material culture into rural Wales. Following the conquest during the middle years of the 70s, three earth-and-timber Roman forts were established in Ceredigion: at Llanio (*Bremia*), to secure the crossing of the Teifi; at Trawsgoed, to guard the crossing of the Ystwyth; and at Penllwyn, above the Rheidol Valley at Capel Bangor. While clearly sited to aid communication and troop movements, the forts were probably also located where they could control pockets of local population.[11]

The numbers were formidable. A regiment of 1,000 men is likely to have been stationed in the fort at Penllwyn. Building work would have required vast quantities of timber to be felled in nearby woodlands, for processing into planks and posts. Fields of view from the new fort site would have been cleared of vegetation. To local communities familiar with the daily, weekly and seasonal calendar of farming, hunting and woodland management, the arrival of a standing army would have been life-changing. Daily military exercises and manoeuvres beyond the confines of the fort, as well as the immediate necessity to procure local food and other resources, would have flooded the former Iron Age landscape with new people, new laws, new restrictions and new languages. The requirements of conquered

Figure 6.4. To experience the full might and majesty of the Roman conquest of Wales one should visit the town wall and turrets – and wider Roman remains – at Caerwent, in Monmouthshire, where the town defences are among the best preserved anywhere in Britain. Named Venta Silurum, *'the market town of the Silures tribe', this Romanised town was the ultimate symbol of the pacification and settlement by the Romans of a once hostile Iron Age tribe. (T. Driver)*

territories like Britain to provide for the Roman army were indeed onerous: 'The more basic needs of the army, of course, were met by requisitioning … and the provision of corn, hides and so on must have been a considerable burden to native farmers.'[12]

Although a number of Ceredigion's hillforts, along with lowland defended farms, must have been occupied when the Romans moved to conquer west Wales, there is no direct evidence of Roman attack on a hillfort in the form of weaponry or physical signs of assault or capture such as the slighting of defences. One authority has argued episodes of burning found at the north gate of the south fort at Pen Dinas, Aberystwyth, could have resulted from different phases of tactical attack by the Roman legions.[13] However, there is no exact dating evidence for any of the burning episodes and the possibility remains that the gates were burnt for other reasons, either accidentally during dry periods or even for the purpose of clearing old structures before building anew.

The Abermagwr Romano-British villa

> Further west [in west Wales] no military installations can be shown to have been occupied within or bordering the putative territory of the Demetae after the 140s … It is manifest that the population of Cardiganshire was now regarded as wholly pacific and reconciled to its lot. There is no hint that this area gave Rome any further trouble.[14]

Until very recently it was thought that Ceredigion, and west Wales more generally, was maintained as a 'military zone' after the major forts were dismantled in or around 130 AD, with only the road networks through mid Wales maintained for communications

Figure 6.5. In south Ceredigion and elsewhere along the coastal plain 'native' defended enclosures with square or rectangular plans seem to reflect Romano-British influence, as with this clearly defined cropmark enclosure at Ty Hen, Penbryn, (SN 286 517) now half-lost beneath the present-day pattern of hedge boundaries. Romano-British occupation was confirmed during the excavation of a similar square enclosure at Troedyrhiw, further to the south. (Crown Copyright RCAHMW, DI2005_0155)

until the end of Roman rule in 410. In particular the lack of Roman villas in west Wales seemed to indicate that the land was too poor to attract agricultural settlements and too unstable politically for wealthy landowners to invest long-term in major building projects. It is now known from excavations between 2010 and 2015, however, that at least one Romano-British villa was established in Ceredigion by the middle of the 3rd century AD, at Abermagwr near Trawsgoed.[15]

The Abermagwr villa was an 'architect-designed' winged villa, undoubtedly developed by a wealthy landowner but still fairly rustic in some of its amenities. The construction effort behind the villa suggests the involvement of a series of specialists including architects, surveyors, quarrymen and slaters. The house or *domus* faced due south to maximize the amount of sunshine enjoyed by the dwelling. The foundations were up to a metre deep, packed with boulders and rounded cobbles no doubt obtained from the bed of the nearby rivers. The stone walls were then built with square-cut stone, perhaps robbed from the ruined military bath house at the nearby Trawsgoed Roman fort. Finally the roof was finished in neatly-cut pentagonal slates in the Roman style, quarried from nearby shale outcrops above the Ystwyth gorge and shaped by professional slaters.

The interior of the villa (Figure 6.7) lacked some of the refinements found at more wealthy villas in south Wales and southern England. There were no mosaics or tessellated floors, although they may yet be found in unexcavated rooms. The far eastern Room 8, only discovered during the 2011 excavations, turned out to be a failed heated room; remains of hypocaust fittings were discovered at the lowest level but the heating system itself seems never to have been fired and the construction pit was in time backfilled with domestic rubbish and building debris. The principal rooms were floored with packed clay and there was evidence for fitted wooden furniture against the walls. A bread oven and central hearth

Figure 6.6. Reconstruction of the Abermagwr Romano-British villa, drawn before the 2011 excavations. Following that year's work on site it was realized that an unfinished or demolished heated room once stood on the east (right-hand) side of the main house or 'domus'. Excavations in 2015 failed to locate any ancillary buildings or pre-villa structures to the west (left) of the house. (T. Driver)

in the main room would have led to fairly smoky, rustic cooking and heating arrangements and suggested that the villa was most likely a single-storey building. However, a small room at the rear produced evidence for furniture fixed with ornate bronze studs, along with glass beads and parts of a rare cut-glass vessel, suggesting a certain level of wealth among the residents.

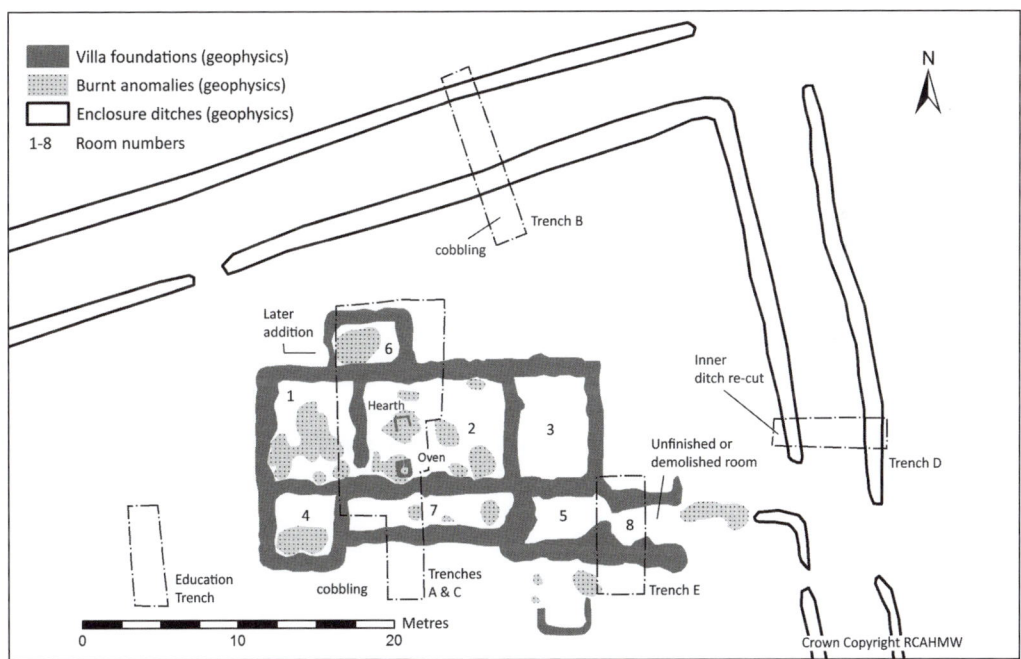

Figure 6.7. Plan of the Abermagwr Romano-British villa following the 2011 excavations, showing excavated areas and the unfinished or failed heated Room 8, on the east side of the house or 'domus'. (T. Driver; Crown Copyright RCAHMW, DD2012_010)

The Abermagwr villa probably sat at the heart of an extensive farming estate, managing lands along the middle reaches of the Ystwyth valley. It seems likely that other villas may await discovery in the hinterland of coastal Ceredigion. Excavations have shown that the Abermagwr villa was occupied until around 330 AD, but after that it then fell into disrepair, apparently following a catastrophic fire. Nothing remains to be seen on site today as the villa lies buried beneath modern farmland.

Coin hoards and late Roman Ceredigion

There is good evidence for the wider use of Roman coinage in Ceredigion during the late 3rd and early 4th centuries AD, suggesting a coin-using population. Roman coin hoards, long since dispersed, have been found at Llangybi, at Nanteos, at Rhiwarthen Isaf near Capel Bangor and at Strata Florida, some containing many thousands of coins. Most of the coins found so far date to the later 3rd century when currency was becoming debased, and so would have been hoarded in great numbers in bowls or pots buried in the ground. There is an outside possibility that the locations of these buried hoards may have related to settlements – or currently unrecorded villas – nearby, with the hoards perhaps being safely hidden close to contemporary local landmarks. Certainly there is fertile valley land at Nanteos and at Rhiwarthen Isaf, entirely suitable for villas like that so recently found and explored at Abermagwr.

The only Roman coin hoard found in modern times in Ceredigion came from Salem, near Aberystwyth. Some 48 3rd-century coins were turned up loose in the cutting of a water pipeline following the tremendous luck of one being found by a small boy on the road alongside.[16] The discovery was subject to the first Coroner's Treasure Trove inquest in Ceredigion in the 20th century. The coins may have been from a dispersed hoard but no evidence for a pottery container was found. It is equally possible that someone on horseback traversing the hills dropped their leather purse of coins. This small hoard is on display in the Ceredigion Museum, with some of the coins still fused together by corrosion. Despite this evidence for coinage in circulation, and being stored, among the later Roman population of Ceredigion it is still not known how and where the bulk of this coin-using population was living, whether in a network of as yet unlocated villas, in Romanised defended farmsteads and small hillforts, or in other forms of settlement not yet recognised in the archaeological record.

As with the Iron Age hillforts and defended farmsteads there is still much to be learned about the ways of life and the nature of the population in the lowlands and hill-country of Ceredigion during the centuries of Roman occupation. The luck and chance which gave us the only known Roman villa in the county, at Abermagwr, may yet yield further discoveries which change our entire view of the early history of the region. It is entirely possible – and indeed very likely – that further Roman forts, signal stations, marching camps, settlements or burials exist somewhere along the wide sweep of Cardigan Bay, awaiting the flash of discovery to bring them to wider attention.

Chapter frontispiece: Along the glorious indented coastline of Ceredigion, bounded by the blue waters of Cardigan Bay, winds the Wales Coast Path. This gives access to a number of Iron Age coastal promontory forts including the curious and inconspicuous coastal fort at Castell Bach, Cwmtydu, seen here in centre-frame with its two lines of curving ramparts facing an isolated rock stack and sheltered bay.
(Crown Copyright RCAHMW, AP_2009_1432)

For the visitor to Ceredigion and Cardigan Bay keen to visit and understand some of the main hillforts of the region, including some of the best examples both large and small, this chapter looks in more detail at ten of the most accessible and interesting sites. Visits to some or all of these will tell you a great deal about the built achievements of the Iron Age communities on Cardigan Bay and the great variety of defended settlements and hillforts in the region. Directions are given, but also assume that the reader will have the appropriate 1:25,000 Ordnance Survey Explorer map for the site showing public rights of way, Open Access land and other information. Descriptions of further hillforts which can be explored along Cardigan Bay are given in Chapter 8.

1. THE LARGEST HILLFORT ON CARDIGAN BAY: PEN DINAS, ABERYSTWYTH

Directions: (SN 584 805) The main south fort at Pen Dinas (or Pendinas) lies within a Local Nature Reserve and is freely accessible at all reasonable times and easily reached on foot from Aberystwyth town centre. The north fort lies on private farmland but can be seen from the south fort. Footpaths are well marked up to Pen Dinas: from Tanybwlch beach car park on the west side; from the side of the main A487 as it leaves Trefechan suburb to the south of Aberystwyth; or via the shortest route ascending from Penparcau on the south-east side, parking in the new housing estates of Cae Job and Parc Dinas and following a path to the summit. The hillfort is best visited in the winter or spring when the bracken is low and the full scale of the enormous terraced eastern defences can be appreciated and explored.

Pen Dinas is the pre-eminent hillfort on the Cardigan Bay coast, outshining any other coastal hillfort from north Pembrokeshire to the Lleyn Peninsula. Described as early as the 1590s as 'Castell Maylor', it is the Ceredigion fort about which most is known, following a five year campaign of excavations before the Second World War. However, these excavations are now almost a century old and caution must be applied to all the conclusions reached, particularly concerning the sequence of development currently understood for this complex hillfort.

Figure 7.1. *The formidable terraced earthworks of the southern part of Pen Dinas hillfort still dominate the skyline of Aberystwyth over two millennia after they were constructed. Originally tall dry-stone walls and elaborate timberwork would have defined the hilltop defences, appearing shocking and new against the natural hillslopes. No other building in the contemporary landscape would have come close to the scale of this hillfort. (T. Driver)*

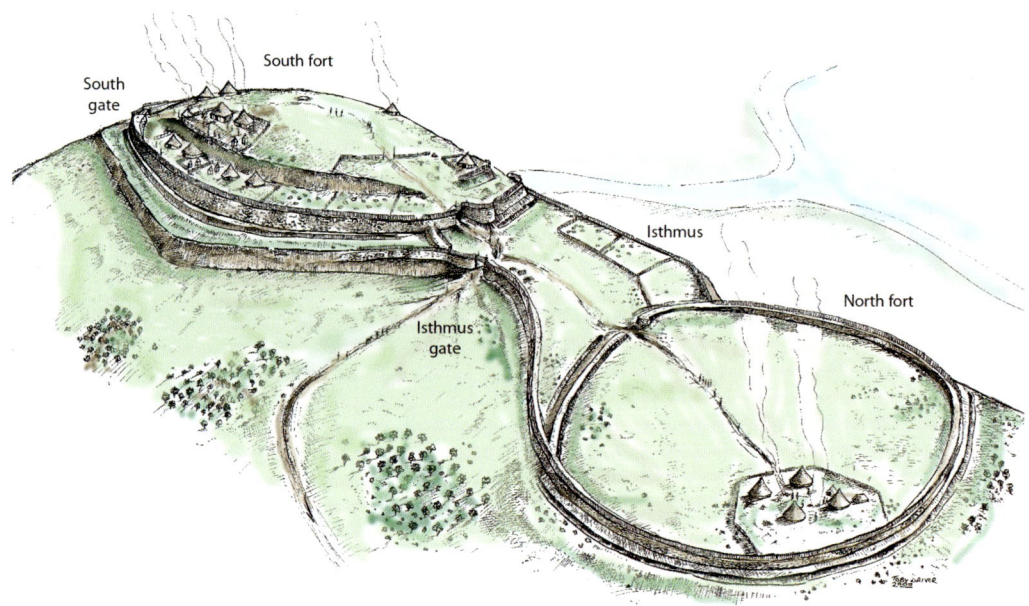

Figure 7.2. *Reconstruction of Pen Dinas, Aberystwyth. Although we do not know how the various parts of the hillfort were used, particularly the older north fort (foreground) which was re-defended when both summits were linked, the drawing conveys some sense of the hillfort in its heyday, perhaps around 50 BC. The central isthmus may have been a public area for markets and fairs, accessed via an outer gate but protected from the 'inner sanctum' of the south and north forts. (T. Driver)*

Landscape setting

Pen Dinas occupies an exceptional position on a coastal hill, which rises towards the western end of a long ridge separating the valleys of the Rheidol and the Paith. A lower and broader summit to the north and a narrower and steeper summit on the south were both enclosed with defences in the Iron Age, and were eventually linked across the intervening saddle of ground known as the isthmus. Pen Dinas is one of the strongest and most readily defensible hills in the region. This coastal hill boasts precipitous slopes on its seaward (western) side and along the south, but is approached by more gradual slopes across a lower lying saddle of ground to the east and north-east. It sits at the coastal confluence of the rivers Rheidol and Ystwyth, allowing exploitation of a variety of resources within easy reach, including marine resources, seaweed, river fish, good grazing land and soils suitable for arable cultivation.[1] The exceptional position of Pen Dinas allowed for visual command and political control of the two vital regional arterial rivers, with an extensive view inland to Plynlimon and a broad coastal vista taking in the entire sweep of Cardigan Bay from the Pembrokeshire coast to the mountains of Snowdonia and Bardsey Island. Mesolithic occupation is attested at its foot whilst finds of a polished axe from the western slopes, and a palstave axe from the Bronze Age, together with an Early Bronze Age round barrow on the summit, show that the hill attracted attention in pre-Iron Age times and may have held some sacred importance.

Excavations before the Second World War

In 1933 Professor Daryll Forde from Aberystwyth University commenced an ambitious programme of excavations which ran for five summers until 1937.[2] The preferred technique of the day was to cut long 'slit' trenches through the hillfort to cross-section defences and establish datable sequences. Wider 'area' trenches were also opened to examine gateways and one house in plan, yet most of the excavation was carried out by relatively unskilled workmen with limited supervision. At the time the work captured the popular imagination, with updates in the local newspaper and contemporary photographs showing visitors at the trench edges. The excavations revealed well-built prehistoric dry-stone walls and gateway passages below the grassy earthworks. Finds included glass and stone beads, spindle whorls and loom weights (evidence for weaving), and a cache of over 100 slingshot, all now lost. The only securely dated find was a Malvernian 'duck-stamped' jar, dating to around 100 BC (Figure 3.21), broken into sherds and discovered against the outer face of the Phase 4 wall (see below) where it intersected with the north fort. When the excavations were finally published in 1963[3] the physical relationships between the lines of walling, and the intercutting of rock-cut ditches and other features, allowed a basic sequence of development to be suggested for the hillfort. This would no doubt be refined, or even entirely changed, if any archaeologists were to return to investigate this lofty hill.

The rise of Pen Dinas

The sequence of development revealed by the excavations suggests that the fort began in the 5th or 4th century BC as a relatively simple oval defended enclosure on the lower north summit (Phase I), with a packed rubble rampart fronted with a palisade fence and ringed by an outer rock-cut ditch. In size and form this would have been similar to Hen Gaer hillfort near Bow Street, and this is probably a contemporary early fort.

Figure 7.4. The great eastern terraces of the south fort at Pen Dinas were quarried by hand from the bedrock, to form an upper terrace with a horizontal area for settlement and craft activities and a lower sloping terrace. In winter when the bracken is low, their vast scale can be appreciated. Note the comparative size of small trees and bushes in this view from below the fort. (T. Driver)

Following the abandonment of this north fort, a new fort was built on the higher and steeper south summit (Phase II). New stone gateways were built at the south and north tips of the fort, both with settings of four massive timber posts up to a metre broad, supporting crossing bridges above surfaced roadways. During this second phase the great eastern terraced defences were also built, partly excavated from the rock, which still represent a colossal engineering feat. There is evidence that these defences also fell into disuse with parts being burnt, while the south gate collapsed and became overgrown.

During Phase III the south fort was reoccupied and extensively repaired with new gateways built over the old. The gateways were sophisticated for Cardigan Bay. The north gate had a great curving buttress or hornwork added to overlook the right-hand side of the approaches, allowing slingers to rain shot down on attackers' unshielded right arms. During Phase IV both summits were linked with the construction of new isthmus defences and a new east-facing Isthmus gate which was successively narrowed from a 12 metre wide gap to a narrow gateway with a crossing bridge. These latest phases of Pen Dinas probably date to the 2nd and 1st centuries BC. There were about a dozen house platforms found within the south fort, mostly clustered in the south-east and north parts; the north fort has long been ploughed but would repay a thorough geophysical survey to uncover the plan of any buried houses or storage structures.

When complete the hillfort would have been striking and awe-inspiring. No other building in the region stood as tall as Pen Dinas. Yet the local shale did not make the most robust building material and evidence for buttresses and props at the foot of some walls and gateways suggests that these dry-stone structures were constantly at risk from bulging or collapse. Worse is the fact that timber components of even the best built gateways will eventually rot. Detailed excavation of the gateway at Castell Henllys, Pembrokeshire, showed

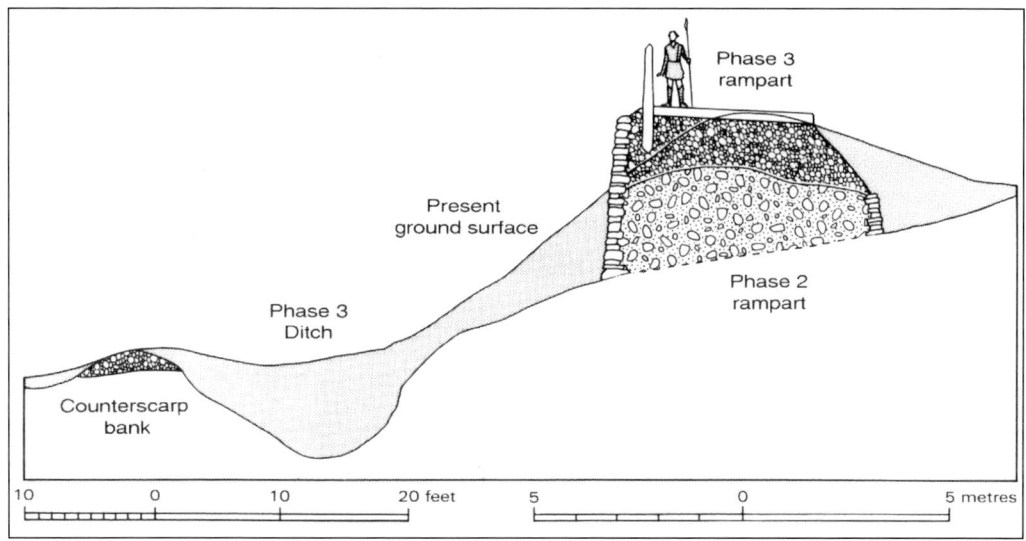

Figure 7.5. Pen Dinas, Aberystwyth. Reconstructed section through the north rampart of the south fort, showing the line of the modern ground surface against the form of the original defences. The guard on the rampart walk towered 5 metres above the heads of any attacker standing on the counterscarp bank below. (Crown Copyright RCAHMW)

that a post-built gateway with integral stone walling will rot and collapse after around thirty years, making it difficult to repair or replace without demolition (see Chapter 4). It is likely that a large and complex hillfort like Pen Dinas was a permanent building site with some parts newly built, some bulging walls propped against collapse and other sections overgrown.

The finished form of the hillfort suggests that the enclosed isthmus could have functioned as a controlled public space for fairs or markets, reinforcing the role of the hillfort as an economic power in the region. However, visitors could be kept away from the protected worlds of the gated north and south forts.

Influence and control over the regional landscape
Something of the regional power of Pen Dinas and its leaders can be learnt by studying the apparent 'exclusion zone' of comparable larger settlements around the hillfort.[4] The closest large hillforts to the north of the river Rheidol, an open landscape within view of Pen Dinas, were Caer Pwll Glas and Darren Camp some 8-12km away. By contrast, the land to the south-east along the Ystwyth valley was visually far more concealed from the coast and difficult to traverse. Here strong, small hillforts were built only 5-10km away from Pen Dinas, hidden from view by rolling hills. Old Warren Hill at Nanteos is far closer, only 3.4 km away, but is potentially an earlier hillfort controlling a distinct territory of the restricted Nant Paith valley. There is also 'clear ground' along the coastal fringes to the north and south of Pen Dinas where no further enclosures have yet been discovered despite sustained aerial reconnaissance. Overall it appears there was a 'zone of influence' to the north and south of this great hillfort covering between 5-12km, where neighbouring hillforts were

not welcome and where those controlling Pen Dinas also 'owned' and controlled the special resources of the coastal belt. A similar 'exclusion zone' was identified around the major coastal promontory fort at Greenala Point on the south Pembrokeshire coast in a recent study by the author and Louise Barker.[5]

The Romans and Pen Dinas

In 1993 Michael Avery[6] argued that episodes of burning found at the north gate of the south fort could have resulted from attacks by the Roman legions. However there is no datable evidence for this, and the gates may have burned for other reasons, perhaps accidentally during dry periods as is still witnessed on this coastal hill today. It is notable that the Ystwyth, or STVCTIA on Roman maps, is one of the few rivers to be named along the western seaboard of Wales. Roman scholars suggest this might be because Pen Dinas still posed a strategic threat at the coastal mouth of the Ystwyth and required identification. No Roman activity is known from the hilltop despite the find of an early 4th-century AD coin of the emperor Maximian. Pen Dinas would have made an ideal location for a late Roman signal station, or even a shrine or temple.

Figure 7.6. A tour party at Pen Dinas, Aberystwyth stand against the skyline on the northern rampart of the south fort, atop the 'command post' to the right of the north gate. The figures give a fair impression of the scale and appearance of a rampart-top palisade, and the scene can be compared to the reconstruction drawing in Figure 4.18. The modern path which enters the fort below them follows the line of the Iron Age entrance track.
(By kind permission of Simon Marshall)

2 & 3. THE QUARTZ-WALLED HILLFORTS OF LONG WOOD, LAMPETER: CASTELL ALLT-GOCH AND CASTELL GOETRE

Directions: Two of the great hillforts of the middle Teifi valley are easily accessible by public footpaths. From Lampeter Rugby Club (SN 579 487), follow the footpath up a stiff ascent towards Mount Pleasant Farm with views of Castell Olwen hillfort below to your left. The path becomes a pleasant ridgeway hike past the Long Wood Community Woodland, and on through fields to first Castell Allt-goch (SN 593 501), then Castell Goetre (SN 603 509). The path can be wet and muddy underfoot.

Here is a rare opportunity to visit and compare two very different Ceredigion hillforts, and to consider ideas of land ownership, chronology and Iron Age prestige display. Look out for a unique signpost in the county, directing visitors to the 'Hill Forts / Cloddwaith Cynhanes'.

Castell Allt-goch is reached first and commands the rounded summit of a knoll set higher than the flatter siting of Castell Goetre beyond. It is an oval hillfort, with opposing east and west gateways and evidence for enlargement from a smaller first phase hillfort. The surviving rampart is impressive in places, standing up to 4m high above the ditch bottom. On the east side low outworks strike through the pasture indicating the position of a once

Figure 7.7. Castell Allt-goch hillfort: a winter aerial photograph from the east. Traces of an early-phase rampart crossing the middle of the hillfort (arrowed), originally identified by Terry James[7] from aerial photographs, suggest the hillfort began as a smaller hilltop enclosure on the left (A) before being more than doubled in size. Some years ago archaeologists thought that the pronounced double outworks in the foreground (B), which still form a sizeable earthwork despite centuries of ploughing, were the remains of a vanished defence encircling the hillfort. This was probably never the case; instead these outworks specifically flank the main gateway (central indent in long side of hillfort) as a way to baffle and slow approaching visitors. (Crown Copyright RCAHMW, DI2009_0901)

Figure 7.8. The multiple eastern outworks of Castell Allt-goch, looking east, still form an impressive defensive feature and would have served to baffle and confuse anyone approaching the gateway. (T. Driver)

Figure 7.9. Castell Goetre, seen from the north-east, is a pear-shaped hillfort with at least two phases. The original 'D' shaped enclosure lay in the foreground (A) before being enlarged to the south-west (top) with the addition of a new outer gate (B). Parchmarks on this 2006 photograph, taken during record drought, revealed the lines of the levelled outer ditches on the east (C - bottom left) of the hillfort for the first time. (Crown Copyright RCAHMW, AP_2006_3839)

formidable double outer defence. Davies and Hogg writing in 1994[8] suggested that cultivation had removed the bivallate outer defences around the rest of the fort, but these were very likely only built to flank the eastern gateway.

Castell Allt-goch may originally have looked quite different. On the south-west side there is an increase in the number of quartz blocks incorporated in an adjacent field wall, no doubt sourced from the fort. Around the rampart large walling stones and quartz blocks have tumbled out of erosion scars, while at the western gateway it is possible to make out intact quartz and stone rampart walling. There was clearly a high use of quartz blocks in the rampart for this fort.

Castell Goetre lies one kilometre further along the ridge to the north-east, reached across a boggy, low-lying stream valley riddled with springs. Perhaps this wet land provided a natural boundary between the two forts, if they were occupied at the same time?

Castell Goetre is one of the county's larger forts, with at least two phases of construction and enclosing nearly 3 hectares. The great sweeping oval hillfort measures 240m south-west/ north-east by 150m north-west/south-east. It is crossed by a curving inner rampart around 6m wide. Once suggested as a late feature, cutting the fort in half and reducing the defended area, it is more likely that this represents an early first phase fort. The cross-bank still has a central gateway. At some point this early oval fort was incorporated into a new bivallate hillfort more than twice the size, with strong gateways sited at the south-west and east.

The inner bank still stands 8-10m wide and up to 2.5m high in places, although it has been cultivated on the west side and almost obliterated along the north. Where the ramparts enter the edge of a forest plantation at the east they stand higher and are more impressive, but are overgrown.

Despite being incorporated in modern field banks, Castell Goetre is a rewarding site to visit as there is plenty of evidence for the original use of quartz- and boulder-walling around the outer defensive circuit. Large quartz blocks lie loose wherever modern breaks exist, or where original gateways have been enlarged by later activity. One can only imagine the original scene of an entirely stone-walled fort, perhaps with broad, squat, quartz-studded walls topped with a strong palisade. The fragmentation of this important fort into several fields and hedge banks today should not detract from its former glory.

Figure 7.10. *A view of the great rampart of Castell Goetre from the south-east, studded with boulders and quartz blocks of the original facing. (T. Driver)*

135

4. A DISPLAY OF POWER ON THE UPLAND EDGE: PEN Y BANNAU, STRATA FLORIDA

Directions: (SN 742 669) Accessible via the Pontrhydfendigaid to Devils Bridge long distance trail, which runs north from Pontrhydfendigaid village or which can be picked up from a footpath alongside Pontrhydfendigaid school (off the B4343 road to the north of the village centre). The waymarked trail heads south-east across farmland north of the village, before turning north and then east, ascending the steep slopes of Pen y Bannau. The route crosses the heart of the fort by way of the triangulation pillar on its summit but the remainder of the hillfort lies on private land.

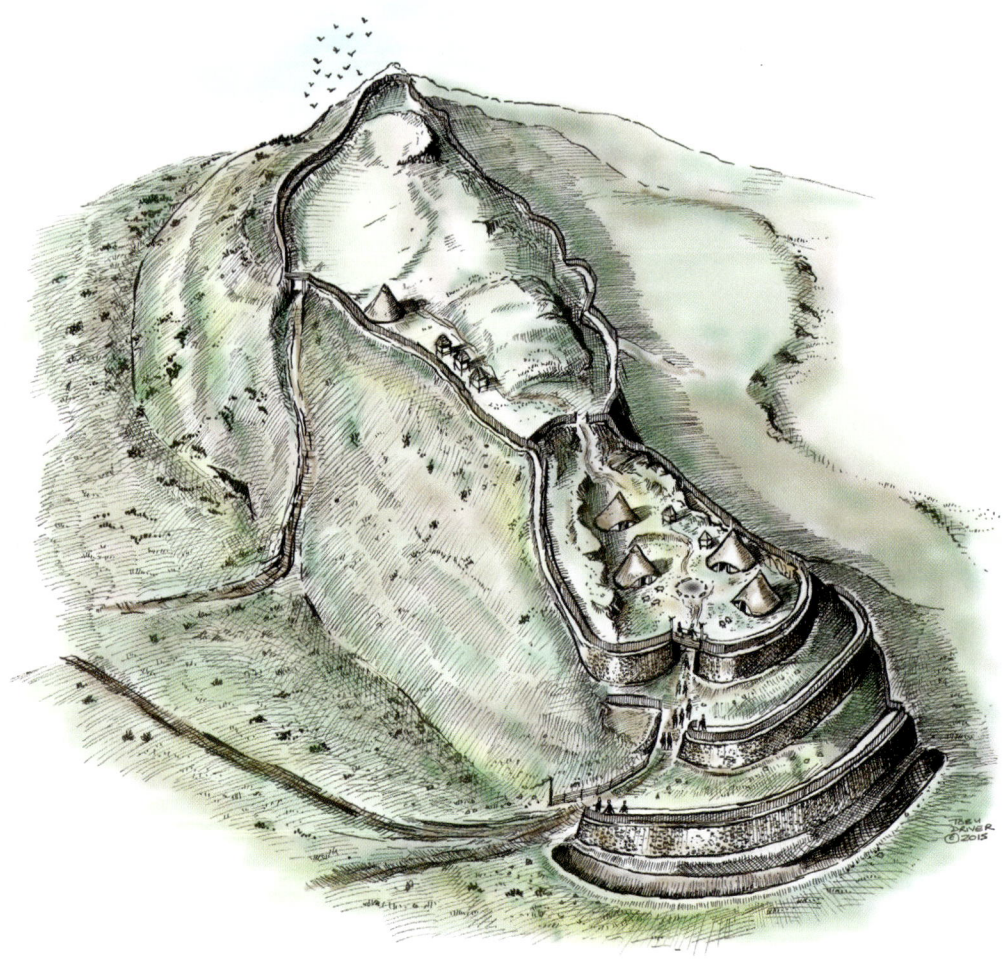

Figure 7.11. An impression of Pen y Bannau in the later Iron Age, showing the main timber gateway crossed by a bridge at the innermost point of the elaborate defensive façade. At least two minor gateways gave access to the 'rear' of the outcrop beyond. (T. Driver)

Pen y Bannau hillfort crowns a high outcrop overlooking the lowlands of Cors Caron/ Tregaron Bog. It has one of the most distinctive and impressive defensive façades in the whole of mid and west Wales. Three steep, stocky banks flank the main gate at the narrow north-east end of the fort. However, these strongly-built defences enclose only a tiny portion of the entire outcrop. The remainder is defended by a low footing wall, probably a foundation for a timber palisade or even – in places – a light fence.

Pen y Bannau occupies a supremely strong position in the regional landscape, its highest point reaching 352m above sea level. The views from the hillfort are extensive, yet the impressive triple façade does not command a wide vista; the full view of the defences is only glimpsed by travellers descending from the high mountain to the north-east from the area around the Teifi Pools. As with other forts in the hill fringe in north Ceredigion, including Caer Lletty Llwyd near Talybont or Tan-y-ffordd in the Rheidol Valley, it is hard not to conclude that the defences faced east to greet visitors arriving over the high ground of the Cambrian Mountains, from distant lands like Montgomeryshire and the Welsh Borders.

Pen y Bannau measures overall c.180m north-east/south-west, but is only 60m wide. The fort is divided roughly in two, with one half comprising the summit of the crag, topped by a concrete triangulation pillar. It is a small hillfort, only enclosing 1.1 hectares, but it makes up for this limited enclosed size with a defended gateway façade which mimics – on a restricted 'budget' – multivallate fortresses like Old Oswestry or Gaer Fawr near Welshpool. Such distant hillforts may well have influenced chieftains, elders or architects who saw them on eastward journeys and wished to emulate the effect of multivallation but with the more limited labour force available on Cardigan Bay.

Figure 7.12. Pen y Bannau has one of the most impressive façades to be seen in west Wales, but it only defends a tiny part of the entire outcrop. Jeffrey Davies[9] likened the effect to a monumental 'boasting platform'. (T. Driver)

Few other hillforts in Ceredigion, or west Wales, possess the build quality, audacity and ambition of Pen y Bannau's gateway, whose steep ramparts still stand 3-4m tall and were once revetted in stone. Any Iron Age visitor arriving for the first time would have been impressed, terrified and humbled. Entering around the eastern terminal of the lowest rampart one climbs uphill along a pathway, probably once surfaced, passing the eastern terminal of the middle rampart and reaching the main inner gateway. Massive stonework protruding through the turf, including a boulder just over 1m long resting on another large stone, suggests the original scale of the gate. The deep passage running in between high gateway terminals (as at Castle Hill, Llanilar and Pen Dinas, Aberystwyth) very likely represents a corridor entrance passing beneath a high crossing bridge on strong timber posts. Inside the fort is a sheltered hollow bounded by outcropping rock, where up to five house platforms can be seen as levelled, grassy areas. The southern part of the hillfort interior is bounded by steep rocky cliffs with two minor gateways. There are the sites of possibly two house platforms together with a small rectangular structure which is probably later.

Figure 7.13. Massive stonework exposed at the original inner gateway at Pen y Bannau suggests the former scale of the entrance here, or indeed the incorporation of boulders within the gateway walling as seen both at Darren Camp and Pen Dinas, Aberystwyth. The scale measures 50cms. (T. Driver)

Figure 7.14. The best view of Pen y Bannau's entrance ramparts is obtained from the north, from the minor road which descends from the hills near the Teifi Pools to Ffair Rhos village. It seems the impressive entrance ramparts were designed to face out towards visitors arriving from across the Cambrian Mountains to the east. (T. Driver)

The distinctive architecture at Pen y Bannau, featuring steep, short lengths of rampart at the gateway, is echoed at two other forts bordering Cors Caron: Trecoll on the west, and Castell, Tregaron to the south. At each one the position of the gateway is not obvious, and must be sought out by passing by or into complicated lines of earthworks. These Cors Caron forts are sufficiently distinctive from any other in Ceredigion to suggest they represent a regional flowering – if only for a generation – of a set of hillforts with common design features. Similar hillforts can be found to the east over the Cambrian Mountains.

5. A remote early hillfort on the high moorland: Castell Rhyfel

Directions: Freely accessible on Open Access land. Just north of Tregaron town centre take a minor road east off the B4343, signposted as a 'dead end', along the valley of the Afon Groes. Follow this single track road towards Penffordd (SN 703 611) and continue until the end of the road near Gwar-castell (SN 719 605). Park safely, then pick up the public footpath – an old green lane – across a ford and out onto Open Access land along the steep-sided valley of the Groes Fawr. After a marked kink in the track (SN 725 599) branch off left (east), diagonally uphill towards a flat summit in the middle distance. Look out for a good Bronze Age cairn, with central cist, on the way up the hill (Figure 2.3). A steep climb between rock outcrops brings you to a grassy summit of Castell Rhyfel (SN 732 599). Beware of sudden inclement weather and hill fog and ensure you are adequately equipped for mountain conditions.

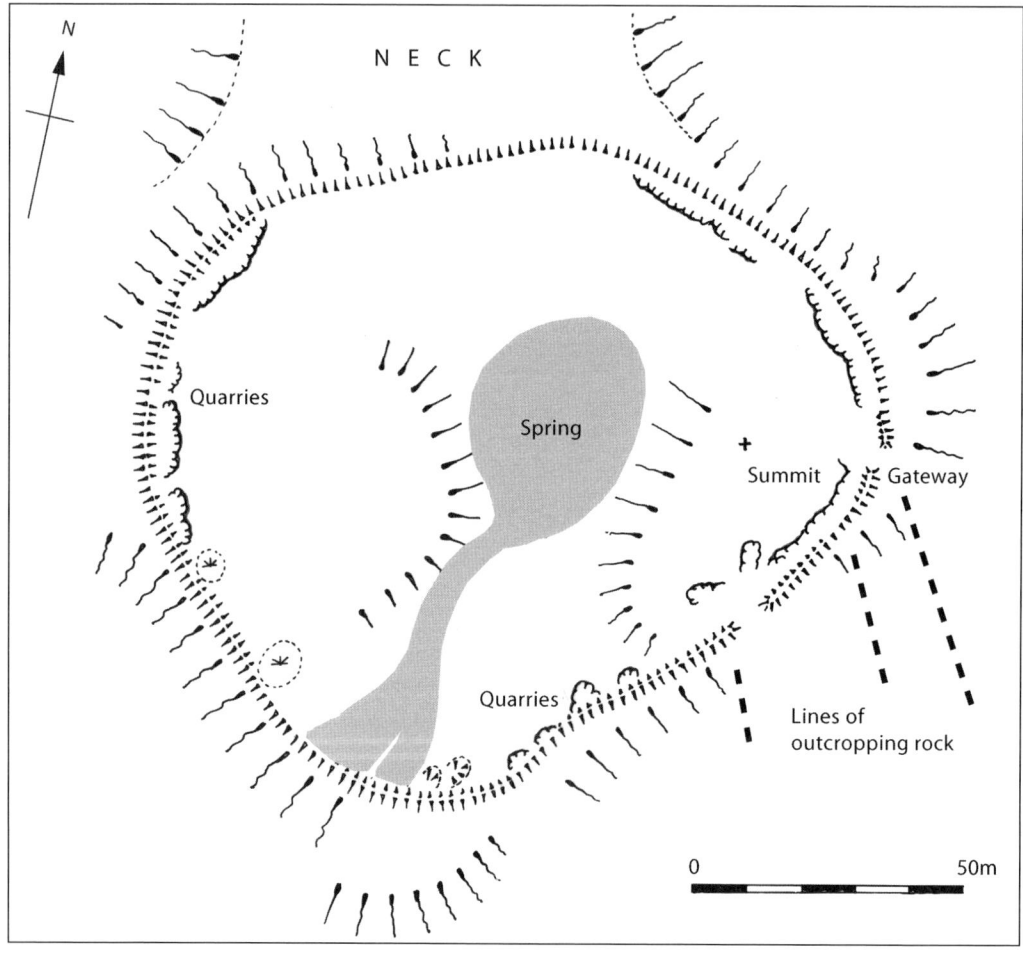

Figure 7.16. Castell Rhyfel. New sketch plan of hillfort compiled by the author.
Note the central hollow and spring, and the natural chevaux de frise caused by lines of upright outcropping rocks to the east. (T. Driver. Sources: various)

Figure 7.15. Castell Rhyfel, aerial photograph looking south-east, with the valley of the Groes Fawr beyond. (Crown Copyright RCAHMW, DI2005_0212)

This is one of the least monumental hillforts in the region, but is included as an accessible example of a potentially early site which is well worth visiting. For some reason, prehistoric people chose to enclose this bare summit with a low perimeter rampart and mark it out as distinct and special among the many rounded hilltops at the edge of the high moorland. Standing on its summit at 500m above sea level one looks west to the curve of Cardigan Bay, from the distant Lleyn Peninsula and peaks of Cadair Idris in Snowdonia in the north-west, to the hills of Pembrokeshire in the south-west. Turning around, one looks out east upon the relentless exposed moorland of the Cambrian Mountains. Like the eroded, remote hilltop enclosure at Lluest y Trafle far to the north near Bontgoch (Figure 2.10), this enclosure may be a Late Bronze Age (or earlier?) meeting place, commanding well-traversed mountain passes. It seems doubtful that this defended enclosure ever functioned as a permanent settlement.

Castell Rhyfel (literally 'war castle') crowns the rounded summit of a ridge, set in an exceptionally exposed position. The defended enclosure is a flattened oval, measuring 133m by 110m. The defences, such as they are, consist of a low earth and stone bank up to 4m in width, but only standing in places up to a metre high. The best sections are found on the south-east side, but the 'rampart' was probably only ever intended as a low footing for a palisade and has clearly suffered from weathering and erosion since it was built. The encircling bank was formed by quarrying material from behind, with the spoil dumped forward on the edge of the slope. This has left a series of irregular, intermittent quarry scoops just inside the perimeter. Some of these are very damp and partly water-filled in the southern

141

half but may have been the most sheltered places to build houses here, if any ever stood on this summit.

The original gateway is at the eastern tip where there is a clear break in the defences with the low rampart ending in terminals. This is one of the few approaches to the fort, which is otherwise bounded by precipitous slopes, except where the ridge continues across a slight saddle of lower ground on the north side.

Two unusual natural features are noteworthy on this summit and may have attracted prehistoric settlers. On the steep south-east slopes are lines of naturally-outcropping upright rock slabs, likened by Helen Burnham of Cadw to a natural 'chevaux-de-frise'. Chevaux-de-frise are strips or areas of upright stones and boulders set around the perimeter of a hillfort, thought to have been an unpleasant defence against mounted attack. A good example can be seen at Castell Henllys, Pembrokeshire. In places the slabs at Castell Rhyfel look like small standing stones, and these jagged rocks protrude from other summits nearby. A further notable feature of the summit is a boggy area in the centre between two spurs of higher ground, which produces two marked lines of run-off to the south. This boggy spring may have provided a water-source, or may even have been a ritual focus. On the southern edge of the boggy area can be seen two or three probable house platforms with their uphill sections cut into the bedrock with shelves of levelled earth below.

Ultimately Castell Rhyfel may have been sited to overlook, and serve, the prehistoric mountain pass along the valley of the Groes Fawr. In historic times the Abergwesyn pass along the Berwyn valley 2km to the south was the busy droving route between Tregaron and the livestock markets of mid and south Wales. In prehistoric times the Afon Groes/ Groes Fawr valley seems to have been the major overland routeway. The potential antiquity of this passage through the hills is shown by the concentration of Bronze Age monuments which line the way; from the two cairns and a standing stone at Nantymaen (SN 761 583) – the stone arguably a 'waymarker' showing the route off the moorland towards the head of the valley – past a cairn at the head of Groes Fawr, and then several more cairns along the Groes Fawr where it winds around the base of Castell Rhyfel and then off along the lower-lying valley of the Afon Groes approaching Tregaron. The Tregaron end of the pass was marked in prehistory by Castell, Tregaron hillfort, which commands the major valley junction between the Afon Groes and the Teifi.

6. Seats of family power, and sibling rivalry? Cnwc y Bugail, Trawsgoed and its neighbours

Directions: (SN 687 740) Cnwc y Bugail is reached via a waymarked public foot-path from Cwmnewidion Isaf farm, alongside the minor road between Abermagwr and Pontrhydygroes, opposite the turn to Cnwch Coch hamlet. Follow the path past the farm, over a footbridge and up through a paddock to a top gate. Follow the path into the next field and keep an eye out for a waymarked gate on your right giving access alongside the hillfort atop its triangular knoll. If you continue following the main path south-east uphill towards Disgwylfa, you will obtain views of two further forts which lie on private land, Castell Disgwylfa and the recently discovered (2005) Coed Tyn-y-cwm on a rise marked by a lone Scots Pine.

Among the three Coed Tyn-y-cwm forts, which command a close set of ridges above Trawsgoed in the central Ystwyth Valley, one can see a splendid example of a small but elaborate hillfort. Cnwc y Bugail ('the shepherd's knoll') has many refining features which mark it out as the former seat of perhaps a single family or individual. Close by, and within sight, are two smaller hillforts. These may be tangible evidence of the Celtic practice of 'partible inheritance', whereby the family's lands were divided equally between siblings who could each build their own homestead or fort. One might be tempted to suggest a father handing land to his eldest sons, but as it is known that the Iron Age had its own native 'queens' and powerful female leaders a male-orientated leadership or line of inheritance cannot be assumed.

Cnwc y Bugail is a triangular hillfort built around an angular, prominent knoll. It commands views to the north over the valley of the Nant Cwmnewydion and out along the Ystwyth valley towards Aberystwyth, but is overlooked by high ground to the south and east.

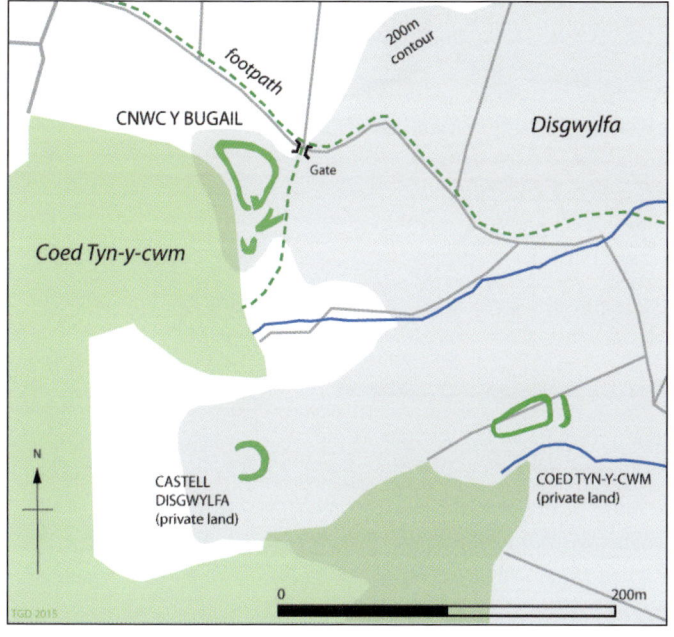

Figure 7.17. Map of the three Coed Tyn-y-cwm forts which are closely spaced together on a series of prominent knolls and ridges, separated by a valley, to the north of Llanafan, Trawsgoed. (T. Driver)

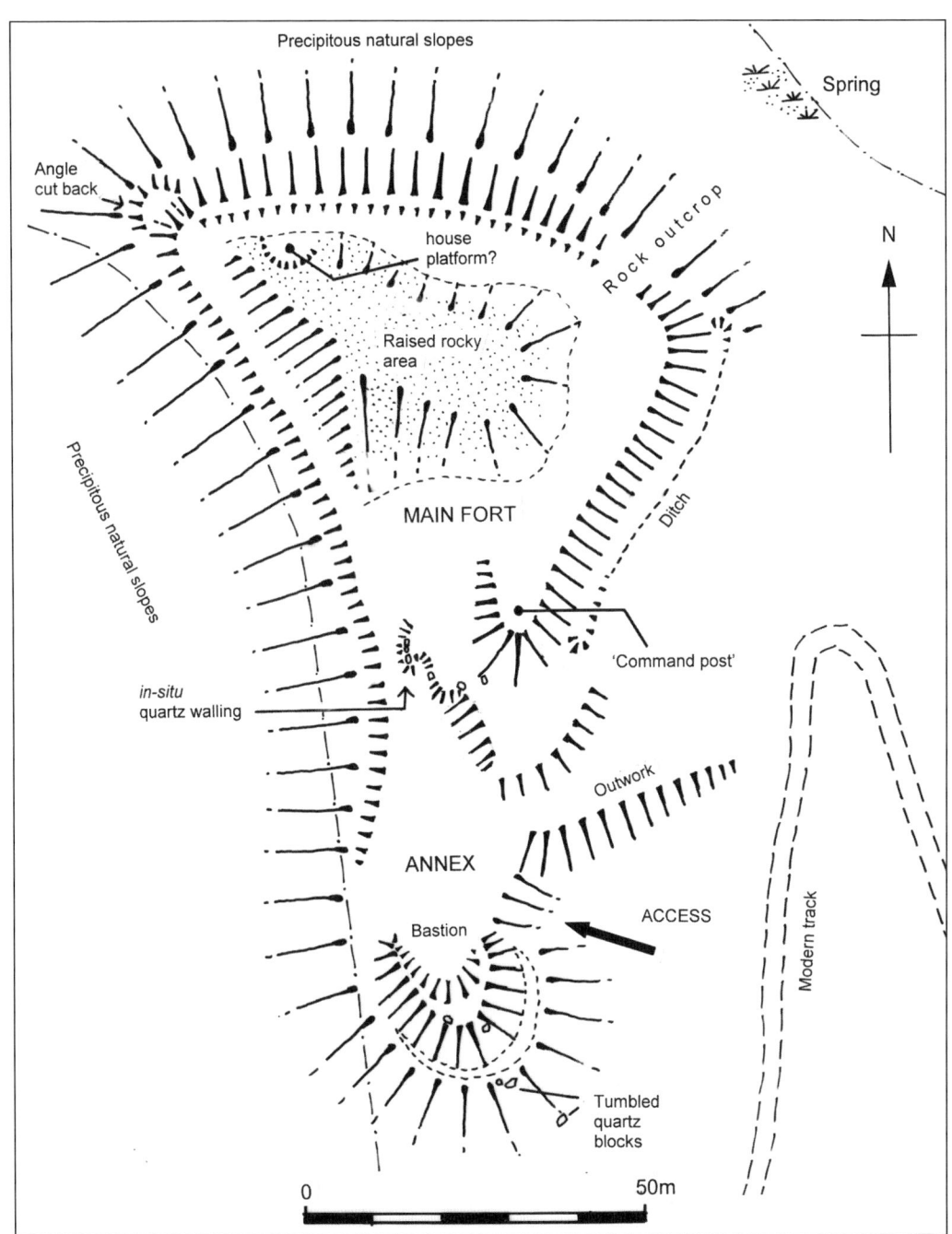

Figure 7.18. Sketch survey of Cnwc y Bugail by the author in 2003, showing the triangular hillfort separated from the southern defensive bastion by the annex. On the eastern side of the annex is the likely position of the outer gate (marked 'Access'), leading to the probable inner gate marked by in-situ quartz walling: without excavation both gateways are speculative. An oblique track also leaves the hillfort to the south-west, running down the slope to the west of the bastion, suggesting different phases of gateways at this small site. (T. Driver)

On a higher ridge to the south of Cnwc y Bugail can be seen the very small second 'fort' of the group, Castell Disgwylfa. Being so small, it is hard to imagine it ever being occupied and perhaps it was simply a 'lookout' to guard over approaches from the south? The third hillfort, Coed Tyn-y-cwm, on a knoll to the south-east and marked at the time of writing by an isolated pine tree, was only discovered during Royal Commission aerial reconnaissance in 2003. It has double ramparts on the west and at least one large house platform.

Cnwc y Bugail is enclosed by a single well-preserved rampart with an outer ditch in places. The neat form of the rampart suggests it was originally stone-walled with a low footing at the top to support a timber palisade. Towards the centre of the interior is a rocky knoll, with at least one probable house platform cut into its northern edge. The likely positions of one or two other roundhouses can be inferred by more level areas within the fort, but traces of medieval or later ploughing within the fort seem to have erased all archaeological traces. Below to the north-east a small spring emerges from a seam of outcropping rock, which may have been useful in the Iron Age.

Quartz walling and controlled access

What picks out this small hillfort as something rather special is the ostentatious use of a particularly showy rock – quartz. Protruding through the grass at the southern tip of the main fort are three substantial quartz blocks, lining what may have been the entrance passage. Other loose quartz blocks can be found tumbled at the southern part of this fort, suggesting quartz walling was widely employed – as it was at other west Wales hillforts including Castell Henllys (see Chapter 4). Moving south of the probable gateway one crosses the annex to the freestanding bastion, where there is further evidence that its front face was originally walled with neat quartz blocks, some of which have tumbled down the slope. On the east side of the annex a low outwork runs down to the dry valley below the fort. This may have been the original main track into the annex, with a secondary gate allowing access to the hillfort interior; however, there also seems to be an old trackway running south-west of the bastion, down a slope into the modern forestry plantation.

Much of the construction of Cnwc y Bugail was about display, together with controlled access. The freestanding bastion is an impressive feature, unique in the county, and stands above head-height on its outer face with an external ditch. Looking at the overall plan of the hillfort, nearly half of the north-south length of the defended summit is given over to the large annex and bastion. This means that public access to the hillfort was important, but carefully controlled. The provision of a large annex may have allowed public events like markets or fairs to be held within the defences without compromising the privacy or elevated status of the main hillfort interior.

Power on the middle Ystwyth Valley

The residents of Cnwc y Bugail were not to be trifled with; on a field visit in 2003 the author picked up a small Iron Age slingshot lying on the ground surface just south of the bastion. Perhaps a cache of stones was stored behind the bastion for times of trouble? As the hillfort is a scheduled ancient monument the slingstone now resides in Ceredigion Museum (but is not on display). Visiting this hillfort it is hard not to be aware of the Abermagwr Romano-British villa which lies in the same valley just under 2kms to the west. It is unlikely the hillfort was still occupied into the 3rd century AD when the villa was first constructed, but both sites are examples of the rising wealth and social status which characterised the central Ystwyth valley in the late Iron Age and Romano-British periods.

Figure 7.19. Cnwc y Bugail as seen from high ground to the east. This view shows the main, triangular defended enclosure occupying a high knoll. Towards the centre of the frame, the east rampart rises and ends at the putative 'command post' which looks down on the gateway to the left. At far left is the south bastion across a saddle of ground – the annex – from the main fort. (T. Driver)

Figure 7.20. Reconstruction drawing of Cnwc y Bugail hillfort as it may have looked around 100 BC. Quartz-rich stone facing enhanced the showy appearance of the bastion (far left) and the 'command post' (centre, alongside main gateway tower). Other ramparts were probably faced with stone and topped by timber palisades. The house locations, positions and forms of both gates and many other details are speculative. (T. Driver)

7. HIDDEN BETWEEN LAND AND SEA: CASTELL BACH, CWMTYDU

Directions: (SN 742 669) Accessible via the Pontrhydygroes to Pontrhydfendigaid section of the Borth to Ystwyth Trail path (tourist leaflet available), which runs north from Pontrhydfendigaid village or can be picked up from a footpath alongside Pontrhydfendigaid school (off the B4343 road to the north of the village centre). The waymarked trail heads south-east across farmland north of the village, before turning north and then east, ascending the steep slopes of Pen y Bannau. The route crosses the fort by way of the entrance earthworks but the remainder of the hillfort lies on private land.

Castell Bach is one of the few coastal forts of Ceredigion and occupies a spectacular but secluded – even hidden – location. Questions remains about why it was built in this particular location and to what extent coastal erosion has reduced the size of the fort seen today. Descending from the high coastal plateau towards Castell Bach a restricted saddle of level ground is encountered at the base of a great 'bowl' in the coastal slopes. The triple ramparts of the fort enclose this entire saddle hemmed in on the south and east sides by steep scarps, on the north by 20 metre high coastal cliffs and to the west by a narrow inlet. Dominating the view, and the coastal inlet, is a freestanding coastal stack which appears to have artificial platforms cut into its pointed summit. Was this originally part of the fort before it was cut away by coastal erosion or was it always separate, perhaps reached by a now eroded land bridge between fort and stack?

The inner fort and outer annex
The bivallate (double-ditched) inner fort currently encloses a quarter of a hectare defined by two close-set ramparts each with an outer ditch; a third rampart and outer ditch are widely

Figure 7.21. View of Castell Bach from the south, showing the coastal inlet and freestanding stack on the left, and the saddle of level ground centre-right occupied by the curving ramparts of the fort bounded by steeper slopes. (T. Driver)

Figure 7.22. Vestiges of substantial stone revetment walling on the outer face of the inner fort at Castell Bach, Cwmtydu. Scale measures 1m. (T. Driver)

spaced some 100m to the east. The whole presently encloses 1.48ha, but may have enclosed nearly 2 hectares before coastal erosion cut away the west side. No artificial defences were required on the south side where the ground rises in a steep scarp.

The bivallate defences of the inner fort swing around to enclose the north-west part of the coastal saddle. The inner rampart stands around 7m wide and 2m tall. The outer is half the width of the inner but stands slightly taller in places and is revetted on its outer eastern face with substantial stone blocks. The intervening ditch, about a metre deep, is water-filled and fed by a spring; here and there former revetment blocks have tumbled into its base. The original main gateway was to the north near the cliff edge where a 3m gap on the inner rampart is matched by a 2.5m gap in the outer, with heightened gateway terminals albeit only standing a metre high.

Cliff erosion through the inner ramparts

Both the inner ramparts are actively eroding on the west side, revealing a cross-section in slumping cliffs. Studies by Keith Ray for the Ceredigion Archaeological Survey in the 1980s, and more recently by the National Trust, suggested that the inner enclosure originally comprised a single inner bank and ditch, but then was remodelled when the outer bank and ditch were built; there was then a rebuild of the outer bank. Despite the appearance of severe coastal erosion, much of the northern cliff line is stable and even stepped-back from the waves. There is no reason to doubt that these are the original northern extents of the fort's defences, with the only losses found on the west side.

The third, outer, defensive bank set apart from the inner may indicate a later expansion of the site. This bank respects the modern cliff edge by ending in an inturned gateway terminal on the north side, leaving a 6m outer gateway. This was clearly the original way

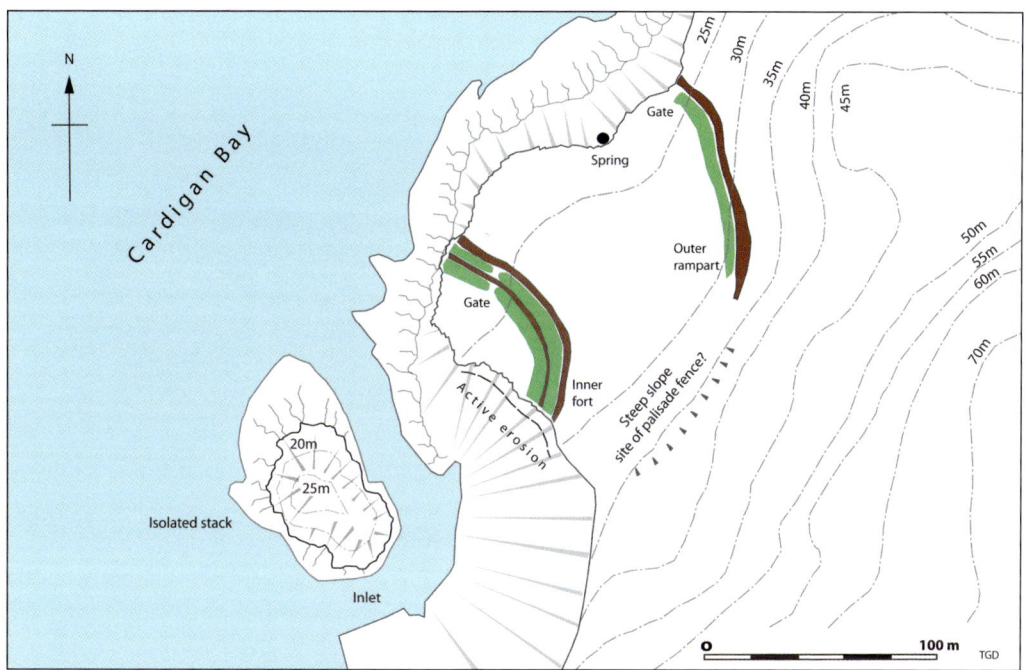

Figure 7.23. Castell Bach. New plan by the author showing the inner and outer ramparts (green), ditches (brown), the isolated coastal stack and the site of the spring in the cliff face. (T. Driver. Sources: various)

into the fort from the east. This wide-spaced outer rampart stands about 7m wide and 2m high in places, with a deep outer ditch making the defence seem more formidable. As with the inner fort, the ditch also encloses an active spring. An eroded modern cut through this rampart shows a span of 2m between inner and outer revetment walls. This great outer-most enclosure to the inner fort is featureless today despite suggestions of an enclosure spotted on aerial photographs in the 1980s. The 'enclosure' probably derives from a series of relatively recent 'herringbone' field drains dug across the centre of the saddle, and visible as parchmarks on aerial photos. A third spring is sited on the cliff edge midway along the annex, walled with small stone blocks which may well be of prehistoric date. Similar walled springs can be seen on Skomer Island, Pembrokeshire.

Landscape setting and remaining questions
Why was Castell Bach built in this location, miles from any similar site? This is the last coastal fort encountered going north until Pen Dinas at Aberystwyth. It is sited on a difficult stretch of coastline, characterized by steep cliffs and few inlets, between the iconic prom-ontory of Pendinaslochtyn to the south-west and the prominent headland of Newquay to the north-east. Only here was there a distinct narrow strip of land defined by two stream valleys, nestled between two coastal bays only 1.8km apart. Inland runs a coherent tongue of land, a coherent 'territory', to Caerwedros village.

The enclosure of three freshwater springs on a coastal saddle may have been significant, especially as two have been incorporated within the Iron Age ditches and a third is stone-

149

Figure 7.24. The eroded southern section through the ramparts of the inner fort, caused by ongoing coastal erosion, clearly shows the structural layers of the Iron Age rampart. Despite the damage being caused to the prehistoric defences, this section has long been a valuable window into the structural history of an otherwise unexcavated site for archaeologists. (Photo: T. Driver)

walled. Perhaps the advantage here was commanding the sheltered coastal inlet, allowing the inhabitants to control shipping out onto Cardigan Bay? The role of the isolated coastal stack in the original fort is open for discussion. Although coastal erosion affects part of the western cliffs of the fort, the stack may always have been an isolated element of the site perhaps reserved for ceremonial purposes. The wide-spaced outer enclosure may have performed a simple farming role for enclosing stock; yet Castell Bach's position in a natural 'amphitheatre' invites speculation as to whether its 'hidden' aspect was part of its role so that ceremonies, markets or other practices within the fort could be observed from the vantage point of the surrounding hills. The siting of a long-lived church, spring and standing stone at St Tysilio's Church on the hill above, a sacred site with origins in the early Christian period, may be significant.

Figure 7.25. The iconic flat-topped conical hill of Pen y Badell, Llangrannog, crowned by Pendinaslochdyn fort, with the low promontory and island of Ynyslochtyn to the right, as seen from Castell Bach to the north-east. In 1860 John Fenton wrote: 'This position overtops all the surrounding elevations, and is conspicuous at some distance along the coast.'[10] (T. Driver)

8 & 9. COASTAL COMMAND: PENDINASLOCHDYN AND YNYSLOCHTYN, LLANGRANNOG

Directions: (Hillfort: SN 315 548; Promontory fort: SN 314 553) Accessible from the Wales Coast Path and in the care of the National Trust, both forts lying within National Trust land. Pendinaslochdyn hillfort is reached via a surfaced public footpath which leaves the road obliquely from the upper part of Llangrannog village (at SN 315 540) and takes the visitor all the way to the summit. Or one can follow the Wales Coast Path direct to both sites from Llangrannog beach.

There are few landmarks on the entire sweep of Cardigan Bay as striking or as recognisable as the flat-topped cone of Pen y Badell. This hill is crowned by the fort of Pendinaslochdyn (with a 'd'), described by Fenton in 1860 as '... the formidable post upon the lofty head-land ...',[11] which overlooks the coastal promontory and detached island of Ynyslochtyn (with a 't'). Dominating the historic shipbuilding village and inlet of Llangrannog from the north-east, and covered by swathes of yellow gorse in late spring, Pendinaslochydyn commands extensive views west to Mwnt and Cardigan Island, north-east to Pen Dinas hillfort at Aberystwyth and beyond to Tremadog Bay, and on the skyline may be seen the Lleyn Peninsula and the silhouette of Bardsey Island. The promontory fort below at Ynyslochtyn raises interesting questions about the relationship between these two very different coastal fortifications.

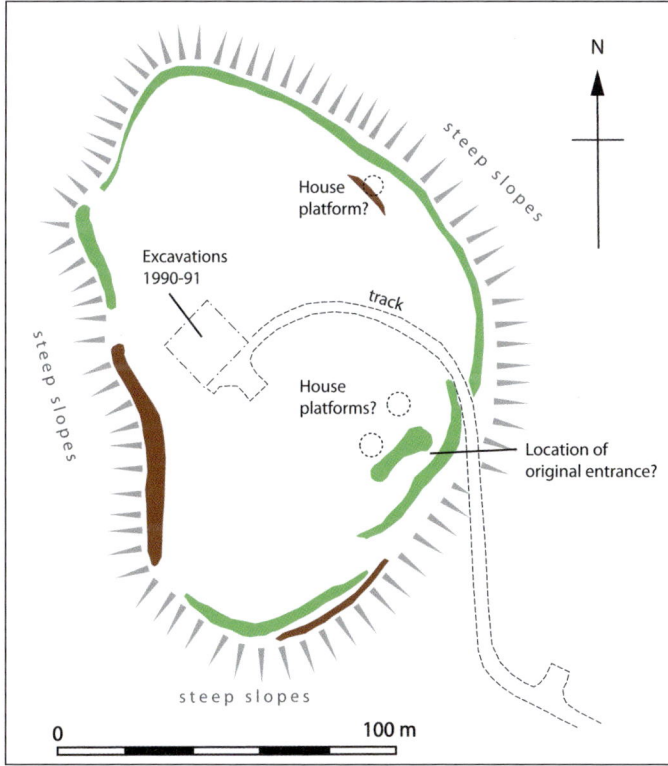

Figure 7.26. Plan of Pendinaslochdyn showing the area excavated by the Dyfed Archaeological Trust in 1990-91, now occupied by a military building. Ramparts and scarps are shown in green, ditches in brown. (T. Driver[12])

Figure 7.27. Pendinaslochdyn hillfort looks down from a towering coastal hill above crumbling sea cliffs near Llangrannog village. (T. Driver)

Pendinaslochdyn

Pendinaslochdyn must always have been an exposed hill summit for settlement, especially in biting winter gales. Yet its visibility and supremacy as a defensible locale on Cardigan Bay means that it probably attracted settlement from earliest times. The kidney-shaped hill summit encloses around 1.5 hectares and is skirted for the most part by a defensive bank 5m wide and up to 2m high, with an intermittent ditch, the defences made by scarping the edge of the natural hillslope. The original gateway probably lay on the south-east side but is obscured by the MoD road serving a modern missile-tracking station on the hill summit.

Excavations by the Dyfed Archaeological Trust in 1990-91,[13] in advance of construction of the MoD installation, discovered part of a roundhouse measuring 7m diameter that was radiocarbon dated to the Romano-British period (85-420AD). Also excavated was a four-post structure about 3m square, the footings of a raised storage building. An isolated post-hole nearby produced a late Bronze Age radiocarbon date, suggesting an early settlement or hillfort on this prominent summit. A cache of twelve rounded beach pebbles – slingshots – was found together on the original bedrock land surface adjacent to the four-post structure. It is remarkable that a cache of slingshot survived intact, presumably as it was left in the Iron Age. They are on display in the Ceredigion Museum.

Pendinaslochdyn looks down upon two Iron Age settlements, Ynyslochtyn promontory fort (described below) and Llangrannog hillfort (SN 311 538) which occupies a narrow, steep promontory to the south-west above the village. This hillfort is not marked on maps, but can be seen in profile from below. Its defining feature is a deep rocky saddle, apparently

Figure 7.28. Ynyslochtyn viewed from the coast path below Pendinaslochdyn fort showing the minor rampart of the promontory fort crossing the last part of the landward peninsula, and the offshore island beyond. (T. Driver)

a natural defensive feature, cutting off the fort from the hillside. The stepped interior, on private land, contains a number of house platforms.

Ynyslochtyn promontory fort

Below Pendinaslochdyn to the north is the rocky peninsula of Pendinaslochtyn, leading to the separate Ynys ('island') Lochtyn. This finger of contorted rock extending into Cardigan Bay is unusual for the Ceredigion coast and is home to a small fort sited at the leading edge of the landward promontory. Sheer cliffs provide the defence on three sides whilst a single rampart around 18m long but only a metre high cuts across the narrow neck of the promontory; the line of an outer ditch can just be made out. Currently the fort encloses an area of around 80m by 50m and Ken Murphy has identified two or three probable house platforms within the grassy interior. Perhaps more intriguing is the archaeology of the offshore island, which may once have formed part of the promontory fort before erosion took hold. Past archaeologists, among them Douglas Hague and Pete Bewers, have suggested there are house platforms and other structures on Ynys Lochtyn which may be of prehistoric or early medieval date. Certainly this remote and dangerous island could have been attractive to early monastic communities.

10. TRADING SETTLEMENT ON THE WESTERN SEAWAYS?
CRAIG Y GWBERT COASTAL PROMONTORY FORT

Directions: (SN 158 502) Accessible from the Wales Coast Path. By car: follow the B4548 minor road to the north of Cardigan towards Gwbert and park near the entrance of the Cliff Hotel. A public footpath takes the visitor along the hotel driveway, around the car park and down into Craig y Gwbert promontory fort. The footpath skirts the perimeter of the fort; the interior is a private golf course.

True coastal promontory forts (as opposed to *coastal forts*) are rare in Ceredigion, largely due to the lack of suitable promontories jutting out along the mainly sheer coastline of Cardigan Bay. By contrast, the Pembrokeshire coast has some 55 promontory forts including many with massive defences.

Craig y Gwbert is a rarity, then, for Ceredigion. The choice of site is excellent. Rather than clinging to the edge of a precipitous and inaccessible cliff as with many Pembrokeshire examples, it is sited very low down – only 10m above sea level – at the tidal mouth of the Teifi Estuary. The Teifi was navigable in medieval times and onwards as witnessed by the two castles at Cardigan, at Old Castle and Cardigan town itself. Sand banks at Poppit Sands must always have been hazardous to shipping and difficult to chart, but Craig y Gwbert sits out beyond these in the open channel. Nor is it buffeted by the full force of the open sea, being set back slightly in the estuary mouth behind the rocky headland of Cemmaes Head. North across the water is Cardigan Island, which has evidence for Iron Age settlement and cultivation. On the landward side of Craig y Gwbert is the fertile coastal farming land of south-west Ceredigion dotted with cropmarks of plough-levelled Iron Age defended farms.

The promontory fort occupies a naturally isolated offshore islet, connected to the mainland only by a narrow isthmus, with sheltered inlets cut in on both sides; the cutting is probably the remains of a prehistoric rock-cut ditch. The inlet on the south would have allowed small vessels to be pulled up on the beach below the fort. Note the splendid rock-cut steps leading down to the northern inlet, of relatively recent date. The fort gate is partly obscured by a small post-medieval limekiln. Stone walling visible through the grass at the main entrance may be Iron Age and the passage itself is floored with bare rock, which must have required the difficult excavation of postholes if a gate was ever provided here.

The interior has been landscaped as part of the golf course and few original features can be made out. Archaeologists have identified pits and postholes cut into the rock on the west side where the grass cover has eroded away, and some of these certain and possible Iron Age features can still be seen today. Broad, expansive coastal rocks defining its western edge could also have allowed occupants to climb down to the water's edge via a series of natural shelves, facilitating the loading and unloading of seagoing vessels at the correct tide.

One is struck by the advantageous position of Craig y Gwbert as a potential coastal trading settlement, jutting out into the seaways but sheltered and backed by a busy hinterland of later prehistoric farms. Its low setting close to the sea may well have contributed to a special role in the Iron Age, which could only be investigated by future excavation.

Figures 7.28 & 7.29: Craig y Gwbert coastal promontory fort is advantageously sited and looks out across the Irish Sea from the mouth of the Teifi estuary. The fort enjoys easy access to a sheltered inlet and beach on the south side, where one can imagine small sea-going craft being tied up and unloaded. (Crown Copyright RCAHMW, AP_2008_0415)
The gully down to the inlet, seen in the photograph below, may have been created in prehistory to serve as a hillfort ditch. The wall of a much later limekiln can be seen to the right.
(T. Driver)

Figure 7.30. The intriguing, isolated island of Ynys Lochtyn, off the tip of Ynyslochtyn promontory fort (site 9), has house platforms and other structures which may be of prehistoric, or early medieval, date. It may once have formed part of the wider promontory fort, before coastal erosion took its toll. (T. Driver)

Chapter 8

GAZETTEER OF HILLFORTS TO VISIT

Chapter frontispiece: Caught in the light of a winter's afternoon, Dinas, Ponterwyd hillfort (SN 743 834) crowns the summit (centre) of a narrow ridge in the foothills of Plynlimon. Accessible on Open Access land, this small hillfort feels barren and remote today. Yet evidence from nearby Bronze Age standing stones (Figure 2.6), and the siting of other hillfort neighbours, suggests that this region was once the focus for prehistoric overland journeys crossing the high ground of the Cambrian Mountains. (T. Driver)

A good number of the county's Iron Age hillforts can be freely visited at any reasonable time via public footpaths and the Wales Coast Path, or on Open Access land designated under the Countryside and Rights of Way (CROW) Act 2000 (indicated on Ordnance Survey Explorer maps (1:25,000)). Many hillforts are marked on Explorer maps, the relevant numbers of which are provided at the start of each section. There are also a number of hillforts which, although not accessed by a public path, are visible from adjacent footpaths or roads and can be rewarding to see.

Many other hillforts lie on private land and out of public view, only to be glimpsed as silhouettes on distant hilltops or remaining completely out of sight. For these sites and others on private land, readers are recommended to make their own enquiries at nearby farms.

Points to remember:
All sites are visited at your own risk and, unless otherwise stated, should be assumed to lie on private land. Readers are advised to follow the Countryside Code (see below). The majority of hillforts are Scheduled Ancient Monuments in the care of Cadw, and are protected by the 1979 Ancient Monuments and Archaeological Areas Act. It is against the law to disturb them in any way or to metal detect over them. If you do find anything of archaeological interest you should report it first to the landowner, then to the Portable Antiquities Scheme (PAS) Finds Liaison Officer for Wales (see below) – or report it to the local Amgueddfa Ceredigion Museum, Aberystwyth. Finds remain the property of the landowner.

Treasure: In England, Wales and Northern Ireland, all finders of gold and silver objects, and groups of coins from the same finds, over 300 years old, have a legal obligation to report such items under the Treasure Act 1996. Prehistoric base-metal assemblages found after 1st January 2003 also qualify as Treasure. Further information can be found by visiting the Portable Antiquities Scheme (PAS) website (https://finds.org.uk/). Finders of potential Treasure in Wales should contact their regional Finds Liaison Officer for help in reporting Treasure and for further advice. By law, finds of potential Treasure must be reported to the Coroner in whose district they were found within 14 days of discovery.

Remember the Countryside Code: Respect. Protect. Enjoy.

Respect other people:

> consider the local community and other people enjoying the outdoors
>
> leave gates and property as you find them and follow paths unless wider access is available

Protect the natural environment:

> leave no trace of your visit and take your litter home
>
> keep dogs under effective control

Enjoy the outdoors:

> plan ahead and be prepared
>
> follow advice and local signs

1. Aberystwyth, Rheidol valley and north

(OS Explorer map 213)

Only two hillforts can be visited via public footpaths. These are **Pen Dinas, Aberystwyth** (see Chapter 7) and **Dinas, Ponterwyd** (SN 743 834) which crowns a moorland crag north-west of Dinas Reservoir on Open Access land. Dinas, Ponterwyd is a pear-shaped hillfort with a single rampart standing up to a metre high. It has a single main gate on the south side, and the traces of up to four house platforms inside the fort. A number of other hillforts in the region can be seen from nearby roads, or observed at a distance from public footpaths, but most lie on private land. These include Caer Lletty Llwyd (SN 651 882) south of Talybont whose terraced defences face an inland mountain pass (on private land but visible from a country lane). Penrhyncoch Camp (SN 658 840) is a simple single-banked hillfort nonetheless commanding a good position on a break of slope on ridge; the fort lies on private farmland but can be seen from the adjacent road. Tan-y-ffordd hillfort (SN 692 798) is sited low down on the Rheidol Valley in private woodland but is passed by a public footpath. In winter the defensive terraces on the north side of the hillfort can be clearly seen through the trees.

2. Central Ceredigion (north), Tregaron to the Ystwyth Valley

(OS Explorer maps 187 (west part), 198, 199, 213 (south part))

Some of Ceredigion's greatest hillforts can be found in this region but most lie well away from public footpaths on private farmland. Eight hillforts can be visited via public footpaths. **Pen y Bannau**, **Castell Rhyfel** and **Cnwc y Bugail** are described in Chapter 7. In the north of the area is **Old Warren Hill** (SN 615 789), near Nanteos House, which lies in a woodland nature reserve in the care of the Wildlife Trust for South and West Wales. This is the largest univallate hillfort in Ceredigion and while the scale of the earthworks is impressive the site is overgrown. Two sites lie in managed forestry plantations close to Trawsgoed and Llanafan. **Coed Allt Fedw** (SN 661 729) can be disappointing to visit within a forest clearing. **Cefn Blewog Camp** (SN 697 724) also lies in managed forestry but is overgrown and can be disappointing. More rewarding is **Castell Bach** (SN 538 688), with Castell Mawr nearby (SN 537 686) on the coast above Llanrhystud village, passed by a public footpath from the village centre although the forts themselves lie on private land. These two hillforts are set on rounded bluffs overlooking the coastal plain. Castell Bach preserves sections of *in-situ* Iron Age stone walling which are worth seeing.

Figure 8.1. Perched on a high crag on the northern escarpment of Cwm Rheidol west of Ystumtuen, Castell Bwa-drain (SN 713 794) is a strongly sited small promontory fort typical of many which dot the hill fringe of Ceredigion. As with many hillforts in mid Wales the site is unexcavated and little is known about its history or archaeology. It is on private land but it is overlooked from nearby footpaths and minor roads. (T. Driver)

3. Central Ceredigion (south), Lampeter and the Aeron Valley
(OS Explorer maps 198, 199)

Two of the largest hillforts in the region, **Castell Allt-goch** and **Castell Goetre** above Lampeter are accessible and are described in Chapter 7. To the east of Lampeter is Caer Cadwgan hillfort (SN 622 479) in Cellan parish, well understood following excavations by the University of Wales Lampeter in the 1980s, but inaccessible on private land. It can be seen at distance from vantage points to the north. Castell Moeddyn or Moeddin (SN 484 519), a well-built small hillfort, lies on private land but is visible from a nearby footpath. A smaller defended enclosure near Cribyn is Gaer Fach (SN 531 514), on private land but alongside a minor road. This is a very small enclosure; it is possible that the Iron Age settlement was reused and rebuilt by the later inhabitants of the adjacent cottage, now ruined.

4. South Ceredigion and the coastal path (OS Explorer maps 198, 199, part of 185)
Inland south Ceredigion

This part of the county, taking in Newquay on Cardigan Bay to Llandysul on the Teifi valley, then west to Cardigan along the winding Teifi valley, is at once the most productive land agriculturally, but also where the majority of Iron Age and Romano-British defended enclosures and hillforts – 60 or so are known – lie buried beneath ploughed fields and are only known as cropmarks. Close to Ffostrasol in central south-west Ceredigion is Caerau, Nant-Barre (SN 360 494), a small inland promontory fort 2km north-west of the village. It can be seen from a footpath which runs north from Pengaer farm on its south side, although the fort itself lies in private pasture. The hillfort is defensively sited and commands wide views to the west and south. There is no public access to Dinas Cerdin (SN 385 469), which is best viewed from a minor road branching east from Bwlch-y-groes hamlet, south of Ffostrasol on the main A486. This strongly-sited fort utilized a splendid vantage point of a raised knoll at the end of an inland promontory, commanding the confluence of two valleys.

Coastal south Ceredigion

Castell Nadolig, Penbryn (described in Chapter 5) lies on private farmland but is visible from the A487. The Ceredigion Coast Path is the best way to visit the remaining hillforts on Cardigan Bay. The great sites of **Pendinaslochdyn** and **Ynyslochtyn**, Llangrannog, **Craig y Gwbert** promontory fort near Cardigan and **Castell Bach, Cwmtydu**, have already been discussed in Chapter 7. Remaining sites south-west of Llangrannog include the unival-late promontory fort of **Castell-bach** (SN 303 536), which overlooks a small bay with an offshore rock, probably a valued landing place in prehistory. Its grass-grown ramparts are crossed by the coast path. Note the absence of any known promontory forts on the great rocky headland of Aberporth. Heading west, the next promontory fort is **Foel y Mwnt** (SN 193 521). This fort is accessible by the coast path, or by car. Pay and display parking at Mwnt is managed by the National Trust. Foel y Mwnt is a commanding promontory fort overlooking a sheltered beach, suitable for beaching ships. Although the defences are denuded and unimpressive, its position is strong and there is a great sense of history at this attractive headland which includes the medieval church below.

5. Cardigan Bay south, north Pembrokeshire

North Pembrokeshire between the Teifi estuary and Strumble Head looks out across the southern sweep of Cardigan Bay. Pembrokeshire is rich in later prehistoric hillforts and defended enclosures, and well over 400 are recorded. Coastal promontory forts also fringe the coast in great numbers; over 55 are currently known and all are easily accessed via the Pembrokeshire Coast Path. There are several notable hillforts to visit. The key accessible site is the excavated and reconstructed hillfort of **Castell Henllys** (SN 117 390), signposted from the A487 coast road and open to the public, including a visitor centre and shop. The roundhouses are among the longest standing Iron Age reconstructions in Britain and are inspiring and instructive to visit. On the high ground of Mynydd Carningli common above Newport is the remarkable and complex hillfort of **Carn-ingli** (SN 062 372), whose multiple walls and scree-built enclosures may date back to the Neolithic. On Strumble Head/Pen-caer two hillforts on the west side are rewarding to visit. **Garn Fawr** (SM 896 388) was one of the first British hillforts to be archaeologically surveyed and has multiple earthen and scree-built ramparts linking outcrops on the summit. Below and to the west is the coastal promontory fort of **Dinas Mawr, Llanwnda** (SM 887 386), where two small ramparts defend a tiny piece of promontory land below a towering rock outcrop. Was this a practical settlement, or the ceremonial enclosure of a dangerous, liminal rock tower?

6. Cardigan Bay North, south Gwynedd

The block of land fringing the northern extents of Cardigan Bay falls between the estu-aries of the Dyfi and the Mawddach and is dominated by the mountain of Cadair Idris. The most rewarding site to visit is **Bird's Rock** or **Craig yr Aderyn hillfort** (SH 644 068) which overlooks the Dysynni Valley and is reached by a waymarked footpath and a stiff climb uphill. Few hillforts in west and north Wales are as impressive. The rocky dome of

Bird's Rock juts out into the Vale with precipitous drops in places. Substantial ramparts defend the landward side of the promontory, with remnants of a stone-walled entrance passage giving access to an interior where roundhouses can be made out. Perhaps this fort – like Castell y Bere medieval castle nearby – controlled the passage of people and livestock between the west coast and the mountains.

Another fort worth seeing is at **Castell y Gaer** (SH 592 090) to the north-west, right alongside a country lane ascending the hill country behind Llwyngwril; the fort is on private farmland. Aerial photographs show prehistoric terraced fields on the hillslopes around the hillfort. A more unusual hillfort is **Pared y Cefn hir** (SH 664 151), actually a high fortified outcrop on Open Access land just on the edge of the National Trust's Cregennan estate on the north flanks of Cadair Idris. A scree-built Iron Age gateway lies at the far north-east end of the crag but there are no ramparts. Was this really a defended settlement, or was it a ceremonial hillfort on the mountain edge? Finally the findspot of the famous Tal-y-llyn hoard (see Chapter 4) lies alongside the present path up to **Cadair Idris** from the Snowdonia National Park's Minffordd car park (pay and display) located at SH 733 115. Follow the steep ascent up from the car park towards the lake of Llyn Cau. Alongside the path in June 1963 a picnicking couple from Llanbadarn Fawr noticed pieces of sheet bronze protruding from under a large boulder. This incredible discovery urges us to think differently about Cadair Idris in prehistory and suggests that parts of the route of the modern path up to Llyn Cau may well date back to prehistoric times.

Figure 8.2. Replica contents of an Iron Age home, displayed inside a reconstructed roundhouse at Castell Henllys, Pembrokeshire. Similar wicker and wooden artefacts from prehistory rarely survive into the modern day, and leave little trace in most archaeological excavations. Such perishable everyday items are only normally preserved in wetland or waterlogged archaeological sites. This view shows how much information we have potentially lost from many of the prehistoric settlements and hillforts of mid Wales and Cardigan Bay. (T. Driver)

Figure 8.3. The next generation: In the summer of 2013, children from Aberystwyth's Young Archaeologists' Club (YAC) reconstructed a classic view of Professor Daryll Forde and his local workmen taken at the Isthmus Gate of Pen Dinas hillfort, Aberystwyth, nearly 80 years previously in 1934. The modern view, taken at the same spot, was recreated by John Ibbotson and Paul Harries of the YAC, guided by the author. Period clothes, long handled spades and flat caps supplied by Anna Evans of Amgueddfa Ceredigion Museum completed the scene. (Upper image: Photo: Crown Copyright RCAHMW DI2010_1293; lower image: photo by kind permission of Paul Harries)

FURTHER READING

Main sources for the hillforts of Cardigan Bay

Browne, D. and Driver, T., 2001. *Bryngaer Pen Dinas Hill-fort, A Prehistoric Fortress at Aberystwyth*. RCAHMW.

Davies, J.L. and Hogg, A.H.A., 1994. The Iron Age. In: Davies, J.L. and Kirby, D.P. (eds.), *Cardiganshire County History. Volume 1, From the earliest times to the coming of the Normans*. University of Wales Press. 219-233.

Driver, T. 2008. Hillforts and Human Movement: Unlocking the Iron Age Landscapes of Mid Wales. In Fleming, A. & Hingley, R. (eds). *Prehistoric and Roman Landscapes, Landscape History after Hoskins*, Volume I. Windgather Press, 83-100.

Driver, T. 2013. *Architecture, Regional Identity and Power in the Iron Age Landscapes of Mid Wales: The Hillforts of North Ceredigion*. British Archaeological Report (BAR) 583. Archaeopress.

Forde, C.D. Griffiths, W.E. Hogg, A.H.A. and Houlder, C.H., 1963. Excavations at Pen Dinas, Aberystwyth, *Archaeologia Cambrensis*, Vol. CXII, 125-153.

Hogg, A.H.A. and Davies, J.L., 1994. Appendix I: Gazetteer of Hillforts and Enclosures. In: Davies and Kirby, (eds.), 239-271.

Hughes, I.T., 1926. A Regional Survey of North Cardiganshire Prehistoric Earthworks, *Transactions of the Cardiganshire Antiquarian Society*, IV, 22-56.

Hughes, I.T., 1933. Some Observations on Hill-top Camps, *Transactions of the Cardiganshire Antiquarian Society*, Vol. IX, 12-25.

Murphy, K. and Mytum, H., 2012. Iron Age Enclosed Settlements in West Wales. *Proceedings of the Prehistoric Society* Vol. 78, 263-313.

Rees, S., 1992. *A Guide to Ancient and Historic Wales: Dyfed*. Cadw/HMSO.

Williams, J.G., 1867. Ancient Encampments Near Aberystwyth, *Archaeologia Cambrensis*, Vol. XIII, Third Series, 284-291.

Wright, F.S., 1914. Some Ancient Defensive Earthworks near Aberystwyth, with Notes on Early Communications, *Aberystwyth Studies by members of the University College of Wales*, Vol. 2, 43-79.

Further reading by chapter
CHAPTER 1

Austin, D., Bell, M. Burnham, B. and Young, R., 1984-86. *The Caer Cadwgan Project Interim Reports*. Archaeology Unit, St David's University College, Lampeter. Unpublished.

Bick, D. and Wyn Davies, P., 1994. *Lewis Morris and the Cardiganshire Mines*. The National Library of Wales, Aberystwyth.

Bowen, E.G., 1936. Cardiganshire in Prehistoric Times, *Transactions of the Cardiganshire Historical Society*, Vol. 11 (1936), 12-20.

Davies, D., (undated). *Welsh Place-names and their meanings*. Cambrian News, Aberystwyth.

Davies, J L. and Hogg, A.H.A., 1994. The Iron Age. In: Davies, J.L. and Kirby, D.P. (eds.), *Cardiganshire County History. Volume 1, From the earliest times to the coming of the Normans*. University of Wales Press, 219-233

Driver, T. And Haylock, K. 2012. *X-Ray Fluorescence (XRF) scanning of three iron age hillforts in Ceredigion 2011-12, Interim report of fieldwork for Cadw, May 2012*. Unpublished.

Forde, C.D., Griffiths, W.E., Hogg, A.H.A. and Houlder, C.H., 1963. Excavations at Pen Dinas, Aberystwyth, *Archaeologia Cambrensis*, Vol. CXII, 125-153.

Grooms, C., 1993. *The Giants of Wales: Cewri Cymru*. Welsh Studies Volume 10. The Edwin Mellen Press.

Guttman-Bond, E. 2014. *Excavation at Penyrheol, Lledrod, Ceredigion (NPRN 308511), May-June 2014, Interim Report*. Department of Archaeology, History and Anthropology, University of Wales, Trinity Saint David. Unpublished.

Hawkes, C.F.C., 1931. Hill-forts, *Antiquity*, 5, 60-97.

Lewis, W.J., 1955. *Ceredigion: Atlas Hanesyddol*. Cyngor Sir Ceredigion.

Murphy, K., 1989. Odyn-Fach Enclosure, Ceulanamaesmawr (SN 648 877) DAT PRN 7463, *Archaeology in Wales*, 29, 43-44.

Murphy, K. and Manwaring, M., 2004. *Prehistoric Defended Enclosures in southwest Wales 2004-5, Report number 2004/100, Project Record Number 52108*. Archaeoleg Cambria Archaeology. Unpublished report.

Murphy, K., and Mytum, H., 2006. Excavations at Troedyrhiw Defended Enclosure, *Archaeology in Wales*, 45 (2005), 92-94.

Murphy, K., and Mytum, H., 2007. Excavations at Ffynnonwen Defended Enclosure, near Cardigan, 2006. Interim Report, *Archaeology in Wales*, 46 (2006), 114-118.

Murphy, K. and Mytum, H., 2012. Iron Age Enclosed Settlements in West Wales, *Proceedings of the Prehistoric Society*, Vol. 78, 263-313.

Mytum, H., 2013. *Monumentality in Later Prehistory, Building and rebuilding Castell Henllys*. Springer.

Page, N., Hughes, G., Jones, R. and Murphy, K., 2013. Excavations at Erglodd, Llangynfelyn, Ceredigion: prehistoric/Roman lead smelting site and medieval trackway, *Archaeologia Cambrensis*, 161 (2012), 285-356.

Piehler, H.A., 1939. *Wales for Everyman*. J.M. Dent and Sons Ltd. Revised edition 1969.

Poucher, P., 2012, Llangoedmore, Cawrence Enclosure, *Archaeology in Wales*, 51, 164-165.

Ray, K., 1987. Ceredigion Archaeological Survey, *Archaeology in Wales*, 27, 8.

Scott, N. and Murphy, K., 1992. Excavations at Pendinas Lochtyn, Llangrannog, Dyfed, 1990-91, *Archaeology in Wales,* 32, 9-10.

Timberlake, S., 2007. Darren Camp and Darren Mine, Banc y Darren, Trefeurig (SN 679 830). The Radiocarbon Dates, *Archaeology in Wales*, 46 (2006), 182-3.

Timberlake, S. and Driver, T., 2006. Excavations at Darren Camp and Darren Mines (opencuts), Banc-y-darren, Trefeurig, Ceredigion, *Archaeology in Wales*, 45 (2005), 98-102.

Timberlake, S., Haylock, K., Driver, T., Barker, L., Andrews, P., Craddock, B., Gilmour, A., Mepham, L., 2014. The strange case of a mysterious lead anomaly: Castell Grogwynion Hillfort, Ceredigion: Iron Age smelting, eighteenth-century pottery or post medieval prospection? *Ceredigion*, Volume XVIII, Number 2, 1-28.

Thorburn, J., 1987. Capel Bangor Camp, Parcel Canol (SN 658 807); Penrhynoch, Trefeurig (SN 658 840); Pen y Daren, Trefeurig (SN 679 830); Pen y Castell, Trefeurig (SN 689 858), *Archaeology in Wales*, 27, 33-35.

Thorburn, J., 1988. *Archaeology in the Capel Bangor-Trefeurig Area*. Ceredigion Archaeological Survey, Saint David's University College, University of Wales. Unpublished.

Wallis, J., Bernard, E., Lister, M. and Ray. J., 1911. Parochialia, being a summary of answers to "Parochial Queries in order to a Geographical Dictionary. Etc. of Wales" issued by Edward Lhwyd, Part III, North Wales and South Wales (continued), *Archaeologia Cambrensis,* Supplement, July 1911.

Wheeler, M., 1943 *Maiden Castle, Dorset. Reports of the Research Committee of the Society of Antiquaries of London 12*. Oxford University Press.

CHAPTER 2

Austin, D., Bell, M., Burnham, B., and Young, R., 1984-86. *The Caer Cadwgan Project Interim Reports*. Archaeology Unit, St David's University College, Lampeter. Unpublished.

Bick, D. and Wyn Davies, P., 1994. *Lewis Morris and the Cardiganshire Mines.* The National Library of Wales, Aberystwyth.

Briggs, C.S. (ed.), 1997. A Neolithic and Early Bronze Age Settlement and Burial Complex at Llanilar, Ceredigion, *Archaeologia Cambrensis*, Vol. CXLVI, 13-59.

Briggs, C.S., 1994., The Bronze Age. In: Davies, J.L. and Kirby, D.P. (eds.), 1994. *Cardiganshire County History. Volume 1, From the earliest times to the coming of the Normans.* University of Wales Press. 124-218.

Burrow, S., 2006. *The tomb builders in Wales 4000-3000BC.* National Museum Wales Books, Cardiff.

Burrow, S., 2011. *Shadowland: Wales 3000-1500 BC.* National Museum Wales, Cardiff /Oxbow Books.

Fleming, A., 2008. *The Dartmoor Reaves: Investigating Prehistoric Land Divisions.* Windgather Press/ Oxbow Books. Second edition.

Gwilt, A., 2011. A sun-disc and mine drain. In: Redknap, M. (ed.), *Discovered in Time, treasures from early Wales.* National Museum Wales Books: Cardiff, 48-9.

Houlder, C.H., 1994. The Stone Age, In: Davies, J.L. and Kirby, D.P. (eds.), 1994. *Cardiganshire County History. Volume 1, From the earliest times to the coming of the Normans.* University of Wales Press, 107-123.

Lankester, E., 1846. *Memorials of John Ray: consisting of his life by Dr Derham. Biographical and critical notices by Sir J.E. Smith and Cuvier and Du Petit-Thouars.* Ray Society.

Murphy, K., 1992. Plas Gogerddan, Dyfed: A Multi-Period Burial and Ritual Site, *Archaeological Journal*, 149, 1-38.

Murphy, K., and Murphy, F. 2013. The excavation of two Bronze Age round barrows at Pant y Butler, Llangoedmor, Ceredigion, 2009-10, *Archaeologia Cambrensis*, 162, 33-66.

Murphy, K. and Mytum, H., 2012. Iron Age Enclosed Settlements in West Wales, *Proceedings of the Prehistoric Society*, Vol. 78, 263-313.

Musson, C., 1991. *The Breiddin Hillfort, A later prehistoric settlement in the Welsh Marches.* CBA Research Report, No. 76.

Musson, C.R., Britnell, W.J., Northover, J.P. and Salter, C.J., 1992. Excavations and metal working at Llwyn Bryn-dinas hillfort, Llangedwyn, Clwyd, *Proceedings of the Prehistoric Society*, 58, 265-84.

Taylor, J.A., 1973. Chronometers and chronicles: a study of the Paleo-environments of west central Wales, *Progress in Geography*, 5, 248-334.

Taylor, J.A. (ed.), 1980. *Culture and Environment in Prehistoric Wales.* BAR British Series 76.

Timberlake, T., 2003. Excavations on Copa Hill, Cwmystwyth (1986-1999); An Early Bronze Age copper mine within the uplands of Central Wales. BAR British Series 348, Archaeopress.

Timberlake, S., Gwilt, A., and Davis, M., 2004. A Copper Age / Early Bronze Age gold disc from Banc Tynddol (Penguelan, Cwmystwyth Mines, Ceredigion), *Antiquity*, Vol. 78, No. 302. http:// antiquity.ac.uk/projgall/timberlake/index.html.

Thomas, R., 1912. A prehistoric flint factory discovered at Aberystwyth, *Archaeologia Cambrensis*, 67, 211-16.

CHAPTER 3

Austin, D., Bell, M., Burnham, B. and Young, R., 1984-86. *The Caer Cadwgan Project Interim Reports.* Archaeology Unit, St David's University College, Lampeter. Unpublished.

Breeze, A., 2005. An Etymology for Dyfed, *Carmarthenshire Antiquary*, 41, 175-6.

Brewer, R.J., 2011. The Porth Felen anchor stock, In: Redknap, M. (ed.), *Discovered in Time, treasures from early Wales.* National Museum Wales Books, Cardiff, 82-3.

Cunliffe, B., 1991. *Iron age communities in Britain: an account of England, Scotland and Wales from the seventh century BC until the Roman conquest.* 3rd Edition. Routledge.

Cunliffe, B., 2001. *Facing the Ocean, The Atlantic and its Peoples, 8000BC – AD1500*. Oxford University Press.

Davies, J.L. and Kirby, D.P. (eds.), 1994. *Cardiganshire County History. Volume 1, From the earliest times to the coming of the Normans*. University of Wales Press.

Davies, J.L., 1994. The Roman Period, In: Davies, J.L. and Kirby, D.P. (eds.), 275-317.

Evans, D.C., 1933. Cribyn Clottas. Some hill-top camps, *Transactions and archaeological record, Cardiganshire Antiquarian Society*. 19-25.

Evans, G.E., 1927. Llandyssul Parish: Part of a Late Celtic Bronze Collar, *The Transactions of the Carmarthenshire Antiquarian Society and Field Club*, Vol. XXI, Part 51, 1-2.

Fenton, J., 1860. Cardiganshire Antiquities, *Archaeologia Cambrensis*, Vol. VI, Third Series, 58-61.

Fitzpatrick, A.P., 2007. 'Druids: Towards an archaeology' in C. Gosden, H. Harrow, P. de Jersey and G. Lock (eds.), Communities and Connections: Essays in honour of Barry Cunliffe. Oxford University Press, 287-315.

Fleming, A., 2008. *The Dartmoor Reaves: Investigating Prehistoric Land Divisions*. Windgather Press/Oxbow Books. Second edition.

Fleure, H.J., 1922. An outline story of our neighbourhood, *Aberystwyth Studies,* Vol. IV, 111-123.

Forde, C.D., Griffiths, W.E., Hogg, A.H.A. and Houlder, C.H., 1963. Excavations at Pen Dinas, Aberystwyth, *Archaeologia Cambrensis*, Vol. CXII, 125-153.

Jones, E., 1962. Tregaron, The Sociology of a Market Town in Central Cardiganshire. In: Jenkins *et. al.,* 67-117.

Mattingly, H., 1948. *Tacitus on Britain and Germany: A new translation by H. Mattingly*. Penguin Books.

Meyrick, S.R., 1808. *The History and Antiquities of the County of Cardigan*. London.

Megaw, J.V.S., 1971. *Art of the European Iron Age: a study of the elusive image*. Adams and Dart.

Mighall, T.M., Timberlake, S., and Grattan, J.P., 2012. *A Paleoecological assessment of the blanket peat surrounding the source of the Severn, Plynlimon*. Unpublished report for the Metal Links Project, RCAHMW.

Moore, P.D., 1994. The History of Vegetation in Cardiganshire. In: Davies and Kirby, (eds.), 26-42.

Murphy, K. 1992. Plas Gogerddan, Dyfed: A Multi-Period Burial and Ritual Site, *Archaeological Journal,* 149, 1-38.

Murphy, K. and Mytum, H., 2012. Iron Age Enclosed Settlements in West Wales, *Proceedings of the Prehistoric Society*, Vol. 78, 263-313.

Nowakowski, J., Gwilt, A., Megaw, V. & La Niece, S., 2009. A Late Iron Age neck-ring from Pentire, Newquay, Cornwall, with a note on the find from Boverton, Vale of Glamorgan, *Antiquaries Journal*, 89, 35-52.

Parkinson, A.J., 1985. Peat, wheat and lead: Settlement patterns in west Wales, 1500-1800, *Ceredigion*, Vol. X (2), 111-130.

Page, N., Hughes, G., Jones, R. and Murphy, K., 2013. Excavations at Erglodd, Llangynfelyn, Ceredigion: prehistoric/Roman lead smelting site and medieval trackway, *Archaeologia Cambrensis*, 161 (2012), 285-356.

Roseveare, M.J., 2012. *Castell Grogwynion, Ceredigion. Geophysical Survey Report. Produced for RCAHMW. CGW121. ArchaeoPhysica Ltd*. Unpublished report.

Scott, N. and Murphy, K., 1992. Excavations at Pendinas Lochtyn, Llangrannog, Dyfed, 1990-91, *Archaeology in Wales*, 32, 9-10

Simpson, M., 1968. A Bronze Mount from Aberporth. *Archaeologia Cambrensis*, Vol. CXVII, 72-76.

Taylor, J.A. (ed.), 1980. *Culture and Environment in Prehistoric Wales*. BAR British Series 76.

Timberlake, S., 2001. Mining and prospection for metals in Early Bronze Age Britain – making claims within the archaeological landscape. In: Bruck, (ed.), *Bronze Age Landscapes – Tradition and Transformation*. Oxbow, 179-192.

Timberlake, S., 2003. *Excavations on Copa Hill, Cwmystwyth (1986-1999); An Early Bronze Age copper mine within the uplands of Central Wales.* BAR British Series 348, Archaeopress.

Timberlake, S. and Driver, T., 2006. Excavations at Darren Camp and Darren Mines (opencuts), Banc-y-darren, Trefeurig, Ceredigion, *Archaeology in Wales*, 45 (2005), 98-102.

Timberlake, S., Haylock, K., Driver, T., Barker, L., Andrews, P., Craddock, B., Gilmour, A. and Mepham, L., 2014. The strange case of a mysterious lead anomaly: Castell Grogwynion Hillfort, Ceredigion: Iron Age smelting, eighteenth-century pottery or post medieval prospection? *Ceredigion*, Volume XVIII, Number 2, 1-28.

Turner, J., 1970. Post-Neolithic Disturbance of British Vegetation. In: Walker and West, (eds.), 81-96.

Walker, D. and West, R.G. (eds.), 1970. *Studies in the Vegetational History of the British Isles (Essays to Godwin).* Cambridge.

Williams, A., 1945. A promontory fort at Henllan, Cardiganshire. *Archaeologia Cambrensis*, Vol. XCVIII, 226-247.

CHAPTER 4

Austin, D., Bell, M., Burnham, B. and Young, R., 1984-86. *The Caer Cadwgan Project Interim Reports.* Archaeology Unit, St David's University College, Lampeter. Unpublished.

Avery, M., 1976. Hillforts of the British Isles: A Student's Introduction. In: Harding, (ed.), 1-58.

Avery, M., 1993. *Hillfort Defences of Southern Britain*, BAR British Series 231, (three volumes).

Browne, D. and Driver, T., 2001. *Bryngaer Pen Dinas Hill-fort, A Prehistoric Fortress at Aberystwyth.* RCAHMW.

Cunliffe, B., 1984. *Danebury: an Iron Age hillfort in Hampshire. Vol. 1, The excavations, 1969-1978: the site.* Council for British Archaeology Research Report 52.

Dodgshon, R.A., 1996. Modelling chiefdoms in the Scottish Highlands and islands prior to the '45. In: Arnold and Blair Gibson, (eds.), *Celtic Chiefdom, Celtic State.* Cambridge University Press. 2nd Edition, 99-109.

Dodgshon, R.A., 1998. *From Chiefs to Landlords, Social and Economic Change in the Western Highlands and Island, c.1493-1820.* Edinburgh University Press.

Evans, D.C., 1933. Cribyn Clottas. Some hill-top camps. *Transactions and archaeological record, Cardiganshire Antiquarian Society,* 19-25.

Gardner, W., 1926. Presidential Address. The Native Hill-forts in North Wales and Their Defences, *Archaeologia Cambrensis*, Vol. LXXXI, Part II, Seventh Series, Vol. VI, 221-282.

Gwilt, A., 2011. The Tal-y-llyn shield fittings. In: Redknap, M., (ed.) *Discovered in Time, treasures from early Wales.* National Museum Wales Books, Cardiff. 76-7

Hogg, A.H.A., 1975. *Hill-forts of Britain.* Hart-Davis, MacGibbon.

Hughes, I.T., 1933, 'Some observations on Hill-top Camps', *Transactions of the Cardiganshire Antiquarian Society*, 15.

Lewis, W.J., 1951. Some Aspects of Lead Mining in Cardiganshire in the Sixteenth and Seventeenth Centuries, *Ceredigion,*, Volume I, Number 2, 177-192.

Lias, A., 1994. *A Guide to Welsh Place-Names.* Welsh Heritage Series No. 3: Gwasg Carreg Gwalch.

MacDonald, P., 2007. *Llyn Cerrig Bach: A study of the copper allow artefacts from the insular La Tène assemblage.* University of Wales Press.

Manning, W.H., 1999. The Use of Timber in Iron Age Defences. *Studia Celtica*, Vol. XXXIII, 21-32.

Murphy, K. and Mytum, H., 2012. Iron Age Enclosed Settlements in West Wales, *Proceedings of the Prehistoric Society*, Vol. 78, 263-313.

Mytum, H., 2013. *Monumentality in Later Prehistory, Building and rebuilding Castell Henllys.* Springer.

Ralston, I., 2006. *Celtic Fortifications.* Tempus.

RCAHMW, 1986. *An Inventory of the Ancient Monuments in Brecknock (Brycheiniog), The Prehistoric and Roman Monuments, Part ii: Hill-forts and Roman Remains.* HMSO.

Savory, H.N., 1964. The Taly-y-llyn hoard, *Antiquity*, XXXVIII, 18-31.

Timberlake, S., Haylock, K., Driver, T., Barker, L., Andrews, P., Craddock, B., Gilmour, A. and Mepham, L. 2014. The strange case of a mysterious lead anomaly: Castell Grogwynion Hillfort, Ceredigion: Iron Age smelting, eighteenth-century pottery or post medieval prospection? *Ceredigion*, Volume XVIII, Number 2, 1-28.

Wenke, R.J., 1990. The Evolution of Socially Complex Cultures. In: Wenke, R.J. *Patterns in Prehistory, Humankind's First Three Million Years.* (Third Edition), Oxford University Press. 277-317.

Williams, G.H. and Mytum, H., 1998. *Llawhaden, Dyfed, Excavations on a group of small defended enclosures, 1980-4.* BAR British Series 275.

CHAPTER 5

Aldhouse-Green, M. and Howell, R., 2000. *Celtic Wales.* University of Wales Press.

Banks, R.W., 1879. On a Wooden Female Head Found at Llanio, *Archaeologia Cambrensis*, Fourth Series, Vol. X., No. XXXVIII, 81-5.

Barker, L. and Driver, T., 2011. Close to the Edge: New Perspectives on the Architecture, Function and Regional Geographies of the Coastal Promontory Forts of the Castlemartin Peninsula, South Pembrokeshire, Wales, *Proceedings of the Prehistoric Society*, 77, 65-87.

Barnwell, E.L., 1862. Bronze articles supposed to be spoons, *Archaeologia Cambrensis*, Vol. VIII, Third Series, 208-219.

Brewer, R.J., 2011. The Porth Felen anchor stock. In: Redknap, M. (ed.), *Discovered in Time, treasures from early Wales.* National Museum Wales Books, Cardiff, 82-3.

Briggs, C.S., 1994., The Bronze Age. In: Davies, J.L. and Kirby, D.P. (eds.), 1994. *Cardiganshire County History. Volume 1, From the earliest times to the coming of the Normans.* University of Wales Press, 124-218.

Boon, G.C., 1978. A Romano-British Wooden Carving from Llanio, *Bulletin of the Board of Celtic Studies*, 27, 619-24.

Children, G., and Nash, G. 1994. *Prehistoric Sites of Herefordshire.* Logaston Press, Almeley.

Craw, J.H., 1923-4. On two bronze spoons from an early Iron Age grave near Burnmouth, Berwickshire, *Proceedings of the Society of Antiquaries of Scotland*, 52, 143-60.

Delaney, C.J. and Williams, G.H., 1982. Cardiganshire: 53. Llanfarian, *Archaeology in Wales*, No. 22, 42.

Driver, T., 1998. Llandre, Geneu'r Glyn (SN 626 862), *Archaeology in Wales*, 38, 94-95.

Fitzpatrick, A.P., 2007. 'Druids: Towards an archaeology' in C. Gosden, H. Harrow, P. de Jersey and G. Lock (eds.), *Communities and Connections: Essays in honour of Barry Cunliffe.* Oxford University Press, 287-315.

Green, M., 1996. *Celtic Art.* The Everyman Art Library, Calman & King Ltd.

Grimes, W.F., 1939. *Guide to the Collections Illustrating the Prehistory of Wales*, National Museum of Wales, Cardiff.

Gwilt, A., 2011. The Iron Age. In: Redknap, M. (ed.), *Discovered in Time, treasures from early Wales.* National Museum Wales Books, Cardiff. 66-81.

James, D.B., 2001. *Ceredigion, Its Natural History.* Cambrian Printers, Aberystwyth.

MacDonald, P., 2007. *Llyn Cerrig Bach: A study of the copper allow artefacts from the insular La Tène assemblage.* University of Wales Press.

Malet, 1859. Cardigan Meeting, report [including Castell Nadolig]. *Archaeologia Cambrensis*, Vol. V, Third Series. 320-352.

Mattingly, H., 1948. *Tacitus on Britain and Germany: A new translation by H. Mattingly*. Penguin Books.

Ross, A., 2001. *Folklore of Wales*. Tempus, 68-69.

Steele, P., 2012. *Llyn Cerrig Bach, Treasure from the Iron Age*. Oriel Ynys Môn, Llangefni.

Williams, G.H. and Delaney, C.J., 1982. A Celtic Head from Llandysul, *The Carmarthenshire Antiquary*, Volume XVIII, 9-16.

Woodruff, C.H., 1904. Further discoveries of Late Celtic and Romano-British internments at Wilmer, *Archaeologies Cantina*, 26, 9-16.

CHAPTER 6

Arnold, C. J. and Davies, J.L., 2000. *Roman and Early Medieval Wales*. Sutton Publishing.

Davies, J.L., 1994. The Roman Period, In: Davies, J L and Kirby, D.P. (eds.), *Cardiganshire County History. Volume 1, From the earliest times to the coming of the Normans*. University of Wales Press, 275-317.

Davies, J.L. and Driver, T.G., 1999. The discovery of a Roman coin hoard at Salem, Trefeurig, Aberystwyth, *Ceredigion*, Vol. XIII, No. 3, 1-4.

Davies, J.L. and Jones, R.H., 2006. *Roman Camps in Wales and the Marches*. University of Wales Press.

Driver, T.G. and Davies, J.L., 2011. Abermagwr Romano-British villa, Ceredigion, mid Wales: Interim report on its discovery and excavation, *Archaeologia Cambrensis*, Vol. 160, 39-49.

Manning, W.H., 2001. *A Pocket Guide to Roman Wales*. University of Wales Press/The Western Mail.

Mattingly, H., 1948. *Tacitus on Britain and Germany: A new translation by H. Mattingly*. Penguin Books.

Percival, J., 1976. *The Roman Villa, An Historical Introduction*. Book Club Associates (Reprint 1981).

CHAPTER 7

Avery, M., 1993. *Hillfort Defences of Southern Britain*, BAR British Series 231, (three volumes).

Barker, L. and Driver, T., 2011. Close to the Edge: New Perspectives on the Architecture, Function and Regional Geographies of the Coastal Promontory Forts of the Castlemartin Peninsula, South Pembrokeshire, Wales, *Proceedings of the Prehistoric Society*, 77, 65-87.

Browne, D. and Driver, T., 2001. *Bryngaer Pen Dinas Hill-fort, A Prehistoric Fortress at Aberystwyth*. RCAHMW.

Davies, J.L. and Hogg, A.H.A., 1994. The Iron Age. In: Davies, J.L. and Kirby, D.P. (eds.), 1994. *Cardiganshire County History. Volume 1, From the earliest times to the coming of the Normans*. University of Wales Press, 219-233

Driver, T., 2013. *Architecture, Regional Identity and Power in the Iron Age Landscapes of Mid Wales: The Hillforts of North Ceredigion*. British Archaeological Report (BAR) 583, Archaeopress.

Fenton, J., 1860. Cardiganshire Antiquities, *Archaeologia Cambrensis*, Vol. VI, Third Series, 58-61.

Fleur, H.J., 1922. An outline story of our neighbourhood, *Aberystwyth Studies*, Vol. IV, 111-123.

Forde, C.D., Griffiths, W.E., Hogg, A.H.A. and Houlder, C.H., 1963. Excavations at Pen Dinas, Aberystwyth, *Archaeologia Cambrensis*, Vol. CXII, 125-153.

James, T. and Simpson, D., 1980. *Ancient West Wales from the Air*. Carmarthenshire Antiquarian Society.

Lynch, F., Aldhouse-Green, S., and Davies, J.L., 2000. *Prehistoric Wales*. Sutton Publishing.

Scott, N. and Murphy, K., 1992. Excavations at Pendinas Lochtyn, Llangrannog, Dyfed, 1990-91, *Archaeology in Wales*, 32, 9-10.

FINDING OUT MORE

The Royal Commission on the Ancient and Historical Monuments of Wales: The Royal Commission is the investigation body and national archive for the historic environment of Wales. Explore the national archive of the archaeology and built heritage of Wales. Find us online at: www. coflein.gov.uk, contact the Royal Commission's free Enquiries Service or visit the NMRW Library and search room in Aberystwyth. Follow the *Heritage of Wales News:* **heritageofwalesnews.blogspot. co.uk**

National Monuments Record of Wales: Telephone: 01970 621200
Email: nmr.wales@rcahmw.gov.uk   **www.rcahmw.gov.uk**

The Dyfed Archaeological Trust: Based in Llandeilo, Carmarthenshire, the Dyfed Archaeological Trust (established 1975) is an independent organisation dedicated to the effective protection, investigation, recording and promotion of the historic environment.
Telephone: 01558 823121/823131
Email: info@dyfedarchaeology.org.uk   **http://www.dyfedarchaeology.org.uk/**

Amgueddfa Ceredigion Museum, Aberystwyth: Amgueddfa Ceredigion Museum is an excellent regional museum which houses the archaeological collections of the county in the Bowen Gallery. Address: Coliseum, Terrace Road, Aberystwyth, Ceredigion. SY23 2AQ
Telephone: 01970 633088   **http://www.ceredigion.gov.uk/index.cfm?articleid=197**

National Museum Wales, Cardiff: At the time of writing the archaeological collections are in the process of being relocated to new galleries at the St Fagans National History Museum, in west Cardiff. **http://www.museumwales.ac.uk/stfagans/**

British Museum, London: The Rhos-rydd Late Bronze Age shield, labelled 'Rhyd-y-gorse, Dyfed, Wales', is on display in Room 51 *Ancient Europe 4000-800 BC*. **www.britishmuseum.org**

Ashmolean Museum, Oxford: The Penbryn Spoons from Castell Nadolig are on display in the *Resisting Rome* case, in the gallery *European Prehistory to AD 100*. The original spoons are well worth a special visit. **www.ashmolean.org**

HISTORIC WALES PORTAL: Search the combined archaeological databases of the Royal Commission, Welsh Archaeological Trusts, National Museum Wales and Cadw at the Historic Wales Portal: **historicwales.gov.uk/**

COFLEIN: Search the database of the National Monuments Record of Wales online: **www.coflein. gov.uk**

ARCHWILIO: Search the databases of the four Welsh Archaeological Trusts online: **http://www. cofiadurcahcymru.org.uk/arch/**

Cadw: Cadw is the Welsh Government's historic environment service working for an accessible and well-protected historic environment for Wales: http://cadw.gov.wales/

Portable Antiquities Scheme*: https://finds.org.uk/

Heather and hillforts (Denbighshire): **http://www.clwydianrangeanddeevalleyaonb.org.uk/ hillforts/**

References

Chapter 1
1. Bowen, 1936
2. Peniarth 118 in Grooms, C., 1993
3. for Cardiganshire see Wallis *et al.*, 1911
4. Forde *et al.*, 1963
5. Piehler, 1939
6. Lluest y Trafle, Bontgoch, and Castell Rhyfel, Tregaron
7. Ray, 1987
8. Murphy 1989, 44
9. Davies and Kirby (eds.), 1994
10. published as a monograph; Driver, 2013
11. Timberlake *et al*, 2014
12. Timberlake and Driver, 2006
13. Poucher, 2012
14. after Dewi Davies (undated) with additions
15. Timberlake and Driver, 2006
16. Mytum, 2013
17. Murphy and Mytum, 2007, 2012
18. Guttman-Bond, 2014
19. Page, *et al*, 2013

Chapter 2
1. John Ray, 5th June 1662 in Lankester 1846, 172-3
2. Houlder, 1994
3. Briggs, 1994 for an inventory of site
4. Briggs (ed.), 1997
5. Murphy and Murphy, 2013
6. Burrow, 2011, 90-96
7. Gwilt, 2011
8. Timberlake *et al*, 2004
9. Briggs, 1994, 158
10. Fleming, 2008
11. Murphy and Mytum, 2012

Chapter 3
1. English translation by Philemon Holland, 1607
2. Parkinson, 1985
3. Jones, 1962
4. Mighall *et al*, 2012
5. Turner, 1970
6. Taylor, 1980, 332
7. Fleming, 2008
8. Moore, 1994, 40
9. Evans, 1933, 20
10. After Williams 1945, Figure 5
11. Austin *et al*, 1984-6, 13

12. Murphy and Mytum, 2012
13. Scott and Murphy, 1992
14. Agricola, 16; Mattingly, 1948
15. Cunliffe, 1991
16. Breeze, 2005
17. Megaw, 1971
18. Nowakowski *et al*, 2009
19. Evans, 1927; Sally Evans pers. comm.
20. Simpson, 1968; Davies, 1994, 315
21. Savory in Murphy, 1992
22. A and B after Williams, 1945, Figure 5; C drawn by Jennifer Foster, Caer Cadwgan Project Interim Report, 1985, Lampeter, Figure 4, in Austin *et al*, 1984-86
23. Roseveare, 2012
24. Williams, 1945
25. Fenton, 1860, 60
26. Agricola, 12; Mattingly, 1948
27. *De Bello Gallico* 3.13 in Cunliffe 2001
28. Brewer, 2011
29. Davies, 1994
30. Fleure, 1922
31. by Timberlake, 2001
32. from Pen Dinas, Aberystwyth, Odyn Fach, Talybont, Pen Dinas, Elerch, Hen Gaer, Penrhyncoch and Caer Cadwgan, Cellan
33. Timberlake, *et al*, 2014
34. Page *et al*, 2013
35. Timberlake and Driver, 2006

Chapter 4
1. Hughes, 1933, 15
2. Dodgshon, 1996
3. Dodgshon, 1998
4. Williams and Mytum, 1998
5. Driver, 2013
6. RCAHMW, 1986
7. Hughes, 1933, 14
8. Ralston, 2006, 182-3
9. Wenke, 1990
10. Cunliffe, 1984
11. Manning, 1999
12. Mytum, 2013, 316
13. Lewis, 1951, 182, citing Hooson's Miners Dictionary (Wrexham 1747)
14. all three lie on private land
15. Murphy and Mytum, 2012
16. Murphy and Mytum, 2012

17. Hughes, 1933, 14
18. Williams, 1867, 287
19. Avery, 1993
20. Mytum, 2013
21. Hogg, 1975, 49
22. Dodgshon, 1996
23. Hogg, 1975
24. Avery, 1976
25. Mytum, 2013
26. Lias, 1994, 31
27. Timberlake, *et al*, 2014
28. Murphy and Mytum, 2011, 40
29. Forde *et al*, 1963, 144
30. Austin, *et al*, 1984-6
31. Evans, 1933, 20
32. Davies and Lynch, 2000, 187
33. Timberlake, *et al*, 2014
34. after Davies and Lynch, 2000
35. after Savory, 1964
36. Savory, 1964, 18
37. Gwilt, 2011, 76
38. Gardner, 1926, 230
39. www.slinging.org

Chapter 5
1. Gwilt, 2011
2. Barker and Driver, 2011
3. Tactitus, Annales XIV, 30-1
4. *Natural History*, 16, 95
5. Fitzpatrick 2007, 289-90
6. Aldhouse-Green and Howell, 2000, 31
7. Gwilt, 2011
8. Davies and Lynch, 2000, 187
9. MacDonald, 2007; Steele, 2012
10. Briggs, writing about the Rhos-rydd, Aberllolwyn shield in the Cardiganshire County History, 1994, 158-9
11. James, 2001
12. George Lipscomb, *Journey into South Wales … in the year 1799*; London, 1802, 170-171
13. Barnwell, 1962, 215
14. after Grimes, 1939
15. Fitzpatrick, 2007, 298
16. Woodruff in 1904, and Craw in 1923-4 (cited in Fitzpatrick, 2007, 294-5
17. F. Lynch pers. comm.
18. Fitzpatrick, 2007
19. Green and Howell, 2000

20. Green, 1996, 140
21. Children and Nash, 1994, 78
22. Ross, 2001
23. Driver, 1998
24. Anne Ross, 2001
25. Williams and Delaney, 1982, 9
26. Williams and Delaney, *Carmarthenshire Antiquary* for 1982
27. Williams and Delaney, 1982
28. Boon, 1978, 620
29. Banks, 1879, 82-3
30. Davies, 1994, 316-317
31. Boon, 1978

Chapter 6
1. Mattingly, 1948
2. Davies, 1994
3. Davies, 1994
4. Agricola, 11 & 12 in Mattingly, 1948
5. Davies, 1994, 280
6. Agricola 18 in Mattingly, 1948
7. Arnold and Davies,, 2000, 14
8. Agricola 29 in Mattingly, 1948
9. Agricola 21 in Mattingly, 1948
10. Davies, *Cardiganshire County History*, 1994, 282
11. Davies, 1994, 282
12. Percival, 1976, 35
13. Avery, 1993
14. Davies, *Cardiganshire County History*, (1994), 283
15. Driver, and Davies, 2011
16. Davies and Driver, 1999

Chapter 7
1. Fleure, 1922
2. Forde *et al*, 1963
3. Forde, *et al*, 1963
4. Driver, 2013
5. Barker and Driver, 2011
6. Avery, 1993
7. James and Simpson, 1980
8. Davies and Hogg. 1994
9. Lynch, Aldhouse-Green and Davies, 2000
10. Fenton, 1860, 61
11. Fenton, 1860, 58
12. after Scott and Murphy, 1992
13. Scott and Murphy, 1992

INDEX